JUST A LITTLE BIT MORE

Barry -
Common Good -
to think includes
Jazz !

T. Carlos

JUST A LITTLE BIT MORE

THE CULTURE OF EXCESS AND
THE FATE OF THE COMMON GOOD

T. CARLOS ANDERSON

Blue Ocotillo Publishing

Austin, Texas

JUST A LITTLE BIT MORE
The Culture of Excess and the Fate of the Common Good
Copyright © 2014 by T. Carlos Anderson

Blue Ocotillo Publishing
Austin, Texas
www.blueocotillo.com

Distributed by ACTA Publications
4848 N. Clark St.
Chicago, IL 60640
www.actapublications.com / 800-397-2282

Library of Congress Catalog Number: 2014902927
ISBN: 978-0-9915328-1-0
Printed in the United States of America by Total Printing Systems
Year 25 24 23 22 21 20 19 18 17 16
Printing 15 14 13 12 11 10 9 8 7 6 5 4 3

♻ Text printed on 30% post-consumer recycled paper

Dedicated to my Mom and Dad

CONTENTS

Rockefeller, Carnegie, Gould, and Morgan

Creating the Middle

God, Money, and Good

Gilded Age Plutocracy, Prosperity, and Poverty

Federal Income Tax: Government versus Big Business

The Raging Bull of the 1920s: The Rich Get Richer

New Permission

Greed—For Better and For Worse

The Lizard Brain

Greed Graduates

Unlimited Growth is Cancer

Greed Management

Madoff's Exclusive Inner Circle (at 18 Percent)

Greed Besieged by United Religious Attack

Survival of the Altruistic

FOREWORD

Writing on behalf of the common good, the author asks how the American economy can benefit all, not a few. As currently structured, it can't. T. Carlos Anderson argues for an egalitarian approach to fiscal matters.

Deftly, he sets the historical scene of how the economy took the form of religion. Money is the new god, actually, the old god in new design. For a god is that in which you put your trust. By tracing the development of the economy from the land of opportunity to the *summum bonum*, the reader gets a perspective as to why we are in the present quagmire.

The new religion comes with priests and bishops known as bankers and investors. The free market evangelists boast of the invisible hand that guides the system. There are even rogue angels like Bernie Madoff and other Ponzi schemers. With money as god, financial worth determines worthiness. Money is no longer "the root of all evil" but the essence of the good life. Excess is the sign of cosmic blessing.

Years ago, psychologist Erich Fromm noted that "greed is a bottomless pit," an apt image for hell. Greed "exhausts the person in an endless attempt to satisfy need," but Fromm contends that the need is insatiable, leading to addictive behavior and the selling of one's soul.

Anderson knows that money talks, but it is a one way conversant. He wants economic democracy to be the new standard to define a system that has lost a sense of proportion.

The reader will benefit immensely in seeing how we have shaped the system we are part of and what can lead to a new way of doing economics that embraces the common good.

Peter L. Steinke

Author and consultant

INTRODUCTION

I want to tell you a story, captivating yet tragic, about a god that has been around for a long time. This deity has staked its claim, oftentimes successfully, in human hearts; through the ages its spirit has been manifested variously in peoples and their events from the Dutch tulip panic to the 2007–08 financial crisis emanating from the US housing market. This god is not new; its inhabited forms and shapes, however, always seem to give the impression of novelty. Its liturgies and incantations allure, its high priests (yes, mostly all male) impress, and burgeoning converts hold fast in the way. For the last one hundred and forty years—what I call the long era—the *new way* of this god has promoted *excess* to the detriment of purposeful common good. Specifically, for the last thirty-five years—the short era—a fundamentalist belief in the powers and ways of the market has pushed excess to new extremes. Excess is not solely the propriety of Wall Street; excess has filtered its way into numerous significant areas of American life.

Common good is a term whose import is not what it used to be. American history testifies to periods when the term was a greater part of societal custom and acceptance. The current day is not one of those periods; the concept, along with others such as egalitarianism and moderation, has fallen out of favor, as I will explore in this book, because of an overarching problem that ails our public life: societal inequality. This specific problem, manifested financially, politically, and economically, has been generated by a propensity for excess. Overconsumption and overcompensation are two apt descriptions of American life since the early 1980s. A great strength of American character through its history has been the ability to risk and push beyond boundaries. American inventiveness, ingenuity, and drive have changed the world for the better—over and again. Yet oftentimes a society's greatest strength can also be its greatest weakness. Sometimes we reach too far with risk or extend ill-advisedly beyond certain boundaries, to the impairment of societal good. Sometimes it's better to accept limits and to reject the allure of unlimitedness.

A pendulum is one of the most beautiful yet simplest of machines: utilitarian, precise, hypnotic. Attributed, by some, with spiritual powers of healing and divination, pendulums traverse the realms of physics and metaphysics. But stripped bare, all a pendulum does, when put into motion, is swing—back and forth, back and forth. There are tales to be told and worlds to be discovered within the arcs of a pendulum.

The stories told in this book, and the thoughts they provoke, are like the arcs created by the fluid tempo of the pendulum. The arc extends to outer reaches and extreme points, but ample space exists for thoughts and experiences within the boundaries. In our current day and time, polemics sell; the political realm is especially poisoned with the compulsion to choose one side or the other. If you don't have a chosen side, or worse, if you are a "flip-flopper," then you are decidedly out of step. This book recognizes the shallowness of gutting out the wide middle regions of certain arguments for what the purging oftentimes is: a hustle, or at least some type of manipulation. Life is made up of many complex parts producing elaborate sums—reducing them to simplistic choices of either-or often makes for an unnecessarily limiting panorama. I don't mean to say that having a point of view or taking a stand is unworthy or untenable. Most all the big issues, however, do not have simple resolutions; in a constantly changing and increasingly complex world, both steadfastness and flexibility are needed. Tunnel vision has its time and place, as does stepping back and seeing the wider view. Both views are limiting and revealing, simultaneously. Perhaps those who are wrongly labeled flip-floppers (some are justly labeled so) actually have a wider view and a greater understanding of reality.

As an example, capitalism is the economic system that has emerged from the figurative and actual battles of the twentieth century as the best structure to provide food, opportunity, and prosperity for great populations. It has boosted millions of people upward from the depths of poverty. Yet, it's not a perfect system: wealth tends to siphon and accumulate upward and disabled and disadvantaged members of society can be easily marginalized. The system needs social accountability, by government and other organizations, for there to be social accord—only a blatant ideologue would say otherwise. And that's precisely the point; critique doesn't always mean rejection. One can participate in a dialogue of critique without an opponent having to make accusations of treason or disloyalty. A wide gulf of common sense lies on the other side of "You're either with us or against us." Preying on societal fears and anxieties to prove a point or make a sale, in the long run, diminishes the common good. When put into motion, the pendulum will swing from side to side—to hold the pendulum in one spot is unnatural. When someone is purposely manipulative, for the sake of winning an argument or procuring unjust financial gain, it's akin to not allowing the pendulum to swing. The pendulum's arc has two end points, and all the other points in between are necessary parts of the whole.

Just a Little Bit More, in addressing personal and societal excesses, including overcompensation, overconsumption, greed, and other exorbitances, doesn't assume that these realities are newly with us. From an evolutionary, biological, or psychological sense, the potential to live out these tendencies has been with us forever. My argument is that these tendencies have been ramped up because of the events of the last one hundred years or so, since the time that John D. Rockefeller Sr. and his peers were making their marks upon history. Their deeds, without judging their faults or merits, simply changed the framework in which we view and understand the world. More than one hundred years ago the pendulum was made to swing in a larger arc than it had before. Instead of wishing it didn't happen that way or that it shouldn't have happened at all, my aim is to contribute an answer to the question, In this new reality, how then do we live together for the common good?

This book will make the argument that part of the founding *American way* was to exalt egalitarianism—more so, certainly, than various parts of European society that many sojourners left behind in coming to the New World. The pall of slavery, of course, immediately casts doubts on such reasoning, but if we accept complexity and acknowledge human deficiencies the argument can continue forward. The oft-heard argument that religious freedom was part of the original American way is legitimate, but it often overshadows the attribute of egalitarianism. The pursuit and development of an egalitarian society, free of the European vestiges of aristocracy and plutocracy, has been forgotten in our day and age, a time of the adoration of wealth and its accoutrements. From the beginning, the founding American way has been shaped, in part, by egalitarianism. I will assert in the following chapters that egalitarianism is significant to our American heritage and is the *necessary moderator of liberty*—a broadly defined term that includes, among other things, the free pursuit of wealth.

In the history of the United States, the common good subsists in the tension created between egalitarianism and economic liberty. Proponents on both sides have pursued and do pursue wealth and its benefits. A significant difference between the two strains of thought is the means by which general society is benefited. The egalitarian viewpoint does not trust isolated individuals to best serve the common good. The liberty side does not trust government to best serve the common good. While the egalitarian side has focused on the goal of a just society lifting up all citizens, the liberty side has focused on the sum of individual goods as the means to best support the common good. The two competing visions are not mutually exclusive; both perspectives envision how to best conduct a society based in certain freedoms, and they serve to balance the other's extreme tendencies. One side fears human propensity to abuse economic freedoms to the detriment of society; the other side fears overregulation and limitations placed upon economic activity that would hinder wealth creation. The two sides can work together, and they have had a lively interchange over the decades and centuries of American life. On the side of pursuing a shared common good have been American figures such as Thomas Jefferson, Andrew Jackson, Abraham Lincoln,

Theodore Roosevelt, Franklin Delano Roosevelt, and Lyndon B. Johnson. On the side of pursuing individual gains as the best way to benefit society have been Alexander Hamilton, John Rockefeller Sr., Calvin Coolidge, Milton Friedman, Ronald Reagan, and Alan Greenspan.

Related to the exchange between these two competing views is the concept of class warfare in American society. The fomenting of class warfare is a charge—during the 2012 presidential debates, for example—that has been bandied about politically, as if it's a brand new phenomenon. This war of words is not new; America has waged this battle from its earliest days. Inherent to capital creation and wealth accumulation is political power; heated conversations producing such grand documents as the Bill of Rights have served to ascertain the best ways to balance freedoms, powers, and limitations for the good of society and individuals. Mandated balancing of powers has coaxed American society from the extremes (those extremes seen in some of the European societies from which early immigrants fled) that can inhibit social freedoms within a society. Balance and separation of powers in multiple manifestations, politically and socially, are the arbitrating principles that serve to keep the playing field as level as it can be. A healthy, verbal interaction on class identity and privilege is necessary for some sense of balance and social justice to be maintained. When political power and economic force merge to become one, the balance can be obliterated. We live in such a time today. Class conflict has existed since the descendants of foragers gathered in settled communities. The much revered and reputed father of modern economics, Adam Smith, lived during a time (eighteenth century) when class differences and accompanying conflict was commonplace, and the economic realities of "workers" and "masters" only exacerbated the struggle. "Those who live by profit" are "an order of men, whose interest is never the same with that of the public, who have generally an interest to deceive and even oppress the public."[1] The fact that some Americans actually consider class warfare to be a societal aberration speaks of America's strong egalitarian roots.

Although not forgotten, the concept of the common good certainly doesn't get the attention that it used to. It's been much more in vogue—for two generations—to speak of individual freedoms and liberties. We have good reason to speak of personal rights; they are one of the vestiges of the civil rights movement, wrested from an era that knew and practiced a common good, yet one generally only for white males. And so the pendulum continues to swing. For a society that has known common good from its very beginnings centuries ago but has wrestled with what that means for its indigenous inhabitants, its slaves, its immigrants, its ethnic minorities, its women, its children, and others, this is a conversation that needs to be continually renewed and understood from all possible perspectives. Robert

Bellah, Maya Angelou, Vine Deloria Jr., Robert Putnam, Parker Palmer, and many others have kept it alive in the last decades; this work joins that conversation from a perspective that blends history, economics, religion, sociology, and philosophy.

I confess to being a practitioner and not a scholar; this work is consequently intended for a general audience. Working as a minister for more than twenty years in Texas and Latin America has given me a good glimpse into the issues dealt with in this book: inequality, poverty, and justice. Other issues, such as greed and polemicization, are topics that are currently contested by politicians and citizens and will be for the foreseeable time to come. Ours is a religious society—*religious* defined as "the search for meaning" (world religion historian Huston Smith, among others)—that for generations now has found its meaning in commerce. For better and for worse, the confluence of commerce, materialism, and consumerism undergird *market fundamentalism,* the true defining American religion. (Chapters 4 and 5 will extensively discuss this position.) Call it the American Dream, or describe it in the way a friend recently did: "America is held together by a desire to acquire more things, to get ahead." This common creed has positive and redeeming social traits, but when lines are crossed and accumulation is excessive and extreme, the common good is compromised. Again, how can we live together, balancing freedoms and limits, for the good of society and for the betterment of the world?

This book challenges one answer to this question, the stock answer that defends unfettered capitalism: Individuals acting in self-interest promote the best interests of a society. (Again, critique does not mean rejection.) This understanding has been a guiding light in capitalism's continued development for more than two hundred years; it is accepted as generally true. However, it is not absolutely true for all times and all situations. For example, criminals (corporate or individual actors) operate in their own self-interest; the majority of us would agree that criminal activity is contrary to the best interests of a society. Some forms of self-interest do need regulation; the best option for such regulation is that of the personal variety—that is, self-control! But do individuals interpret self-control differently? Of course they do. Consequently, we live with communal agreements (spoken and unspoken), social contracts, and laws. Freedoms are limited; unlimited freedom is a fallacy in most areas of life. Life is shared communally; no one lives in a vacuum where his or her actions are of no consequence to anyone else.

Driving a car on the freeway entails freedoms, limitations, and self-interest. Freedoms are enjoyed simply by being able to travel the route of one's choosing from one place to another. But infinite choices of routes to one's destination do not exist, and cars are best driven where roads have already been constructed.

Freedom is balanced by limitation. Self-interest serves all drivers sharing the road; we rightly assume most everybody is planning to arrive at their destination in an efficient manner: driving at an accepted speed for the particular road, not crashing their car into another car, and so forth. The rules and expectations of the road are commonly agreed upon; furthermore, some of those rules are enforced by civil authorities—police and sheriff's deputies. There are many other common expectations, of course, such as acceptable driving habits and proper working conditions of vehicles. When all drive according to the rules, freeways work wonderfully well for our individual and communal transportation goals, with their rightful mix of liberties and restrictions.

But every so often, there are motorists who don't drive by the rules. Whether they aren't obeying traffic lights or they are speeding excessively (barring cases of emergency), they drive with the "freedom" of doing what they please. Their motivations to do so can range from plain carelessness to rigid ideology. They *can do* what they are doing; it's risky, but it can be done. But they do so to the detriment of everyone else sharing the road. This type of behavior writ large and what it does to our society is the purpose of this book. Our freeways are arenas of human social contract, and so are the arenas of economics, politics, and markets. How banks, investment firms, and other businesses operate is part of the contract, because the actions within and of those organizations affect how society gets along. We all are truly in this together, for better or for worse.

We live in a time when the concept of freedom is championed. This book will do some of that, but from an entirely different direction than what is most typically current. Beside the freedom from unjust authority or rule, there are also the freedoms of being liberated from wants and unhelpful desires, along with the freedoms of choosing the best interests of others or the society. And yes, just like other choices, these choices are not necessarily without hazards. Guidelines and markers, individually and communally negotiated, help us do what's best for the common good.

The familiar phrase "All things in moderation" is the proper ying to excess's yang. In a sense, excess and moderation are complementary opposites. Stated as such, we understand excess, like moderation, to have good and bad qualities, at one and the same time. One or the other is not wholly evil or wholly good. The two concepts rely upon each other as if they were two parts of the same system. One part—excess—has taken for the last thirty-five years its greater portion in that shared system. A destructive societal inequality has been one result of that imbalance. Nobel Prize–winner Muhammad Yunus states that the social ill of poverty belongs "in a museum" alongside other vestiges of antiquity, such as slavery, racism, and sexism (unfortunately, which still have some vitality today).[2] This book serves to join the chorus through the ages that says great economic disparities are unacceptable; it's especially true in this day and age of advanced human endeavor. I am not arguing for economic equality—the equal distribution of resources and goods—which is unrealistic and untenable. I am lifting up the idea that *economic democracy*—a newer term, but solidly within the American canon of ideas related to egalitarianism and opportunity—be examined and advocated. We don't have to live in a society where the rich get richer by design and boast more political power in the wake of their good fortune. This type of status quo, going strong for some thirty-five years now, has once again become unacceptable. We've seen it before in the Gilded Age and during the 1920s, the latter manifestation eventually bringing on the Great Depression. It's time for the pendulum to swing in the opposite direction. The supposed new god of excess has had a long enough run; it's time for the common good, based in egalitarianism, to once again flourish.

CHAPTER 1

ROCKEFELLER AND THE NEW PERMISSION

When John D. Rockefeller Sr. retired from the helm of Standard Oil in 1913, he had accumulated a fortune of $1 billion.[1] His wealth stood apart from that of peers Carnegie, Gould, and Morgan. Not only was he significantly wealthier than his contemporaries but he also had attained more wealth than predecessors Vanderbilt, Astor, and Girard. By the early part of the twentieth century, Rockefeller was the wealthiest person the world had ever known.* Legend has it that around this time Rockefeller was asked the following question about wealth accumulation: "How much is enough?" His reputed answer: "Just a little bit more."

Without question, Rockefeller was incredibly focused, innovative, and relentless as a worker and business titan. Standard Oil, its development and domination of its field, stands out as a progenitor of a new era in world events. Where did Rockefeller get his drive and determination that fueled his desire to attain "just a little bit more"?

Rockefeller, Carnegie, Gould, and Morgan

John Rockefeller's father is one of the more interesting characters revealed in the history of public Americans. William "Big Bill" Rockefeller (he stood close to six feet tall, which was quite rare in the mid-1800s) was a confidence man who lived a double life for most of his adult years. As a teenager in New York State, he would drift from town to town posing as a deaf-mute, communicating his deception with the help of chalk and a small slate. He sold cheap novelty items, and preyed on townspeople's sympathies for monetary gain. Like a Ponzi schemer, his ruse required him to exploit wider and wider territory, lest he be recognized by one previously beguiled. John Rockefeller's biographer Ron Chernow writes bluntly about Big Bill: "Throughout his life, he expended considerable energy on tricks and schemes to avoid plain hard work."[2] In his own way, Bill was just as relentless as his first-born son would turn out to be.

---

* It could be argued that the House of Rothschild, mid-nineteenth century Europe, controlled more wealth than Rockefeller. The Rothschild dynasty, however, consisted of a father and his five sons.

Big Bill married Eliza Davison in 1837—apparently he saw Eliza's father, John, as someone who had extractable cash. John Davison was to give Eliza $500 when she married. In order to marry Eliza, Big Bill broke off his engagement to a Nancy Brown (who worked as Bill's housekeeper), a relationship that had no promise of remuneration. John D. Rockefeller was born to Big Bill and Eliza in 1839; he followed the birth of sister Lucy and preceded the birth of four siblings. Big Bill, however, was not content to have left Nancy Brown jilted. She continued to work as a housekeeper in Bill and Eliza's humble home and bore Bill two daughters, their births sandwiching the birth of John D. At the birth of the second illegitimate daughter to Nancy Brown, Eliza's family intervened on her behalf and forced Big Bill to put Nancy Brown and the two daughters out of the house.*

Big Bill then began a pattern that would define his marriage to Eliza for the next two decades. He abandoned her for months at a time, returning in due season to provide for her and the children. The Rockefellers were not poor, and Big Bill did an admirable job providing for his growing family. Yet they themselves and all others who knew the family were completely unaware how he secured the greater portion of his income.

"Doc" Bill Levingston was Big Bill's alter ego when he left the environs of his family life with Eliza and their children. Levingston was a traveling physician, selling pills, potions, and the requisite snake oil. Not only that, he met a young woman, Margaret Allen, whom he married. The bigamous relationship was unknown to both Margaret and Eliza. Big Bill would eventually leave Eliza for good, and he managed to keep his double life hidden to most members of both families for decades. One great irony of Big Bill's life in his later years is that he was not able to tell his "patients" about his rich son lest his ruse be exposed.

When a teenager, and as the oldest son, John D. was responsible for maintenance of the family house and farming their land due to Big Bill's wanderlust. Being a quite sober lad, he seemed to handle the additional burden very well, while pining for the opportunity to strike out on his own (and to be liberated from his father's vagaries). Rockefeller attended school until he was sixteen, at which time he left the household to live and work in Cleveland, Ohio. It was there that Rockefeller began his ascendancy in work and business that continually gathered momentum. His was a driven success from early on. Father and son were significantly different in character and practice, yet they shared a relentlessness to achieve and strive for that which was within reach, whether by

---

* Nancy Brown would eventually marry, bear other children, and provide for a respectable upbringing for her two daughters fathered by Bill Rockefeller (Chernow, 8–10).

hook or crook (father) or by plain hard work (son), outdistancing and outsmarting their competitors. For both, money was the prize.

John D. was brought up as a Baptist, albeit a strain of the denomination that emphasized moral rectitude for a transformed world (more so than for heavenly rewards). Toward the end of his life, Rockefeller explained to interviewer William Inglis, "I was trained from the beginning to work and save. I have always regarded it as a religious duty to get all I could honorably and give all I could."[3] His vocational attributes of thrift, reliability, and honesty were by-products of his religious upbringing.* Accumulating wealth was not frowned upon as long as it did not lead toward pompous and garish display and a miserly attitude in Christian charity. Rockefeller would live faithfully by these demands.

His first job, in 1855, at age sixteen, was as an assistant bookkeeper at a dry goods firm in Cleveland. Rockefeller had a great gift for organization and financial management. Having helped his mother with household management and balancing the family ledger book, Rockefeller's orientation to detail and affinity for structure suitably served him in his new world of formal employment. Ledger books were almost sacred for Rockefeller; he was not confused by them and understood their meaning at a glance. As long as they were honestly prepared, ledgers were brutally revealing for a business, exposing inefficiencies and uplifting achievement and accomplishment. Rockefeller came to work early and sometimes left as late as 10:00 p.m. (the early mornings and late nights dully lit by whale-oil lamps). Yet he loved his new environment; he was energized and liberated by it, and his self-identity was befittingly established. His attraction to numbers led him to other duties at the firm, including the collection of delinquent accounts, at which he was adept. The experiences in his first job guided the rest of his working days; the early Rockefeller—ardent, efficient, and hard working— had much in common with the later colossus Rockefeller.[4]

Recall that at this time in the United States there was much clamor, opportunity, and struggle to make one's fortune. The year 1848 saw the advent of the California gold rush—which Mark Twain declared to be the event that brought about a new era of money worship in American society. A decade later, Pennsylvania would be awash in a darker and stickier gold as oil was discovered and another mad rush was spawned. Then the bloody Civil War, beginning in 1861, gave occasion for the opportunistic to profit via weaponry, food and provision supply, and uniforms. Historian Niall Ferguson points out that because of America's unique history of conquest and westward expansion, the American spirit of entrepreneurship has

---

* His sense of honesty was questioned later on in his life, especially during antitrust investigations.

always been robust, even and especially after failure. Natural-born risk takers have had favor and encouragement for creating new businesses and not being ruined by past failures.[5] The Bankruptcy Act of 1841 was the first law of its kind to establish voluntary bankruptcy, a historical shift that helped to bring an end to age-old reprisals such as debtors' prison. Debtors' and creditors' rights were now squarely balanced against each other as never before.[6] In nineteenth century America, expansion, battle, and fortuity combined to reward those who saw success and risk to be two equal sides of the same coin. The value placed on the growth of commerce, small and large scale, was worth the risks inherent to it. The ability to walk away from debts and start all over again helped to settle the vast American frontier.

Andrew Carnegie, born in Scotland in 1835, some four years before Rockefeller, immigrated with his family to Pittsburgh in 1848. Carnegie was said to be a tireless bundle of energy who worked hard on Americanizing his accent and grammar. His work experience as a teenager and an adult was boundless, from clerking to telegraphy to railroads to bridge building to oil to steel. His is the classic American tale of rags to riches. His mother, Margaret, imparted to her son the unfailing desire to work, to avoid shameful poverty, and the ambition to dominate within the working environment. Carnegie did not marry until he was fifty-one, only months after the death of his beloved and commanding mother.

Carnegie, not unlike many human beings, was beset with public and personal contradictions. His legacy is well known today for many excellent philanthropic pursuits: libraries, music and performance halls, and educational facilities, all still alive and vigorous generations past his death. Yet, his treatment of workers (the deadly Homestead Strike of 1892 as prime example), conniving of associates, and propensity to lie in order to personally profit paint a gloomier portrait of the man.[7]

Jay Gould was diminutive—barely five feet tall—and did not boast of physical strength. His ambitious mind, however, made up for any physical shortcomings. Born in 1836 as the only brother to five older sisters, Gould was on his own by his thirteenth birthday in rural New York State. Like Carnegie, the young Gould was skilled enough to carry out a diverse set of tasks to survive: bookkeeping, surveying, writing, and tanning. Gould suffered periods of overwork throughout his life, which coincided with poor physical health. Upon marriage in 1863 to Helen Miller, the daughter of a prominent New York merchant, Gould bought into a small New York railroad. His fortunes grew from that transaction, yet he suffered a number of financial setbacks, all due to his fearlessness toward risk. More than anything else, Gould was a skilled manipulator and speculator of stocks and bonds—a financial technician who worked in gold, wheat, railroads, and telegraphy. Bribery was part of his handbook; he had a bigger yacht than J. P. Morgan, but Gould's was not admitted to the New York Yacht Club because of his robber baron reputation.[8]

John Pierpont (J. P.) Morgan, unlike Gould, commanded great respect in various sectors of society. He was not nearly as wealthy as Rockefeller, Carnegie, or Gould; he essentially continued on the vocational path set out by his father, albeit on a much grander scale. Morgan was born in 1837 in Connecticut; unlike his three aforementioned peers, he was connected. His grandfather was a founder of Aetna Insurance Company; his father, Junius Morgan, was a prominent banker, midcentury, working in London. John Pierpont represented his father's firm in New York, and in 1871 J. P. partnered with Anthony Drexel to establish his own firm. By 1895 the banking firm was in his name exclusively, and his reputation was firmly settled nationally as he orchestrated bailouts on behalf of the US government during the gold panic of 1895 and the stock market panic of 1907. (The US Federal Reserve System was established in 1913, in part out of unfavorable reaction to the perceived power that Morgan, a private citizen, held on the national scale.)

Morgan possessed an incredibly intimidating presence. Broad shouldered and fearsome of face, with a large, purple nose (due to rosacea, a skin disease that can result in the enlargement of the nose), Morgan insisted that all his professional portraits be retouched. He was quite capable of putting in twelve- to fifteen-hour workdays, his personal workplace authority matching that of his physical ubiquity. While the three aforementioned peers reveled in the competitive possibilities available to the capitalistically favored, Morgan was weary of the "ruinous destructiveness" characteristic to the market system. Morgan tired of the "bitter, destructive competition" that would lead to "demoralization and ruin" for those involved, who depended upon business success to care for and feed their families.[9] While he did openly donate to charities, churches, hospitals, and schools, Morgan did not leave a grand legacy of philanthropy. Rockefeller and Carnegie significantly outdistanced him in benevolence.

Rockefeller changed the world not only by his business acumen and monetary accumulation, but by giving the world a new permission. According to historian Charles Morris, before the Civil War, outside the Deep South, Americans had more goods and more food equitably distributed than any other society in the history of the civilized world.[10] Whereas Europe was still defined by staid hierarchy—elite status conveyed by patrimony—and its grandiose cathedrals, America lent status to its citizens by the degree of their labor and acquisition. The pauper was not constrained in the New World as he would have been in the old. Rockefeller,

Carnegie, Gould, and Morgan were the main protagonists of the Gilded Age, an epoch of previously unimagined growth, capital formation, and advancements that would foster further material gains for both privileged and working classes. As to how equitable the distribution of these gains was, Rockefeller and his peers helped to forge a new permission toward grand inequalities also previously unimagined.

Creating the Middle

Throughout history there have been the supremely and emphatically wealthy, living in the midst of the poor. Grand inequalities, of course, were not a novel creation in the new era brought about by Rockefeller and his peers. King Croesus of Lydia (modern-day Turkey) was reputed to be of tremendous wealth; his governance is credited to be the first to make and use coins (sixth century BCE). When he was put to death on a pyre by the invading king of Persia, legend says he cried out three times to Solon, the Greek poet and reformer, who had warned Croesus of the fickleness of wealth.[11] Marcus Crassus (115–53 BCE) is said to have been the wealthiest citizen of ancient Rome.* He commanded in the army and traded in slaves and land (he would purchase, on the cheap, sections of Rome as they burned, and then bring in firefighting brigades that would wall off the destruction). Trophies won in battle were another of his pursuits of acquisition; he died, however, in battle against the rival Parthians. Legend has it that his conquerors mockingly poured molten gold down the throat of his corpse to satiate his uncompromising desire for attaining more wealth.[12] The legend, of course, is dubious; yet it communicates a sense of the injustice that exists in some historical literature toward those whose accumulative holdings were almost beyond conceiving.

The travails of the economically poor are not well documented throughout recorded history. It was of much more interest and concern to chronicle the unique, wealthy, and powerful and their affairs, travails, and battles. Extremely wealthy individuals, along with Croesus and Crassus, have been present throughout history: Alan the Red (England, eleventh century), Musa I (Mali/Ghana, fourteenth century), Jacob Fugger (Germany, sixteenth century), Heshen (China, eighteenth century), among others. In the last 250 years, as mercantilism gave way to free trade–based economics, the tally of the exceedingly wealthy has

---

* Crassus's nickname was "Dives," the same legendary name given to the purposely unnamed wealthy character in the parable of the rich man and Lazarus in chapter 16 of Luke's Gospel in the Christian New Testament.

increased exponentially. Modernizing developments in Britain, Western Europe, and North America beginning in the early 1800s brought about a new era of credit creation and increased money supply. Niall Ferguson maintains that, in part, this financial revolution preceded the Industrial Revolution.[13]

Consequently, the quality of life experienced by a vast majority of earth's inhabitants today (and for the past two hundred years or so) is arguably much better than it ever has been.* Life expectancy, literacy, and food security for the majority have greatly improved. Eradication of certain diseases, increased biological knowledge, and greater understandings of the workings of the physical universe have made certain tasks of life much more manageable. Social gains for women and historically marginalized peoples have enabled many more to experience a fuller and more meaningful existence. And not only that, a new phrase began to be used around the 1850s, distinguishing a new class of people distinct from the privileged and working classes: the middle class.[14] This development preceded the Rockefeller era, yet Rockefeller and his peers helped to exacerbate its growth significantly.

God, Money, and Good

The evolution of Rockefeller's work and leadership in turn creating what would become the world's most powerful corporation is a fascinating study. The young Rockefeller slowly crept toward involvement in the oil craze that started in Titusville, Pennsylvania, in 1860. By 1863 Rockefeller had gotten into the refinery business as "a little side issue" in Cleveland, and by the end of the decade he had bought or squeezed out nearly all of his ample refinery competition in and around Cleveland. As previously mentioned, his ascendancy from that point was practically unimpeded.[15] Rockefeller made his fortune with Standard Oil selling kerosene (for lighting and heating purposes); gasoline would not become a Standard staple until the early 1900s when Rockefeller was essentially retired, his fortune compounding in voluminous holdings of Standard stock. (Thomas Edison's improved light bulb, thereby eliminating Standard's oil lamps, was finally practical and inexpensive enough for home use [in turn dependent upon newly built power stations] in the 1890s; and Henry Ford and other early carmakers did not see their new gasoline-powered engines become popular until 1905, thereby making gasoline, a mostly unused by-product of the refining process of oil, a newly significant commodity.)[16]

---

* Excluding, of course, bouts of slavery, child labor, and employment practices where working conditions have been overly harsh or deadly.

Rockefeller's business shrewdness, aided by fortunate timing, was enhanced by a piercing ruthlessness directed toward his competition. As is well documented, Rockefeller used several means, some legal and others not, to enhance his positions and holdings. Secret agreements with railroads for shipping advantages, the intentional placing of other names on subsidiary businesses to hide the fact that they were Standard holdings, and price undercutting actual competitors were the regular business tactics of Rockefeller and his loyal associates.[17] The need to win out over his competitors was paramount for Rockefeller;* the combination of human and divine will to carry out the mission was potent. "I believe the power to make money is a gift from God . . . I believe it is my duty to make money and still more money, and to use the money I make for the good of my fellow man according to the dictates of my conscience," Rockefeller exclaimed to a reporter. This quote helps to understand how Rockefeller was not fazed by the widening income gap that industrialization had brought about—it was all part of God's plan.[18]

Rockefeller's God talk was not religious babble or cover-up. He was deeply religious in thought and practice. He and his wife, Cettie, were faithful to the Erie (later changed to Euclid) Avenue Baptist Church, located in downtown Cleveland, for decades. A plain and humble congregation, it was not populated by the well-to-do, save the Rockefellers. Rockefeller taught a Bible class for adults and most likely covered a large portion of the annual budget with his regular offerings.[19]

When I was a graduate student in the Twin Cities (Minnesota) area, I joined a few classmates to make summer money working on a painting crew. One job had us painting the exterior of a two-story house in a fairly affluent suburb of St. Paul. Because we were seminary students, we sometimes entered into conversations with our clients about church affiliation and practice. The couple who owned the house was Baptist. Cresting middle age, their kids were grown and out of the house, yet the husband still worked. It was midday and midweek when we finished the painting job, so as we cleaned up, we conversed with the wife, who told us of her and her husband's commitment to God and their local congregation: they both sang in the choir and went to Bible class, and her husband served as an elder. So that we wouldn't get the wrong idea about her husband—God forbid he be a quaggy believer incapable of conquest—she informed us, with the squinted eyes of conviction, that he was the "best damn businessman you'd ever see." We understood: he was really good at making money. Faith in God and making as much money as possible were not oxymoronic for our patrons; it was the exact strain of Rockefeller's creed rearticulated most accurately a century later.

---

* Rockefeller occasionally overpaid when buying out competitors; attaining greater market share was worth the extra cost.

Rockefeller was, arguably, the best businessman the world had seen, using a strict definition of the term geared toward wealth generation. There is no question that he was also the best philanthropist the world had seen up to that time. He lived up to both parts of his creed, making as much money as possible and redistributing it as divinely commanded. Rockefeller gave away some $530 million in his lifetime (his son, John D. Rockefeller Jr. eventually gave away the same amount as had the foundation bearing the family name). The University of Chicago, the Johns Hopkins School of Public Hygiene and Public Health, the General Education Board (assisting education in the South, eradicating hookworm, and modernizing agricultural practices), the Rockefeller Institute for Medical Research,* the Rockefeller Foundation, and Spelman College were the main creations and recipients of his benevolence. There, of course, were many more. The development of Rockefeller's humanitarian efforts is one of evolution from parochial charity directed toward individuals to innovative advancement of research and programs, led by experts in their particular fields, affecting broad categories of peoples. A longtime Standard Oil associate and an ordained Baptist minister, Frederick Gates was instrumental in shepherding Rockefeller toward his seasoned views on how best to "make good." Essentially, Gates helped Rockefeller move from reactive benevolence, responding to individual requests, to proactive philanthropy, where greater focus is given to prevention rather than to relief.[20]

In 1889 Andrew Carnegie published an essay entitled "Wealth" (republished in the United Kingdom as "The Gospel of Wealth"). As previously mentioned, Carnegie dutifully embodied the saint and sinner dual nature congenital to most human beings. In that new era of greater available wealth, Carnegie strongly suggested that wealthy individuals donate large sums of money to worthy causes during their lifetimes so that their heirs would not frivolously waste their inheritances;** this course of action simultaneously allowed for the working classes to share in some economic benefits of the age. (Higher wages, of course, were not at the crux of the Carnegie credo; his steel plant workers routinely put in twelve-hour days, seven days a week.)[21]

Rockefeller was duly impressed with Carnegie's words and acknowledged Carnegie's influences in his own philanthropic efforts. While Rockefeller's devotion to family (he and Cettie had five children, one dying as an infant) would not allow him to abide by the same conviction toward familial inheritance as that of Carnegie, Rockefeller called on fellow tycoons (including Marshall Field

---

* Ironically, it helped to put quacks, like his father, out of business.
** Carnegie and his wife, Louise Whitfield Carnegie, had one daughter, Margaret. She served for many years as a trustee to the foundation bearing her father's name.

and Philip Armour in Chicago) to follow their philanthropic leads. However, if there was one thing Rockefeller and Gates disapproved of concerning Carnegie's efforts, it was the occasional display of vanity that accompanied his charitable gifts. Rockefeller and Gates wanted their own efforts to be free of any attachment to self-promotion; during his lifetime Rockefeller strongly insisted that any buildings constructed with his money not bear his name. Rockefeller, in his mature philanthropic development, was now mostly interested in getting to the root of problems. "If anything can be done to remove the causes which lead to the existence of beggars, then something deeper and broader and more worthwhile will have been accomplished."[22]

Gilded Age Plutocracy, Prosperity, and Poverty

The causes that lead to "the existence of beggars" and the forces creating grand disparities of wealth accumulation have been with us forever; they gained unforeseen momentum and grand sweep, however, when Rockefeller and his peers ruled their day. *Plutocracy* is a term that historically has meant "rule by the wealthy." The ancient Greeks coined the word *ploutos*, meaning "wealth," and *kratos,* meaning "to govern." Our modern-day usage of the term refers to the influence a wealthy minority has over the political arena in a society. It also can be indicated by the (high) concentration of assets accumulated by the wealthiest members in a society. Historian Kevin Phillips identifies the Gilded Age of Rockefeller, Carnegie, Gould, and Morgan as the first of America's plutocratic eras. He quotes the late American political scientist Samuel Huntington to describe the era: "Money becomes evil not when it is used to buy goods but when it is used to buy power . . . economic inequalities become evil when they are translated into political inequalities."[23]

When a broad brush is used to summarize early American history, the general perception is that new European arrivals desired to freely express their religious convictions. While there is ample truth in that statement, it doesn't tell the whole story. Particular colonies had religious allegiances (for example, Maryland was Catholic and Massachusetts was Puritan), and there was plenty of religious persecution to go around. Eventually, the desire for free religious expression was guaranteed in the Bill of Rights, under the First Amendment of the United States Constitution, where government is prohibited from establishing a state religion. Incidentally, a citizen's right to express no religion is also assumed in the First Amendment. Often overlooked today is that many of the pioneers arriving to the colonies, and later to the newly founded country, *sought escape from the economically stratified societies of their aristocratic European homelands.* Nobility, heredity, and tight class strictures were prevalent in their native lands; "America" somehow promised opportunity and egalitarianism. Historian Morris says that "America was the only country where 'worker' was a job description rather than a badge of class."[24] Outside the urbanized areas of New York, Philadelphia, and Boston, and the South with its plantation districts, it was generally true that American society avoided aristocratic European stratification with its own republican (rule by the people) institutions. Eighty percent of the population (in the 1830s) lived outside the big urban areas and the slave-holding regions; thus, the wealth concentration of the urban and plantation areas affected relatively fewer people than might be expected. The rich-poor gap was significantly less pronounced in the early American heartland where the majority resided.[25]

But this reality would soon change as the large cities continued to grow and as wealth creation and economic discrepancies were amplified. In 1850 the United States had some 150 to 200 millionaires; by the turn of the century there were 4,500.[26] The incredible growth and development of American manufacturing, ingenuity, and mechanization in the last half of the nineteenth century is unparalleled. It wasn't all hard work, sweat, and honest labor, however. The history of the railroad industry's rise is infamously peppered with graft, greed, and swindle—including government coaction and largesse. Even though the term itself was used rarely at the time, *social Darwinism* was alive and in the air.* The spirit of laissez-faire ("let it be") dominated economics and sociology. The progress of child labor laws, which had their origins in the industrial era, stalled during the last quarter of the nineteenth century. Government was less active interfering on the behalf of the downtrodden. "The survival of the fittest" held sway in a number of human relationships—labor, social, economic.[27]

The US Senate, at this time, was chosen by state legislatures. It consisted, as it does today, mostly of those who were financially well-to-do. Nelson Aldrich, who served thirty years for the state of Rhode Island, married into wealth and while in office amassed a fortune. He dutifully served the trusts (his daughter Abby married John Rockefeller Jr. in 1901), built a ninety-nine room chateau on seventy-five acres of prime shore along Narragansett Bay, and sailed a 200-foot yacht.** As his power grew and his critics took notice, he stood by his business and political credo "Deny nothing, explain nothing."[28] The journalist David Graham Phillips exposed some of Aldrich's unspoken corruptions and those of

---

* Darwin's *On the Origin of Species* was published in 1860. The term *social Darwinism* was first used in the late 1870s.
** Oil, sugar, steel, meatpacking, and tobacco were the prominent trusts.

his colleagues; not long thereafter the Seventeenth Amendment was ratified and senators were then elected directly by popular vote.

Phillips's exposé of corruption in high places was, of course, not an isolated work. Before Ida Tarbell famously exposed some of Rockefeller's merciless methods for profit, he was publically blasted by the writer Henry Demarest Lloyd, who called Rockefeller the "czar of plutocracy." Lloyd was a singular character: a preacher's son who married into riches; a lawyer, journalist, unabashed campaigner for social justice, and political activist called the "millionaire socialist." Lloyd occasionally was vulnerable to hyperbole in some of his rants, but he typically spoke with perceptive clarity.[29] "Liberty produces wealth, and wealth destroys liberty" from his book *Wealth Against Commonwealth* still commands contemplation and reflection from those who earnestly desire capitalism to do its utilitarian best.

Lloyd was among the first wave of the muckraking journalists and reformers of the late nineteenth and early twentieth centuries, reacting to the conditions of increasing disparity between rich and poor. Jacob Riis, documenting slum conditions in New York City, and Ida Wells, chronicling lynchings of African Americans, also used their writing skills to implement change in American society. Tarbell, Upton Sinclair, Frank Norris, Lincoln Steffens, Joseph Pulitzer, and others also raised protestations that unveiled to the public the new era of ruinous excess that suddenly had become status quo. The open and thriving economic atmosphere in an era when personal income was yet not taxed, coupled with the existence of few but nascent regulations upon business,* made for an environment that rewarded the aggressively avaricious (and the honest). Save for Union veterans from the Civil War, the American populace had no social safety nets; systems for "old age" pensions in Germany and Great Britain were embryonic.[30] Labor unions, in existence from the beginnings of the industrial era, were still in their younger stages of development, localized, and without much legal support. Economic liberty was good, but it needed supervision—desperately. That the revelations of the muckrakers and reformers were widely popular is no surprise; they struck a chord with the experience and suspicions of a public that quite often was on the short end of the bargain.

The underside of progress—poverty, disability, early death—was experienced by many of the first generation immigrants (and native-born Americans leaving rural areas seeking work) living in the now burgeoning urban areas of the Northeast

---

* The Sherman Antitrust Act of 1890, although widely popular upon passage, was not put into practice until the administration of Theodore Roosevelt, 1901-09.

and Midwest. The largest migration the world had known was in progress. From 1870 to 1900 the population of the United States almost doubled; the 1900 census records more than 76 million residents.[31] Cheap labor was plentiful and helped fuel the continued growth of factories and industries. It was a time of terrible upheaval for American families and communities; homelessness increased significantly, and multitudes of children were orphaned or half-orphaned as both husbands and wives abandoned their families. Yes, upward mobility was achieved by immigrants (as textbook surveys on American history convey to schoolchildren), but downward mobility was a most common reality as well—whether one was old, young, rich, or poor was no cause for immunity.[32]

While vast numbers suffered, many prospered. For residents and immigrants, but less so for recently freed slaves and their offspring, the societal roots of opportunism and egalitarianism were influential; they helped to foster the unique American talents of discovery, inventiveness, and improvement. Unsettled lands, available natural resources, and a common obsession to get ahead (sometimes by whatever means necessary) made for a brave new world that, in terms of production and consumption, was now pacing itself ahead of the old world of Europe.

Consumerism started in earnest in America in the 1870s. John Wanamaker's Grand Depot opened in Philadelphia in 1876. A converted railway station, it was arguably America's first department store. Seventy thousand people attended its grand opening—the majority of these were women as was the sales staff that attended them. Clothing, fabrics, sheets, pillowcases, household items, toiletries, and perfumes were showcased. Wanamaker had his vision set on the class of consumer newly coming to the fore in American society—the middle class. He guaranteed a cash refund on returns and catered to their values of thrift and austerity. Wanamaker's new conception for consumption anticipated a wave that has hardly abated since: consumer wants seemingly without limit.[33]

Chicagoan Aaron Montgomery Ward's catalog "Wish Book"—150 pages long by 1876—was a godsend to rural folk living anywhere within the tentacle reaches of the railroads emanating from Chicago; they could shop in the city, as it were, without having to leave their rural outposts. Ward also promised his customers satisfaction or their money returned, which endeared him to a skeptical clientele that bought from his business sight unseen. Richard Sears and Alvah Roebuck soon followed in Ward's wake with their own Chicago-based catalog of a "vast department store boiled down." The mail-order business was another unique and effective American innovation.[34]

"History had never seen an explosion of new products like that in the America of the 1880s and 1890s," writes historian Morris. The branding of national food products from meat (Armour) to cereal (Kellogg) to beer (Pabst) to flour (Pillsbury) to soda (Coca-Cola) coincided with the advent of national advertising. Other products, now more readily available, made life simpler as the turn of the century neared: Bissell carpet sweepers, Gillette safety razors, Levi work jeans, rubber boots, and zippers. Yet other products, newly available to the middle classes because of mass production, such as bicycles, sewing machines, and pianos, made life grander and less constricted. Middle-class parents, instead of sending their kids to work in the second industrial era's factories, now kept them in school. Leisure time was a new reality for quantities of youth, who would spend nickels at the corner soda fountain drugstore where they listened to new gramophone proto-jukeboxes, thanks again to the availability of electricity.* Not only were the privileged classes clamoring for and obtaining more things, but so were the middle classes, including their children.[35]

The proliferation of consumer goods and products made life better in many ways, but there was an accompanying downside: anxiety.[36] The tremendous growth in the complexity of American society—the highest of the upper classes attaining heretofore unimagined quantities of wealth, the creation and establishment of middle classes, and the abject conditions of squalor endured by many of the immigrant and urban poor—made for a population vulnerable to the worries of status and class: struggling for position and fighting to maintain it. Competition is good and can tend to bring out the best, but too much of it can crush and destroy. And grand inequalities are antithetical to the maintenance and progression of the common good.

It was precisely at this Gilded Age crest that Thorstein Veblen, an American economist and sociologist, wrote his yet influential book *The Theory of the Leisure Class* (1899). He coined the phrase "conspicuous consumption" to describe spending by the richest Americans to build up their own prestige and image. For Veblen, this wasn't progress—it was a return to the aristocracy and decadence of stratified Europe.[37] Furthermore, it helped to strengthen and perpetuate an atmosphere where people tended to *compare up* rather than down; the material ideal for one to attain resided in the class above. Certainly this desire did and still does inspire positive motivation for upward mobility, but it can also feed a consumerist urge that narrowly defines life satisfaction by the accumulation of material goods. Positional goods (yesterday's phonograph, today's iPhone) have their own practical uses and values, but they can also assign prestige and

---

* The availability of residential electricity would not be standard in American homes until the 1920s.

image relative to time and place, and unintentionally, anxiety, if they are used to differentiate oneself from others.

Historian Sven Beckert tells the story of a monied Gilded Age couple whose anxiety (and fear) compelled them to leave the country after their fancy costume ball caused a public outcry against their opulence. Lawyer Bradley Martin and his wife, Cornelia, hosted J. P. Morgan, John Jacob Astor IV, and other influential guests in February 1897 at the fairly new, thirteen-story Waldorf Hotel in New York City. The guests were instructed to dress as European nobility, kings and queens—monarchists, aristocrats, and plutocrats—on parade. Apprehensive even before the gala started, they hired Pinkerton guards to surround the hotel to protect themselves and their guests against "men with socialistic tendencies." The tension of projecting an aura of upper-class privilege in a society yet nominally egalitarian was too much for the Martins; after the party, they left to live in England, evacuating to escape further conflict and criticism. England was the logical choice for the Martins; they owned another home there.[38]

A generation or so before Rockefeller, Stephen Girard and John Astor were the wealthiest Americans. Historian Kevin Phillips has charted the fortunes of America's wealthiest as compared to the median family income at particular points in time. Girard (1830) and Astor (1848) held fortunes 17,000 to 1 and 50,000 to 1 greater, respectively, than the median family income of those particular years. Rockefeller's ratio, in 1912, was an astounding 1,250,000 to 1. (According to Phillips, only Bill Gates's ratio of 1,416,000 to 1, in 1999, has surpassed Rockefeller's.)[39] The time had come when too much was enough, with the common good under attack like never before. The muckrakers and reformers in their continual calls for change enlisted the middle classes and others to their crusade, and a shared cause was created in what we now call the Progressive movement.

The Federal Income Tax: Government versus Big Business

The *Mayflower*, blown off course to the north by the onset of Atlantic Ocean winter weather in 1620, dropped anchor in Cape Cod in November. The arduous passage followed by a harsh winter killed off half of the 102 passengers; "God's good providence" (the description of *Mayflower* leader Edward Winslow), in the form of stashes of maize found in nearby Indian habitations and burial sites temporarily abandoned for the winter season ensured survival for the rest. Whether one calls it stealing or survival, the unintended generosity of the indigenous peoples saved the Pilgrims during their first winter on new land.[40] These pilgrims, adherents to the Church of England and King James, were Puritan separatists seeking religious freedom not from the crown but from the dominant political group within their common church (the separatists wanted less Roman Catholic influence in the Church of England).* Upon their arrival, the journeyers signed a covenant that was to serve as a guide for their communal life. Summarized, it said they voyaged to new land to establish "a civil body politic" including "just and equal laws . . . for the general good of the colony." The Mayflower Compact was signed as the ship harbored offshore of today's Provincetown, Massachusetts; the general good was the common good.

On August 20, 1907, President Theodore Roosevelt was invited to Provincetown to lay the cornerstone for the Pilgrim Monument, commemorating the *Mayflower* Pilgrims' first landing in the New World. This was the occasion on which the president laid blame for the country's financial woes upon "malefactors of great wealth." In the buildup to the Panic of 1907, Roosevelt drew a line between republicanism and plutocracy: "I regard this contest as one to determine who shall rule this free country—the people through their governmental agents, or a few ruthless and domineering men whose wealth makes them peculiarly formidable because they hide behind the breastworks of corporate organization."[41] The Progressive movement, ongoing for some two decades by this point, was now hitting its stride; the pendulum was swinging back in the other direction as societal change proliferated.

The movement was a culmination of various forces: civic, religious, and scientific. Women's suffrage, temperance, governmental reform, and medical and engineering modernization were all Progressive agenda items, as was the rejection of surfeit advantage and profit for the excessively well-to-do, which the socially Darwinist Gilded Age had produced.

The goals of the Progressive movement were in line with what had been agreed upon by the Pilgrim antecedents some three hundred years earlier: just and equal opportunity for the *common good*. (Certainly, some achievements of the era were overreaching and resulted in unintended complications, the clearest example being Prohibition.) Again, while the aspect of religious freedom is continually (and correctly) emphasized in review of early American development, the aspect of freedom from economic tyranny must also be equally remembered and underscored. A great measure of the Progressive movement was a recovery of this egalitarian aspect of the American way.

---

* King Henry VIII, in 1534, established the Church of England separate from the Roman Catholic Church as the result of Pope Clement VII refusing to annul the first of his eventual six marriages.

Teddy Roosevelt himself was among the American citizens of his day who had significant wealth. That distinctiveness, however, did not keep him from seeing society with a sense of parity. And while his rhetoric as a politician was often fiercer than his actions, he was a committed reformist. He was obsessed with fairness; his concept of "square deal" was evident in his efforts to head off conflict between labor and ownership, to forge agreements with opponents within his own political party, and to protect the welfare of society and nature against the machinations of big business. In 1903, two years into his presidency, Roosevelt was in the midst of a late spring tour of Rocky Mountain country when he arrived in Butte, Montana, and found himself thrust into the middle of a labor dispute at the mining city. In a memorable speech, Roosevelt prevailed upon the warring sides to work out their differences, using the two words—square deal—that he would subsequently use again and again. He left the copper and silver hub with three gifts: a silvered-copper vase and a silver loving cup from the belligerents, and a pair of silver scales of justice from the minority blacks who also worked the mines. Roosevelt cherished the silver scales; they beautifully symbolized his doctrine of square deal and reminded him of the place where he had coined the phrase that would endure as one of his principal legacies.[42]

Roosevelt drew on his sense of balance and fairness as he presided over a country in the midst of political storms brought about by the abuses and inequalities of the day. Socialism, anarchism, and other political options were bandied about by reputable principals (DuBois, Debs, Goldman); Roosevelt was most interested in fixing the excesses of capitalism for its own good, which, among other things, provided a hedge against political extremism.

As a younger man serving in the New York State legislature, Roosevelt exhibited reformist tendencies, but at times they resulted from less charitable considerations. In 1882 twenty-five Democratic members of Irish ancestry served on the other side of the aisle from Roosevelt and his fellow Republicans. One of them, "Big John" McManus, was particularly distasteful to Roosevelt. McManus was a saloon owner, and saloons often served as the pivot point for urban political machines. The politically and socially corrupt culture Roosevelt and his colleagues witnessed in the saloons was antithetical to their reformist tendencies and more refined tastes. Roosevelt described McManus as "unutterably coarse and low," and once chased off the larger man, threatening to "kick [him] in the balls."[43] The future "trust buster" was obviously adept at busting more than trusts.

For those of us living in these post-Prohibition generations, we might catch ourselves wondering how in the world did the Eighteenth Amendment see the light of day, much less hang on for some fourteen years? Historian Daniel Okrent explains that a number of forces gathered in the first two decades of the 1900s, perfect storm–style, to bring about Prohibition: the temperance movement, women's suffrage, growing momentum for a federal income tax, racism, and World War I.[44] Teddy Roosevelt was not a "dry," but he was a Progressive. Progressives saw what alcohol (much of it paid for and quaffed at saloons) did to workers and their families; it destroyed them and put the lives of their families in peril and into poverty. "When the laboring man works eight hours and spends none of his time at the saloon, he will save up more money and better his economic status," wrote renowned Kansas newspaper editor William Allen White. "When the workingman spends his evenings at home or at the library, and has good books and a gramophone and an automobile, society will be better off."[45] White, an early twentieth-century Progressive to the core, spoke for millions of his fellow Americans who wanted a better society (on their own terms, of course). Prohibition started in 1919. The pendulum, slow and steady, continued to swing in a new direction.

For many years the women's suffrage movement stood firmly upon its own merits and goals, yet it was buttressed significantly, after the turn of the century, by the temperance movement. Many women (and men) wanted saloons to be regulated if not closed down entirely, and they were ready to vote for politicians who agreed with them. Besides hoping to reduce family and social destructiveness caused by alcohol,* they shared other common goals as well: basic improvements in health and hygiene, reductions in crime, and reduction in prison and poorhouse populations. A pragmatic synergy emerged between the two movements that helped carry each to approved legal status.

The emergence of the federal income tax (Sixteenth Amendment, 1913) paved the way for the government to eventually shut down the fifth largest industry in the land: the producers of beer, wine, and hard liquor. The taxes on their products accounted for close to 30 percent of all federal revenue in 1910.[46] Yet the success and efficacy of the new tax revenue stream cleared the way for Prohibition, even with the country's foray into World War I. The Progressives were having their day, and their reach was extensive.

When Democrat Woodrow Wilson, a reformist in the spirit of Teddy Roosevelt, was into the second term of his presidency, the country's approaching entry into World War I necessitated further advancement of the new tax code. The new federal income tax was highly progressive; in 1918 only 15 percent of

---

* The Ku Klux Klan was also in favor of Prohibition, as were most southern states. That the despised black man could no longer procure alcohol meant fewer abuses and rapes of white women, according to their point of view.

American families paid personal federal taxes, with the wealthiest 1 percent paying 80 percent of all revenues collected. Economic historian W. Elliot Brownlee claims that Wilson and his Treasury Secretary, William McAdoo, "embraced taxation as an important means to achieve social justice according to the humanistic ideals of the early republic." That meant taxing the very wealthy first and foremost, since they had the "ability to pay"; it was Wilson's way of guiding the country on a middle course between socialism and unmediated capitalism.[47] Even so, the social milieu continued to be one where alternative political and economic options were being espoused; Wilson, like Roosevelt before him, strove to move the country toward a capitalist, shared common good that would help mitigate the forces of political extremism.

The wealthiest Americans—business leaders especially—responded to the revised tax code with outrage. They fought government's growth (a result of the power and implementation of taxation) and the accompanying potential to restore and keep alive the egalitarian ideals of the society's earlier days. At this point in the country's political history, the Democratic Party had a strong tradition of representing the disadvantaged, exhibiting hostility to special privilege (as represented by accumulated wealth) and opposition to taxation based on consumption. Republicans, on the other hand, championed reduced taxes and called for less government interference in business—and rode those ideals to clear-cut victories in the 1918 elections.[48] Two years later, Republican Warren Harding was elected to the nation's highest office and Andrew Mellon, one of the wealthiest of Americans, was appointed secretary of the treasury. This change of leadership, after twenty years of Progressive Era political power, brought about significant revisions. Mellon advocated that reduced taxes, especially for the wealthy and corporations, were needed to further economic expansion and increase prosperity.[49]

He was right—for the wealthiest of Americans. Tax rates fell throughout the 1920s, and the wealth gap between the very richest and the rest of Americans grew exponentially.[50] Plutocracy was reborn; a generation after it had crested and was felled by Progressivism, it was back. Historian Frederick Lewis Allen had a special name for the period of 1923–1929: "the seven fat years."[51] He saw Mellon as the dominant figure of that day; banker and industrialist, Mellon held the post of treasury secretary from 1921 to 1932. Only a loyal family member, expecting a choice inheritance, could have claimed that Mellon was not guilty of conflict of interest. Mellon was the third wealthiest American after Rockefeller and Henry Ford.[52] In January 1932 impeachment hearings were held against Mellon; he was accused of corruption, granting illegal tax refunds, and favoring his own business interests in Treasury decisions. He resigned the very next month, before a vote was taken on the proceedings.[53]

"Throughout the seven fat years, business—and especially financial business—was king. The overwhelming majority of the American people believed with increasing certainty that business men knew better than anybody else what was good for the country, and that government had better keep its hands off their affairs and thus permit economic nature to take its course."[54] These are the words of Allen, written in 1935 from the other side of the Great Crash, which had started in October 1929. Reading Allen today, on the other side of the financial blowout of 2008, is like reading critical commentary on our own time. Allen talks about numerous issues we are currently very familiar with: national and state capitals thick with lobbyists advocating support for bills to increase their own profits by restricting competitors; publically appointed regulators who have little interest in enforcement; newspapers with friendly attitudes toward business and finance executives; and the adulation of Wall Street by political and business leaders.[55]

The emergence of Wall Street as the preeminent financial district in the country (and later to rival London) dates back to the late 1860s and early 1870s. Private banks, trust companies, and brokerage firms proliferated in the years immediately following the resolution of the Civil War. Life insurance business burgeoned as well. In the 1880s and 1890s, a number of industrial and business titans, including Rockefeller, Armour, and Carnegie, moved their headquarters to Manhattan.[56] By the turn of the century, J. P. Morgan's buyout of Carnegie Steel served as the bellwether merger transaction among hundreds in the ten years between 1895 and 1904, financed in large measure by Wall Street. The panic of 1907 notwithstanding, the number of individual investors from 1900 to 1910 using the exchanges and firms of Wall Street almost doubled, growing from 4.4 million to 7.4 million.[57] Wall Street was ascendant, but its growth and popularity attracted the beginnings of a watchful eye from Washington. Rockefeller had to answer to a federal subpoena in 1907, the Supreme Court ordered the monopolistic trusts of Standard Oil and American Tobacco to break up in 1911, and Morgan sat before the Pujo Committee that had been charged with investigating the money trusts in 1912. The struggle was on—who determined and controlled the nation's present movements and future destinies: corporate big business conglomerated in Manhattan or the federal government?

Establishing a permanent federal income tax was, in part, the government's way of wresting control over big business. There had been income tax collection previously in the country's history, during the Civil War, but it was phased out a few years after the war ended. Property had been taxed, without cessation, since the colonial era. In addition to property taxes, revenues principally came from consumption: excise taxes on domestic items (alcohol, for example) and tariffs on imported goods. Part of the Progressive Era philosophy was that consumption taxes hurt the poor and favored the wealthy; an income tax—especially a progressive one (the greater the income the greater the tax rate) focused on the wealthy's ability to pay—would favor the middle and lower classes. Furthermore, a progressive federal income tax would punish and discourage monopolistic power and recover the egalitarian values of the early republic.[58]

The Revenue Act of 1916 imposed increased personal and corporate income taxes, excess business profits tax, and the country's first federally imposed estate tax.* President Wilson's infamous overreach prior to the midterm elections of 1918 (essentially, "Vote in a Democratic majority in both houses or Germany is aided") backfired, and a Republican majority was achieved in both chambers of Congress. The end of World War I, coming after the elections in November 1918, added to the momentum that eventually brought the Progressive Era to its end. The war, which lasted four years, required only a year and a half of US military involvement. US financial involvement, on the other hand, absolutely crucial to Allied victory, was unequivocal from beginning to end. While much of Europe laid waste and in need of renovation, the United States' homeland was unscathed and its financial coffers, from loans privately and publically made during the war to Europe, were overflowing. Among the United States, France, Germany, and the United Kingdom, the United States held some 75 percent of aggregate gold reserves, more than double the amount before the war. Working out debt payments and reparations agreements, even with or, better, *because of* the Treaty of Versailles, was laborious and slow. In 1922 Andrew Mellon led a newly appointed World War Foreign Debt Commission, deputized by the US Congress to play hardball with the Europeans. Newspapers in Europe began to call Uncle Sam by a new name: Uncle Shylock. Andrew Bonar Law, British prime minister who lost two of his sons in the war, was incensed at the American rigidity and accused the war profiteers of worshiping "God Almighty Dollar."[59]

The Raging Bull of the 1920s: The Rich Get Richer

As previously mentioned, Mark Twain called the California gold rush the watershed moment in American history, when the pursuit of wealth became the newly ordained credo of the land. The following words, written primarily

---

* Following the reasoning of no less than Thomas Jefferson, progressive estate taxes were enacted as a way for the "abolition of hereditary distinctions and privileges" (Brownlee, 48).

about the notoriously corrupt New York politician "Boss" Tweed, indict a society moving farther away from its egalitarian origins.

> What is the chief end of man?—to get rich. In what way?—
> dishonestly if we can; honestly if we must. Who is God, the
> one only and true? Money is God. Gold and Greenbacks and
> Stock—father, son, and the ghost of same, three persons in one;
> these are the true and only God, mighty and supreme . . . [60]

Twain, of course, was not atheistic toward the religious pursuit he describes. His own financial foibles, including bankruptcy, however, didn't spoil his pejorative evaluation of the developing spirit of the nation: the "pursuit of happiness" was more and more related to mammon, its pursuit and procurement.

While the Gilded Age saw a relative few live out and attain the credo, the 1920s witnessed to a movement that, although secular, was not unlike the Great Awakening revivals that had earlier swept the colonies and country. Within the money trust were the priests and prophets of the movement, New York City was the holy ground of the sacred pursuit, and Wall Street was the inner sanctum. We already saw the prolific increase of participants in Wall Street–based investment (or "speculation," for dissenters) in the '20s; one of the best-selling books (nonfiction) of the decade, *The Man Nobody Knows*, describes Jesus as a business genius who conquered the world with twelve men of questionable business acumen. Bruce Barton, the author, was an advertising executive. As had happened before in the history of this unique land and people, religion was yoked to business success and used as evidence that God was looking down on the proceedings with not only guidance but also approval.

For some, Wall Street's aura (as if religious) began to rival that of the church's (US church attendance waned in the 1920s),[61] as it gave adherents the assurance of confidence and control in the face of an uncertain future. The beneficent stock market would provide for the young and the elderly, and it would abolish the need for charity and end poverty. The promised land was within reach; God's plan was destined to be fulfilled. For a civilization dedicated to doing business—one (unlike certain European countries) that lacked a royal court, an established church, and staid hierarchies—the stock market stood over the landscape as the steeple calling and gathering the faithful to the temple in devoted adulation. To not be bullish on America's ascending market was akin to burning the flag; good Americans believed in the market and prosperity was the payoff.[62]

One gets the sense that this first ride of Wall Street's bonanza absolutely intoxicated those garnering the previously unrealized gains. The phrase *playing the market* comes from the 1920s; the stock market was now accessible to regular folk, as were the statistics of the national pastime. Understanding how a good baseball team worked by the numbers—pitchers having low ERAs, batters having high averages, and fielders having low error percentages—was akin to being able to manipulate (now no longer frowned upon) the market. "Management science," a product of the second industrial era, furnished the impression of mathematical sophistication to speculation, nay *investment*, in the stock market. "Players" were now encouraged to assess the worth of their holdings, not only on current book value but also on their prospects for future earnings.[63] The ticker tape parade, celebratory and American to the core, originated in New York—using the paper output from the Wall Street machines that printed out the joyous numbers signifying victory and prosperity.

The prosperity of the 1920s was real; one part of it was well earned (due to American ingenuity, inventiveness, and increased productivity) and benefited American workers: some larger corporations initiated pension, stock ownership, and profit-sharing plans for their employees.[64] Another part of the prosperity was simply good timing (the events of World War I shifting wealth to the United States from Europe). Yet another part needs to be added into the mix: overreach. Historian Steve Fraser describes three periods in American political history as moments of "crony capitalism": (1) the Gilded Age, (2) the 1920s, and (3) the period that started in the 1990s and continued on into the new century.

> The 1920s was that . . . era during which the government bent its efforts to serve the narrowest interests of the business classes, and especially its peak institutions. Crony capitalism implied more than mere corruption; or rather it raised corruption to the level of state policy, to a form of extra-legal mercantilism in which one could no longer easily tell the difference between the representation of a political constituency and the servicing of a corporate client.[65]

The Mellon tax cuts for the wealthy, easy credit (similar to the boom era of the 1990s–2000s), and increased consumption all contributed to inflate the economic bubble. Not all Americans were sharing in the prosperity, however. Worker wages, incredibly, in 1927–29 were only slightly higher than they were in 1919–20. Nearly all the increased profits—from efficiencies, mergers, and amplified productivity—were enriching the owner classes and stock market participants. For decades Wall Street had experienced the same rate of growth as the rest of the economy; now the Street was outpacing the gross national product by leaps and bounds. The raging bull market saw the Dow Jones average quadruple during the 1920s.[66]

Some Americans used access to easier credit (installment plans, mostly) to purchase products: cars, radios, electric irons, vacuum cleaners, washing machines, refrigerators. Other Americans were left out, however, and missed the rising tide entirely. One-fifth of the nation's citizens—many of those living in the South, in urban and industrial ghettos, in mining regions, and in some rural farming areas—lived in contemptible conditions. Poverty was just as rampant as prosperity. Stuart Chase's 1929 critique of the era, *Prosperity: Fact or Myth*, published just as the stock market began its descent, analyzed how the rising worker productivity of the decade, due in part to elimination of certain jobs, overrewarded the wealthy. "The dictators of destiny," according to Chase, were the businessmen of the 1920s. They replaced "the statesman, the priest and the philosopher as the creator of standards of ethics and behavior."[67] The true religion of the land—commerce—was pushing other venerations to the side. But the god that brightly offered prosperity in one hand had a dark offering in the other. The setup for the Great Crash was for the most part in place: speculative excesses carried out by the wealthy, and a greater supply of newly produced goods than underpaid Americans could afford in the long run.[68] Starting from the artificial heights attained by the end of the decade, the collapse would have significant downward momentum.

The Dow Jones average reached 381 in September 1929. By July 1932, it bottomed to 41. The overheated and top-heavy economy finally bubbled over and crashed. The fears a very few had about excess speculation in stocks, commodities, and real estate were finally and unfortunately realized. The era of New Economics, where stock prices had reached "what looks like a permanently high plateau," according to Yale economics professor Irving Fisher, turned out to be a complete sham. "Too much"—tax cuts for the wealthy, goods purchased on easy money by regular Americans, and speculation by Wall Street—was simply not sustainable. At the Crash, the wealthiest 1 percent of Americans had some 40 percent of overall US wealth, including 83 percent of the liquid wealth; and the top one-third of that 1 percent—40,000 people out of a national population of 120 million—held 30 percent of all U.S. savings. These figures of gross inequality would go unmatched for seven decades.[69]

New Permission

"Just a little bit more," whether actually verbalized by Rockefeller, well describes a strong social imprint in the United States vibrant since the turn of the twentieth century. The economic crashes that started in 1929 and 2008 have multiple commonalities, the most crucial being the excess trust, idolization, and pursuit of wealth. We all need money to get by—but when money becomes an end in itself, the common good, somehow, is diminished.

Rockefeller and those others who accumulated the vast sums of wealth never before realized in the maturing and developing society gave a *new permission* to leave the egalitarian foundations of American society behind. The strain of American thought that believed society was better off through the pursuit of individual gains, a society of the sum of individual goods, was further established, but with an important enhancement. The new permission further bolstered an idea that persists strongly in our day: great accumulations of wealth will eventually make all members of the society prosperous. Of course, debates about wealth distributions are age-old, but the new permission from the Gilded Age gave accumulation a renewed legitimacy. Unimaginable sums of wealth held by an individual were no longer an embarrassment or something to conceal; they were validation and proof of the virtues—hard work, efficiency, intelligence—now recognized as foundational to the world's leader of commerce, the United States of America.

But how much of a good thing is too much?

CHAPTER 2

GREED

The small Texas town of Pontotoc, geographically located as the bull's-eye of the state, has experienced its share of tough luck through the years. Formed as a community in 1878, Pontotoc was nearly wiped out nine years later by a typhoid outbreak. The local contamination was so severe that a new cemetery had to be established on the other side of the town—the town doctor suspected rotting corpses as the deadly contagion affecting the town's water table. But the community persevered; a private school soon educated more than 200 students from the surrounding area, and local producers traded in cotton, cattle hides, and pecans. Vibrancy, however, was fleeting for Pontotoc; proposed railroad lines never made it to the community; the school, the San Fernando Academy, eventually closed its doors; and the town's population topped out at 300 in the 1920s. A fire wiped out the majority of the town's commercial buildings in 1947, sealing its fate as a town of little consequence. Pontotoc—a Chickasaw word meaning "land of hanging grapes"—is now a small town of fewer than 150 souls in Mason County, off of Texas state highway 71, about 100 miles northwest of Austin and 120 miles south of Abilene. The brick wall ruins of the school still stand, impervious to the constant winds and scorching summer sun.[1]

On May 16, 2013, the body of Mark Powell was discovered in the Pontotoc cemetery. He died from what appeared to be a "self-inflicted gunshot wound," according to a Mason County attorney. Powell was fifty-three years old—his death tragically leaving behind his wife and their three children. Powell had pedigree; his father is a well-known former hospital administrator and CEO. Mark Powell grew up in Abilene and played on the Abilene Cooper High School golf team. In 1981 he graduated from Baylor University, majoring in economics. Moving to Austin in 1983, Powell began his thirty-year run working for the first of four investment firms. He made his mark and worked hard on contacts, both business and civic. He was a committed churchgoer; he served on the boards of Dell Children's Hospital, First Tee of Greater Austin, Young Life, YMCA of Austin, and others. He was well known and respected in circles of influence and riches. He lived in a well-to-do part of the city, in a house valued at more than $3 million.

No one may ever know why Powell chose to end his life in a remote cemetery located halfway between his childhood and adult hometowns, but we do know that he had borrowed (and claimed to have invested) a substantial amount of money, more than $28 million. Nearly ninety entities—banks, companies, and individuals—have filed claims against Powell's assets. Powell was no Bernie Madoff—but he did live large, thanks in great part to other people's money.[2] Worldwide travels included golf at the best and most exclusive clubs and to other expensive venues to fish, hunt, and ski. His daughter was one of forty-six young ladies presented at the ultra exclusive International Debutante Ball at New York City's Waldorf Astoria Hotel in December 2012.* Inclusion in the presentation list is strictly by invitation *and* ability to pay—upward of $20,000.

Powell's tale is tragic, but its outcome is not entirely surprising as the details come to light. He's not the first to have overextended his financial wherewithal, and he won't be the last. He secured at least thirteen loans in the two weeks before his death.[3] He obviously was at a point of extreme desperation. The discussion of his death here is not to trivialize it but to raise an important point about the pervasive nature of greed.

Powell graduated from Baylor and went to work in the financial industry right at the beginning of the short era of excess. The "good life," as promoted during this era, treats material excess as desirable, attainable, and deserved. Where was the balance or brake to Powell's sense of entitlement?** Rockefeller's permission has turned into a prerogative for some. Not only was Powell's debt out of control, so also was his ability to experience a sense of fulfillment. *How much is enough?* It would be interesting to know if Powell ever heard at the churches he attended over the years the admonition from the Hebrew wisdom teacher of Ecclesiastes: "The lover of money will not be satisfied with money; nor the lover of wealth, with gain."[4]

The influences that coerced Powell to his fate were certainly diverse; greed did not act alone. During Powell's formative years, greed yet cowered as a sinful and deviant social value; it was in the early 1980s that it underwent an image change. For many in the United States born after 1980, the world they have grown up in is one where greed and excess are not aberrant but normal. Today, the societal forces that glorify materialistic gain are truly commonplace and all-encompassing; neither rich nor poor are resistant to their penetration. Greed is useful; but, as I will argue, it can become deadly when *endorsed* by a society.

---

* The same hotel—predecessor building—that hosted the Martins' aristocratic costume ball in 1897
** As will be discussed later in this book, it's often the underprivileged in American society who are excoriated for their sense of entitlement. It's more accurately said that a sense of entitlement is vibrant in all Americans—rich and poor, and those in between.

Greed—For Better and For Worse

Greed is a many-splendored thing; it is useful in certain and specific situations. Humans wanting *more* food, security, and opportunity—motivated by greed or not—is usually a good thing. Without a doubt, however, greed can bring forth tangential problems and, more so, can be toxic in and of itself. Greed is not just a feeling but also a combination of thought, desire,* sentiment, and passion. It can be developed into an action—sometimes with intricate planning, other times at a moment's notice. Greed is a "selfish and excessive desire for more of something than is needed."[5] Greed run amok obliterates the distinction between wants and needs.

Greed is infectious; it typically encourages and creates more of itself, extending its reach. Greed is competitive; it can bring out the best in certain situations and the worst in others. "We need greed," writes British satirist Tony Hendra (he played Ian Faith in the movie *This Is Spinal Tap*). "Greed makes the world go round. Greed drives history. The greedy fish wriggled up onto shore, looking for more, and its greedy spawn grew feet and arms and waddled about looking greedily for food, becoming in the fullness of time Rush Limbaugh."[6] The nationally syndicated radio host, who makes an extravagant living spouting polemics to a large and loyal core of listeners, is on record claiming that "greed" or "self-interest" has "fed more mouths than charity ever could."[7] Limbaugh, no savant of balanced information, is right, in this case. The motivation of self-interest inherent to capitalist economies has triumphed over the ability of centrally planned economies to feed the masses, and for that matter, of charitable acts to feed the hungry. Greed has always been a determining factor, whether small or large, in eating, the basic animal need and function.

Older animals in the evolutionary time frame, such as reptiles like snakes and alligators, don't have to eat all that often to persevere. Yet when they do eat, they tend to go large—a big snake swallowing a chicken whole, for example. Survival of the fittest favored reptiles that were able to make it longer between meals, which was possible because their body temperature adapted to their surrounding environment. Greed in procuring food, we assume, played a role for survival. But it wasn't the only factor; predation, abiotic environment, and genetic advantage also determined sustainability.

---

* *Desire* is differentiated from *greed*; desire gets us up in the morning and serves as positive motivation for myriad human tasks and endeavors. Desire, unlike greed, only occasionally hurts its bearer and others.

Conversely, mammals, younger in evolutionary terms than reptiles, eat more often, using food as energy to maintain a constant body temperature. As a result, regular eating is more crucial for mammals, including the human variety. We don't need to eat every day, but doing so is advantageous. Food gathering and procurement by our ancient ancestors determined who survived into the next generation. Greed—"desire for more"—certainly was good and necessary for survival. Without question, greed played a decisive role in evolutionary development. We wouldn't be here without it.

Animals and humans seem to have a built-in preference for *more*. In the 1950s, Dutch ethologist Nikolaas Tinbergen studied the oystercatcher, discovering that when given a choice between incubating its own small egg or the giant egg of a much larger bird, it preferred the much larger one. Even though it was biologically impossible for the oystercatcher to have laid such a large egg, it was nonetheless her preference. An evolutionary understanding of the phenomenon makes sense: within the sexually dimorphic oystercatcher species, the female is generally larger than the male, which shows that a larger egg generally has greater viability than a smaller one. In a similar sense, the human gene pool still vibrant today harkens from our ancestors who, most likely, secured or fought for the biggest portions of sustenance available.[8] Sometimes bigger and more are better.

For all of us who are dog lovers, good luck with trying to teach your dog to eat slowly. It's simply not possible for most of the species—to do so would be to work against millennia of evolutionary development. Not only does the early bird get the worm, but the greedy pup gets the bone.*

Greed is useful, and sometimes necessary, for *survival*. In certain situations, one's survival dictates death for another; greed prolongs life for some and the very same greed cuts off life for others. Greed is effective for survival: for individuals, families, communities, and species. In matters of life and death, greed is part of both the winning and the losing hands.

However, when basic survival is assured and no longer an issue, greed can become something less than useful, if not held in check. For example, when I've gathered enough food for myself and my family for the foreseeable future—do I keep at it? Do I continue to gather for myself even if my neighbor looks to be in need and my continued gathering of food would hurt my neighbor? When basic survival is not at stake, greed can cross the line into areas that harm the common good.

---

* Greedy Pup, LLC, sells the Eat Slow Bowl to help your canine avoid bloating. I'm not kidding: www.greedypup.com, (retrieved February 7, 2012).

The Lizard Brain

Peter Whybrow, a British neuroscientist who teaches at UCLA, describes human passions—including greed, among others—as controlled by the primitive portion of our brain, the reptilian part of the brain. Pledged to ensure our survival, this part of the human brain is similar to the brain of the average lizard. Our hearts push blood about and our lungs exchange carbon dioxide for oxygen instinctively, not because we think to do these tasks but because they are directed by this elemental part of our brain. Our fully advanced brains, thanks to evolutionary development, are enhanced with a mammalian cortex, allowing for rationalization and abstract thought; but at the core, our primitive lizard brain is what keeps us breathing while we sleep and drives us to acquire more and more of those things we perceive to be scarce. The reward system in the brain—where dopamine, serotonin, and endorphins reside—is based in our primal lizard brain as well. Sex, safety, and food are at the top of the scarcity list; the modern eras of excess (the long era since the time of Rockefeller, the short era since 1980) have made for an intriguing new reality to which our brains—consciously and subconsciously—are entirely unaccustomed.

Whybrow claims that excess, or the "orgy of self-indulgence," has contributed to the erosion of our natural abilities to self-regulate. When *more* was primarily a matter of survival, limited resources helped keep our reward systems in check naturally. Future reward was discounted for immediate reward, but usually, enough was understood to be *enough*. Our reasoning abilities—the main difference between mammals and reptiles—helped us balance future and immediate rewards, distinguishing between needs and wants usually within the context of an immediate community of fellow human creatures. But now in the post-Rockefeller era, when *more* is a lifestyle ideology, our primitive reward systems are oftentimes overloaded and confused. The result: the ancient desire linked to our cerebral reward system becomes an addictive greed that co-opts our advanced ability to reason and act out of common sense. Greed, like a destructive drug habit, has the capacity to seek *more*—unreasonably and impulsively.[9] Lizards and other reptiles have no ability to reason; we do, however, and at times we use that ability to rationalize our greed and convince ourselves that wants and needs are indistinguishable. Yesterday's luxuries have become tomorrow's necessities; today's understanding of survival, smothered in excess and greed, would be unrecognizable to most of our forebears who survived on necessities such as food, water, shelter, clothing—and, common sense.

Greed Graduates

Ivan Boesky, the infamous 1980s arbitrageur, gave a commencement speech at the University of California, Berkeley, Haas School of Business in 1986. He wasn't an inspiring speaker; the invite, of course, had everything to do with his stature as the premier Wall Street partisan of the moment. After the requisite platitudes about America as the land of opportunity and a favorable retelling of his own rise in Detroit as the son of Russian immigrants, Boesky, departing from his prepared notes, remarked: "Greed is all right, by the way. I want you to know that. I think greed is healthy. You can be greedy and still feel good about yourself."[10] Later that same year he was indicted for insider trading and eventually fined and jailed. The Gordon Gekko character—"greed is good"—famously played by Michael Douglas in the *Wall Street* films is loosely based upon Boesky. Whether or not Boesky felt good about himself is his own judgment; writer Jeff Madrick describes Boesky as someone who, "hungry for a fortune," sought money "because he believed it conferred esteem and glory."[11]

Risk arbitrageurs, like Boesky in his day, make some of their best money on corporate mergers and takeovers. They buy up the stock of a target company with the goal that the price will rise, or they sell the stock short with the conviction the price will fall. If an arbitrageur is able to buy enough stock of a target company, she becomes more than an interested third party in the proceedings; she becomes a player, able to dictate new ownership or management terms. Large sums are at stake, fortunes to be made or lost.

More is at stake, however, than the bottom lines of financial players in the game. When the situation in question involves a hostile takeover of a business, also at risk are the livelihoods of people and the well-being of their families. Granted, takeovers of publicly traded businesses are entirely legal and can serve to modernize, bring new efficiencies, and increase productivity. But when business assets are plucked by a third party (directly or indirectly assisted by arbitrageurs) strictly with the intent to sell them off for maximum profit—this is where greed can ravage the common good. Perhaps Boesky, after his conviction and subsequent debarment from the financial services industry, did have a change of heart and conscience: before his sentencing he enrolled in seminary classes at the Jewish Theological Seminary in New York.[12] Whether or not the federal judge who sentenced the disgraced arbitrageur took Boesky's scripture studies into consideration for less jail time—only God knows.

Corporate takeover waves occurred during the 1890s and 1920s—coinciding with the excesses and inequalities of those eras—followed by a handful in the late 1960s, and starting again in the 1980s and continuing to our current day. Most debatable is what social good mergers and acquisitions serve. Critics charge that a company's wealth is transferred from workers to financiers and that company funds to be used for research and development (and sometimes pensions) are typically jettisoned. Proponents talk mostly about market-share gains and increased revenues for stockholders. The irony is that the best-run companies— with low stock values or idle cash or both—have been takeover targets more often than failing companies. Obviously, more money can be made for arbitrageurs, bankers, and investors from a company that is doing well. Madrick argues that the "mere threat of takeovers changes corporate values." Long-term corporate health is sacrificed for short-term gains; threatened corporate environments discourage new ideas, and employee benefits are generally curtailed.[13]

Yet in the mid-1980s, value began to emerge from failing companies, thanks to an old strategy—firing employees—newly named "downsizing." "Chainsaw" Al Dunlap (the nickname used by both admirers and critics), the newly hired CEO of Philadelphia's Scott Paper in 1994, fired 35 percent of the company's workforce before overseeing its sale the following year. After his twenty months of leadership, having ended the company's charitable giving in the community, its support of the Philadelphia Museum of Art, and cutting the research and development budget in half, Dunlap left the company and came out of it $100 million richer. The price of Scott stock soared on Wall Street (up 225 percent), but it was essentially a redistribution of company funds from employees to stockholders and, especially, executives. Dunlap soon thereafter was hired as a new CEO again, for Sunbeam, but his old tactic—downsizing—had already been utilized at Sunbeam the year before he arrived. His challenge would be to make money the old-fashioned way: shepherding new and better product development. Dunlap was not up to the task. Share value plummeted and the board of directors, after two years of his leadership, gave him the ax. The Securities and Exchange Commission (SEC) eventually filed suit against Dunlap and four other Sunbeam executives for accounting fraud. They were charged with cooking the financial books in order to inflate the stock price with the goal of personal enrichment. Dunlap agreed to settle a Sunbeam shareholder suit; by that time the company had gone into bankruptcy, snowed under with $2 billion worth of debt amassed under Dunlap's reign.[14] Greed, not always as good as Gordon Gekko claims, damages the common societal good, sometimes including that of stockholders!

Unlimited Growth Is Cancer

As of this writing in 2013, the effects of toxic greed still linger in America and throughout the world from the 2007–08 economic crash. Various factors contributed to the crash: a foolish overextension in the market of housing sales, easy money and credit in general, and, as we saw in the 1920s, an overheated stock market. The unenlightened self-interest of a few has once again made things worse for the many. Just like self-interested drivers on freeways, everything works beneficially for all when certain rules and regulations are followed. When rogue operators think they can get away with flaunting the rules, accidents happen and the system is compromised. From the people who bought more house than they realistically could afford to the loan originators and financial backers of those transactions, to Wall Street securitizations of those loans, to the rating agencies that endorsed the securitizations, to US Federal Reserve Chair Alan Greenspan, the primary player who made money and credit acquisition easy for an extended period, to overleveraged Wall Street firms—there's plenty of blame to go around. Every single one of us who thought the boom economy that carried over into the twenty-first century was legitimate—we also shoulder some of the blame. That's precisely what economic bubbles do—they get a majority of people thinking that the good times will continue, that we've entered a new era, and that we can have it all. We were fooled. Our time is no different than previous times when economic bubbles got out of control and *limitation*—self and societal—became a bad word. We were overextended financially and overabsorbed with consumerism; the concept of restraint for many was as anachronistic as US savings bonds.

Unmitigated greed is like cancer. The defining characteristic of a cancer cell is its inability to self-regulate. Healthy cells, as part of normal cell life span, divide and multiply. There is a favorable balance between cell proliferation and cell death. Genes that regulate cell growth, division, and death function to maintain the vitality of larger organs and tissues and the organism as a whole. DNA mutations that lead normal cells to become cancerous essentially take over the regulatory processes in those cells. Cancer cells are committed to one thing and one thing only: unlimited growth. Uncontrolled and rapid growth of these newly transformed—cancerous—cells creates tumors; these malignant tumors will invade other organs and areas of the body. Ironically, these renegade cells meet their death (barring interventions) as their unlimited growth eventually kills the entire organism. Unlimited growth is not sustainable. Cancer, not entirely but in part, is like an economic bubble: lots of growth, but none of it good for the organism. Biologically, limitation is natural and healthy; it's part of the way organisms survive and how all things are kept in some sense of harmony and equilibrium. Unlimited growth, on the other hand, is pathological and not natural.

Unlimited growth and unmitigated greed have this in common: they don't know when to stop, and they do not serve the common good.

Enron Corporation had cancer. Enron expanded on Rockefeller's permission and took it to new extremes. The growth that Standard Oil experienced in the Gilded Age was due in great part to opening and developing new markets. Kerosene and then gasoline were products that met with an ever-increasing demand during Rockefeller's lifetime. Rockefeller's business acumen was of the highest level; the good fortune to come into the world when he did was entirely capricious. Rockefeller's greed, as he saw it, was blessed and infused from on high. The genuineness and scope of his philanthropic efforts were and is, for the most part, unquestioned. Enron, in comparison, dabbled in what it thought to be new markets (cable and broadband, deregulated natural gas, power plants in India and Brazil), but the capricious timing of becoming a "great company" was simply due to the 1990s' bull market. It was a company riddled with cancer, due to its lobbying for and adoration of the deregulation of all business opportunities. Unlimited growth was its great goal, and Enron did its best to act as if goal and reality were fused into one.

Ken Lay, Enron's founder and longtime CEO, like Rockefeller, was an observant Baptist. His faith was important to him and was not, by self-admission, separate from his business values and ethics. He was charitable and philanthropic; he had a doctoral degree in economics. What really got him excited, however, was the conviction that guided the work of Enron—in the words of Enron chroniclers Bethany McLean and Peter Elkind, "the dogma of deregulation." Lay kept it pretty simple: free markets trump government-controlled markets every time. Lay was the face of the company, the revered business sage who was not overly exigent; he was the rare CEO who valued listening and defusing conflict. Like a philosopher, he roamed the environs of Enron, sharing the good news: free markets create opportunities to make money. And just like Rockefeller, Lay loved to make money.[15] Unlike Rockefeller, however, that love proved to be his downfall. His religious faith and accompanying values and ethics became subsumed into his business practices—and consequently vaporized.

Lay's number-two man, Jeff Skilling, also liked to make money. Beating Goldman Sachs's Lloyd Blankfein to the punch by more than a decade, Skilling sermonized that he and his Enron colleagues were doing "God's work" by creating opportunity and wealth. Whereas Lay's understanding of the divine was fairly traditional, Skilling's was much more avant-garde. Greed was the greatest motivator of all, and generating profits was the meaning of life. A co-worker reported Skilling saying, "I've thought about this a lot, and all that matters is money." Skilling's doomed contribution complicit to Enron's eventual death by cancer was his getting Lay to agree to use *mark-to-market* accounting. Revenues and profits in traditional accounting are recorded as they materialize; mark-to-market records potential value and profits based on current market value of the asset or liability. Mark-to-market is a legitimate system of accounting, befittingly used by futures exchange markets. Skilling, pushing the envelope, knew that attaining Securities and Exchange Commission approval for Enron to use mark-to-market accounting (for Skilling's finance division) was an absolute coup: his staff of fifty celebrated with champagne toasts.[16] With Enron's myopic focus on profit margins, SEC permission served as an authorization for Enron DNA to be transformed from that which allowed for desired growth to that which engendered unlimited growth. Like a cancerous tumor that grows and grows undetected, Enron's core allegiance to unmitigated growth made itself blind to problems that came up. The company would simply bring in more profits and outgrow whatever trouble came its way. Enron's fate was sealed. To quote Bob Dylan, "It's not dark yet, but it's getting there."[17]

"It had become a culture of excess, where nothing was too over-the-top," according to McLean and Elkind. Wall Street, generally, and Enron's stock price, specifically, were company obsessions. A headquarters lobby ticker featured updates of the company stock price for all employees and visitors to see; the elevators were equipped with TV monitors locked into CNBC. Through Enron, Wall Street had an outpost in Houston. To the outer world Enron's stock price was its facial appearance, yet no one saw what was destroying and eating away the inner workings of the corporate body. *Fortune* magazine named Enron its Most Innovative Company six years in a row. Such acclaimed economic and social commentators as William Kristol and Paul Krugman would regularly come down to Houston to share their wisdom with Lay in the posh fiftieth floor boardroom, pocketing $50,000 for their time and savant expertise. Three weeks before Enron crashed in 2001, Alan Greenspan accepted the Enron Prize for Distinguished Public Service (granted in part by highly regarded Rice University); Nelson Mandela and Mikhail Gorbachev were previous recipients.[18] Despite the number of awards or recognitions given, applause and mutual admiration won't cover up a nagging truth in the world of commerce exchanges and interactions: unmitigated greed is cancer. Greed is useful for survival, but it can be deadly when one already has plenty on which to survive. Lay and Skilling were both arrested and convicted on conspiracy and felony fraud charges. Lay died in 2006 awaiting sentencing; as of 2013 Skilling languishes in a Colorado prison.

Consider also the former Big Five accounting firm Arthur Andersen, tasked with keeping Enron's books clean and legal. The money trail was too good;

Andersen went down as Enron pay and subsequent profits clouded its leaders' and managers' judgment. Excessive greed, which doesn't ask the question, How much is enough? can take a company down, no matter how big. Company founder Arthur E. Andersen (1885–1947), who prided himself and his business on integrity and honesty, must have been doing flip turns in his grave. The company motto "Think straight, talk straight"—inherited from Andersen's Norwegian immigrant mother—was no match for 1990s-era consultancy fees.*

Greed Management

Just before the beginning of the subprime mortgage meltdown was detected in the summer of 2007, political commentator Michael Kinsley wrote a piece for *Time* magazine entitled "Private-Equity Pigs." The short article questioned the morality of certain ultra-rich Americans (for example, Henry Kravis, Stephen Schwarzman) petitioning members of Congress to maintain the provision that allowed them to pay a 15 percent rate, rather than 35 percent, for federal income tax on capital gains. His comments on greed, even before the taint of the crash, are insightful.

> Ordinarily, the concept of greed isn't very useful in terms of trying to understand the economy. We are all greedy. We'd all like more . . . But maybe an especially virulent strain of greed is spreading, something like bird flu. Maybe this is a greed so profound that it blinds its victims to their obvious self-interest. Maybe this greed can turn the brightest into fools. It's hard not to think of another explanation.[19]

Every single one of us, by evolutionary dictate, is greedy, for better and for worse. The idle rich seeking tax breaks and street-surviving drunkards seeking to attain cheap booze get what they need by greed. Again, greed has helped all of us survive thus far this side of the Pleistocene divide. Functional communal life as we know it can be described as *greed management*. Our greed, collective and individual, cannot run rampant or it contributes to our demise. Laws, customs, mores, and codes make for a livable society in that these help define what acceptable behavior is and what it is not. Greed management is part of our social contract, part of advanced civilization. Nearly all aspects of communal life are subject to regulation—baby food and diapers, roadways, house building, NCAA athletics,

---

* Andersen's company was founded in 1913; when he died in 1947, at sixty-one years of age, he was still leading the company.

medications, restaurant food preparation, manufactured items—for good reason: to ensure quality, safety, and equity. A robust give and take between opposing camps for more and fewer regulations fosters a workable balance. Food poisoning deaths from restaurants are (thankfully) rare, with profits from successful eateries realized by owners, cooks, and servers alike. New home structures are made sound and generally affordable for many; these homes are electrically wired safely and properly fit with reliable plumbing. Cholera is extremely rare in the United States, thanks to proper management of water supplies. Regulation—in moderation—protects and extends life. Of note, one area of American commerce that continually advocates less regulation is the financial industry. Less regulation and more risk add up to greater opportunity and wealth creation. What is often understated is that the same formula can also bring great losses and create instability, as we saw with the economic swoon that began in late 2007. There is a sense that the ideological call for fewer regulations, purposely ignorant of the problems it has created over and again in more than two hundred years of modern financial history, is an unknown harkening back to our more primitive days and selves.[20] Greed management is a fairly modern concept for group and communal flourishing. Greed management serves as a brake on the notion that more and more is always better. Highly competitive situations, like financial markets, need plenty of smart regulation lest primitive appetites rule.

Madoff's Exclusive Inner Circle (at 18 Percent)

Bernie Madoff has been rightly excoriated since his arrest for securities fraud in December 2008. The deception and greed that contributed to investor losses of $18 billion (some $65 billion when paper losses are included) is brazen. Madoff admitted his fault—he pled guilty to federal felony charges and he has accepted that he will die in prison. His grand Ponzi scheme worked for years; as soon as the 2007–08 swoon dug in, however, he was done. Madoff doesn't deserve a whole lot of pity. His story is somewhat compelling; he claims to have worked his way up from "little guy" status, establishing his trading firm in 1960 with a mere five hundred dollars, borrowing office space and additional money from his father-in-law. He took on trading jobs that the big guys—Bear Stearns, Goldman Sachs—weren't interested in. He wasn't in their class or league. His father-in-law helped him additionally by steering business Madoff's way. Madoff did plenty of legitimate work before he started his Ponzi scheming; in 1970 he pioneered a form of automated-trading technology (with the help of his brother Peter) and the Wall Street bluebloods took notice. Soon enough, Madoff was making decent Wall Street money, as more investments funneled in his direction. But the chip he had on his shoulder about the big firms—Madoff was from pedestrian Queens, his tongue never losing its distinctive accent—got a bit bigger with the stock market crash of 1987. Some of his higher profile clients pulled out their investments, and Madoff's capital was depleted. "They betrayed me." This, allegedly, was the impetus and the timeframe in which Madoff started his scam.[21]

Madoff's actions have taken an enormous toll, causing much human sadness: life savings depleted, charity funds lost and charities closed, pension funds drained, dreams and expectations squandered. Without question, Madoff's treachery damaged the common good considerably. And while the heartbreaking stories of the cheated are plentiful and compelling—some 13,500 total individuals, unions, and charities invested with Madoff—another side of the story has not been trumpeted: the desire for more and more. As the saying goes, every story always has (at least) two sides. The managers of charitable organizations serving humanitarian ends aside, many Madoff investors felt as if they were part of an exclusive inner circle; in the heady bull market days of the late 1990s and early 2000s, investors demanded a prime return. With Madoff Investment Securities, returns of 10 percent, and even up to 18 percent, were normal year after year. Other investment options—legitimate securities—did not perform up to the bogus standard set by Madoff's firm. As his reputation grew, he worked only with big investors and got to the point where people sought him out. The Jewish boy from Queens, whose father and mother in 1963 were investigated and reprimanded by the SEC, had made it. He was a Wall Street god; his brother and his two sons, along with other family members, were in his employ and his name was as good as gold.[22]

"Everyone was greedy" he told interviewer Steve Fishman in 2011, while imprisoned at the Butner Federal Correctional Institution in North Carolina. Madoff was a moneymaker; to get some Madoff action, you had to have plenty of money to begin with and boast of good connections. Orphans and poor widows were not Madoff victims. Upon gaining audience with the prince of steady profit, some investors simply begged Madoff to take their money. Others would have loved to beg Madoff to take their money, but they never gained access—a temporary sour luck. Other investors, already ensconced within the inner circle, mortgaged expensive homes and liquidated other options in order to invest even more money with Madoff. Of course, he nearly always complied. Madoff didn't act alone—it takes two to tango. Madoff's victims were taken advantage of, but measures of greed contributed to their blindness to Madoff's ways.[23] This is what greed does to us: we have what we have, but like Rockefeller, we want "just a little bit more." Enough is not enough, and we become oblivious to the pangs of our own consciences and to the dysfunction of the common good.

Greed Besieged by United Religious Attack

In the upcoming pages of this book I will discuss religion at length. My definition of religion is practical—*ultimate importance* (Jeff Skilling's pursuit of profits, for example)—and will be explored in greater detail in chapter 4. In this chapter, I will reflect on traditional philosophical and religious treatments of greed. Religious systems, and in particular certain ethical viewpoints, are human traditions that speak of collective experience. While significant disagreements about various practices and beliefs within the major religious systems exist, there is absolute agreement on the following two issues: unmitigated greed is toxic and excessive greed creates inequalities that impair the common good.

The traditions of the great religious systems of the world give voice to the divine imperative to protect the poor and to the duty of the religious to include the poor and powerless in the life of greater society. Not only do Buddhist, Christian, Islamic, and Jewish thought condemn excessive greed and its inherent difficulties and damaging repercussions for individuals and the community, but many indigenous belief systems also warn against the human tendency to want more and more.

Jewish tradition calls for a "jubilee year" when outstanding property debts individuals hold within the community are to be retired. Buddhism calls for a desire to want what one has, not what one doesn't have. Christianity urges greater attention to the treasures of the heart rather than those of material nature. Islam encourages individuals to be free from want in order for the community to be more equitable and just. Indigenous sacred strains warn of evil spirits with appetites that run riot, causing protracted harm to the greater community.[24] And, it is worthwhile to recognize that opposing the overwhelming desire to acquire more and more, which damages communal life, doesn't require a religious belief system.

Aristotle, eminently influential upon Western thought and theology, wrote of (Greek) *pleonexia*, commonly translated as greedy, overreaching, or desire for excessive gain. Scholar Charles Young, commenting upon Aristotle's writings, says that the philosopher took the common understanding of the term to a deeper level. For Aristotle, pleonexia is "the absence of a certain restraint on the desire for gain. A just person does not want gain when it involves taking what belongs to another. An unjust person is similarly not restrained."[25] Whether the acting agent is a cancer cell or a business titan, the effects of greed are manifest when self-limitation is expressly absent.

Self-restraint, as a hedge against greed, is a fundamental axiom of Buddhism. The six mind states or realms of Buddhism include one referred to as the "hungry ghost." This craven figure is typically depicted with a long pencil neck, pinhole mouth, and an oversized paunch. The wandering ghost, due to anatomical deficiencies, is unable to satiate its unquenchable desires. This mind state is associated with compulsion, addiction, obsession, and greed. Understood metaphorically, the hungry ghost can be present in any one of us.[26]

Buddhism targets individuals for change or enlightenment; it does not have a strong history of collective social activism. Islam, on the other hand, places a strong call upon adherents, individually and collectively, to be wary of the ways of greed. The Qur'an recounts the tale of a man whose greed brings his life to a brutish end. Qarun (not to be confused with the name of the holy book) lived in Egypt during the time of the pharaohs. He was of the tribe of Musa (Moses),* and his riches were the cause of his own arrogance and pretentiousness. His showy lifestyle created envy among the poorer in his own community—a further detriment to the common good. Qarun was warned that "God doesn't love people who gloat" or "corruptors." But this wealthy one paid little heed. In the end, he and his house with all his possessions were swallowed up in an earthquake. Qarun was done in by "arrogantly believing that all his possessions were earned of his own accord."[27] If only Qarun had been born into the Gilded Age or later, his self-belief would have been status quo, at least, among his peers.

Islam recognizes that money in itself is not an evil. Throughout history, many Muslim societies have allowed for the ownership of private property, prescribed rules for inheritance, encouraged private enterprise and investment, and recognized the legitimacy of reasonable profits. However, limitation and restraint, to check and curb greed help maintain a sense of balance. There is ample historic evidence of economic practices in Muslim communities that seek distributive justice as a primary goal rather than profit and its pursuit.[28] The concept and practice of limits is part and parcel of Islamic economy and piety; a well-known saying from the holy book is "Do not exceed the limits" that Allah has put in place.[29]

Islamic economic jurisprudence prohibits *riba*, collecting interest on loans. From its beginnings in the 600s CE, Islam has strictly outlawed riba. In the post-Enlightenment world, Islamic banking practice has modernized, and various financial transaction arrangements have been developed that respect the prohibition of riba. In most cases the precepts require the lender (bank) and borrower to share the risk involved in the transaction through a partnership arrangement (*musharakah*

---

* The historical prejudice of Islam (and Christianity) toward Jews cannot be ignored in reviewing this tale.

and *mudarabah* are but two examples). For example, instead of a bank lending money to a prospective home buyer in the form of a mortgage, the bank will buy the property sought by the potential buyer and then resell it or work out a lease-to-own agreement with the buyer. Lariba American Finance House of Pasadena, California, is the largest Islamic mortgage lender, riba-free, in the United States. Even in the midst of the economic downturn, Lariba's customers have had extremely low foreclosure rates. Bank founder Yahia Abdul-Rahman attributes this to Lariba's partnering with customers; they know their customers and choose carefully with whom they will work.[30] Lenders actually knowing their customers is quaint and old-fashioned—possible for Lariba since their client pool is relatively small; it worked for George Bailey (the banker in *It's a Wonderful Life*) and seems to serve the common good better than did the practices used by mortgage companies such as Countrywide, Washington Mutual, and others that flamed out in the 2007–08 subprime loan crisis.

Judaism, predating Islam, also prohibited lending money for interest, called usury. The Hebrew Bible book of Deuteronomy disallowed lending for interest within the Israelite community; outside the community—with foreigners—it was permissible. Usury was prohibited within the community mostly so that the poor would not be exploited by those with money to lend. The financially well-to-do lending to poorer members within the community was seen as a form of philanthropy, ultimately supporting the communal common good. An interesting historical note: most all the competing religious systems and secular codes from the ancient Near East, from which Judaism emerged, did not forbid usury. Israel, a smallish community dwarfed by Egypt, Assyria, and Babylonia, forbade usury most likely to protect and unify a poor community that needed to do all it could to stay together and survive. Demanding interest on a loan to a neighbor was understood to be an act of hostility.[31] The Hebrew word *anawim*, a plural noun translated "the poor" or "the marginalized," can be understood to have an unexpected antonym: brutality, untamed anger; *the violence of the rich*.[32] The expected antonym—the rich—is not specific enough; the actions of one group directly affect the state of another within the community. Their fates are united, for better and for worse.

The Christian New Testament is decidedly ambivalent about prohibiting usury. A handful of Gospel stories told by Jesus (who, of course, was Jewish) concern the lending of money and the collecting of interest, giving the impression that the latter was a common practice. Yet, the Gospel of Luke quotes Jesus encouraging his hearers to "lend without expecting anything in return." This moral injunction was coupled with the contrarian charge to love one's enemies.* Both exhortations mostly have been relegated to the realm of private faith as opposed to that of public practice in churches. Later on in Luke's account, Jesus famously loses his temper with the moneychangers and lenders doing business in the Jerusalem temple court, condemning their unscrupulous practices and driving them out. This narrative is like others in the New Testament that condemns greed and blinding devotion to riches: Lazarus and the rich man; the rich fool; the rich young ruler; and, the oft-quoted "love of money is the root of all evil."** Riches are not condemned in the New Testament, but the early church decidedly rebuked the honor and prestige they seemingly extend to their holder.

"Those who are characterized as unfaithful in Luke use wealth and possessions to acquire honor, status, and power," writes New Testament scholar Ray Pickett. These unfaithful types, usually isolated from their community, are contrasted with the faithful who are concerned that material resources are distributed to those with material needs. It's a continuation of the Jewish notion of philanthropy within the community—the rich not taking advantage of the poor but creating a sense of equity, helping keep the community together. Pickett continues, "The use of wealth for self-aggrandizement is seen to deprive others with insufficient material resources. Such behavior is criticized in the light of the law and the prophets [Hebrew scriptures] as greed, idolatry, and hubris, and, more importantly, as diametrically opposed to the justice, love, and purpose of God."[33]

The church increasingly exhibited disdain for usury, banning clergy and eventually the laity from its practice. By the 1300s in the Roman church, the consequence for a Christian practicing usury was excommunication. The Christian ban on adherents practicing usury, combined with the Jewish admission to lend to those outside the community, led to Jewish *ghetto* ("casting") communities establishing themselves just outside larger European cities. A Jewish presence in Venice, as an example, dates back to 1509. The Jewish communities were useful to the larger cities for financial services and taxation. Their presence in the various cities was regulated; their business was essentially restricted to financial services. Banking wasn't limited to Jews, however; the Roman Catholic Medici family of Florence, *banchieri* ("bankers") because they did business seated on banks or benches, were foreign-exchange dealers. The Medici worked closely with the Vatican, which had various currencies flowing in and out of their coffers. As would the Rothschilds centuries later, the Medici family spread its services to vital points within Europe, including London. Currency exchange, potentially very lucrative,

---

* Luke 6:34–35.
** Respectively; Luke 16:19–31; Luke 12:13–21; Matthew 19:16–22; 1 Timothy 6:10.

was chiefly carried out without resorting to usury. Within their point cities, working with merchant creditors and debtors, the Medici would work around the proviso of no usury by using bills of exchange. Bankers acted as brokers providing cash at a discounted rate for bills of exchange when necessary. Still, even with partner supporters, no overt interest rates were involved; depositors were given a portion of the annual profits of the firm as compensation for risking their money.[34]

The Protestant Reformation, starting in the early sixteenth century, eventually changed the way the church treated usury and its practice. It became acceptable, Geneva's John Calvin leading the way, to lend money at a reasonable rate of interest; usury was newly understood to refer to lending money at exorbitant and unjust rates.[35] The Roman Catholic Church adopted a similar view in the early part of the eighteenth century—not coincidental with the modernizing effects of the industrial era, including the realization that wealth could be created. All major church bodies today participate, through their financial investments, in the modern understanding of utilizing money to make more money.

This chapter began with the concession that greed is both for better and for worse. It's useful and necessary for survival; yet one's survival narrative often involves the tale of another's death. Greed is not innocuous; greed tips the scales one way or the other, often to the point of instability. However, because greed is as commonplace as night and day, *the key is to keep it in some sense of proper balance.* Both day and night have their allotted times; one does not dominate or eliminate the other. Greed run amok can be extremely harmful; greed managed and restrained helps the common good.

The Jewish understanding of good and evil *yetzer* (inclination or desire) is apropos to the challenge of keeping greed in check. The Christian teaching of original sin, humanity's first parents falling into evil, affirms that all of Adam and Eve's subsequent offspring are stained with sin. A Jewish interpretation of humanity's beginnings, on the other hand, tells how both good and evil yetzer were given by God in the creation of man and woman. *Yetzer harah* is inclination toward evil, and *yetzer ha-tov* is inclination toward good. The good inclination is to keep the evil one in check, but not entirely. Yetzer harah is necessary for human ambition, progress, and procreation; without yetzer harah humanity would not survive. But Torah (God's law) has also been given to keep yetzer harah in its proper place. "The Holy One, blessed be He, spoke unto Israel, 'My Children, I created the evil yetzer, but I created Torah as its antidote.'"* The proper attention and study of Torah keeps the evil yetzer, even though dealing in yearnings such as

---

* Talmud Kiddushin 30b.

envy and rivalry, on a positive path. When the evil yetzer is unchecked, however, things are different: it can consume its bearer to the point of ruling its activities, leading eventually to self-destruction.[36]

Destruction is a hallmark of the Native American mythical tradition of the Wendigo. Known to various people groups, including the Algonquin and Ojibwe, the Wendigo is primarily understood to be a malicious cannibalistic spirit into which humans can transform, if they themselves participate in cannibalism. The legend most likely was employed to reinforce taboo against the practice. The Wendigo, similar to the hungry ghosts of Buddhist tradition, are envisioned to be gaunt and emaciated, but with a voracious appetite. The embodiment of greed, gluttony, and excess, Wendigos were never satisfied with annihilating one victim—new victims were constantly needed.* In some Wendigo traditions, the monster grew proportionally according to the (human) meal it had most recently consumed. Thus satiation was never attained; gorging and deprivation two strange bedfellows. In the Wendigo tradition, not only was cannibalism taboo but greed as well. An overly greedy person ran the risk of transforming into a Wendigo; via its inherent warning of excesses the tradition encouraged moderation and communal cooperation.[37]

Throughout human history various people groups, by their philosophical, religious, and cultural traditions, have striven to keep greed and excessive desire under control. In the last hundred years or so, these traditions have been challenged by a competing outlook and practice: more is better. This idea is not new, but it is newly accepted by ever-expanding numbers of practitioners. And while it does contain certain truth—its truth is neither general nor universal. There are many times and situations where more is not better. The classic traditions convey that the "more is better" credo does have a grave dark side, especially when it gets out of control. We've been warned: attempts to gratify the hungry ghost only bring on more hunger and craving. And we have only so much in this world by which to survive and prosper—how to keep the ghost in check?

Survival of the Altruistic

Thanksgiving Day, November 24, 2011, was the day that a number of big American retailers—Kohl's, Target, Best Buy, and Walmart—extended the biggest shopping day of the year, Black Friday, with a prelude. Their doors would open at 10 p.m.

---

* Sounds like a Ponzi scheme.

Thursday night and stay open through Friday.* The big, bloating turkey and trimmings meal that begets tiredness be damned; employees would need to report to work early Thanksgiving evening to prepare for the onslaught of shoppers.

That evening at a Walmart in Los Angeles, a woman doused fellow shoppers with pepper spray in order to get her hands on one of a few discounted Xbox video-game players available. The woman was accused of "competitive shopping," using the spray to gain preferred access to merchandise in various parts of the store. She left after making her purchases; twenty people were eventually treated for minor injuries from the pepper spray. A Los Angeles police lieutenant described the melee as "customer versus customer shopping rage."[38] That same evening in six additional states other retailers witnessed similar violence.[39]

Research shows that the same area in the brain is stimulated and rewarded when the following tasks are involved: making money, having sex, getting a good deal, and using cocaine. Dopamine receptors in the primitive brain light up when one "scores"—financially, sexually, or chemically. In one study, laboratory rats, when wired to receive electrical stimuli in the dopamine centers of their brains, opted to continually press a lever facilitating the stimulus—this "hit" eventually became more important than all other activities, including eating and drinking: death by dopamine.[40] We humans are infinitely wiser than rats, but the options that titillate our lizard brain dopamine centers are more expansive as well. Thankfully, Black Friday Eve—rather, Thanksgiving—comes only once a year.

Rockefeller and Carnegie—neither of whom grew up with excessive wealth—knew that they and their world had arrived at a new place of material and financial procurement unforeseen in the scope of history. Their good fortune was due to a potent combination of hard work, skill, luck, good timing, industrialization, and greed. Both knew inherently that the greed component of that amalgamation somehow had to be kept in check. Both chose to *give back* via philanthropy, with Carnegie even encouraging his wealthy peers toward disinheritance of their children. They somehow knew intrinsically that keeping all they had acquired was wrong; philanthropy, for them, was the antidote to greed's bounty.

Greed and selfishness are archetypal human traits. But like the balance between night and day, altruism, fairness, and charity have moderated greed and selfishness for millennia. Brain scans on experiment subjects who were given a series of choices either to keep money or give it to a charitable cause revealed

---

* Malls are following the trend to open their doors on Thanksgiving for shoppers, cooperating with the big retailers to essentially annex the holiday for commercial purposes. Chapter 5 further explores the role of malls in what I call America's mythic religion.

that those dissimilar actions engaged different parts of the brain. The typical dopamine-based reward centers lit up for those choosing to keep the money; for those choosing charitable options, a different portion of the brain—relating to attachment and bonding—lit up. It's not just greed that helps us survive; altruism and other nonselfish traits help individuals and communities carry on. Altruism is not simply, as its critics imply, a form of "selfishness in disguise"; altruism—unselfish concern for another's welfare—is a vital part of the network of social relationships that help us survive.[41] These networks are the communities and societies that help keep our own greed from consuming us.

The greedy Wendigo—the evil spirit that devours—continues to prowl. Do we acquiesce, in the spirit of people like Ivan Boesky and Jeff Skilling, naming greed a good thing? Or do we call greed what it is—destructive—and fight its presence and influence by building upon the traditions that aim to keep it in proper balance and its proper place? Greed helps us to survive; cooperation helps us to thrive.

CHAPTER 3

WHAT HAPPENED TO EGALITARIANISM?

"All animals are equal" read the final and seventh commandment that the new leaders Snowball and Napoleon promoted at the newly christened Animal Farm. Control of the land had been wrested from human hands; oppression and injustice suffered by the farm animals would be mere memories of days archaic. Opportunity! Ownership! True community! Boxer, the literal workhorse, vows, "I will work harder." Other animals do their part; education, cooperation, and production rule the early days of animal administration. All is good, perhaps too good. The two aforementioned leaders, both pigs, begin to distance themselves from the rest and reward their own grand leadership efforts. Soon, however, these two begin to struggle with each other for sole leadership of the farm. Difficulty, conflict, and betrayal ensue. One, Napoleon, emerges as the exclusive leader—the other, Snowball, is banished from the property and subsequently demonized as having been a traitor all along. Napoleon consolidates his power, begins to walk on his two hinds legs like a human, and intimidates now subordinated fellow animals with a pack of trained attack dogs. The seven original commandments eventually pass away, leaving only one, modified: "All animals are equal, but some are more equal than others."[1]

George Orwell's masterpiece, *Animal Farm*, is admired and cherished by both political conservatives and political liberals. Written during World War II as a critique of totalitarian and communist governments, it is one of those rare works that continues to speak truth to new generations of readers decades after its original publication. Stalinism, certainly, and communism, for the most part, have not outlasted the judgments of the novella. *Animal Farm*'s allegorical treatment of timeless issues—power, greed, and corruption—apply to all societies and forms of government. The message of the "fairy story" has something to say to twenty-first century adulation and pursuit of wealth: human (and animal, for that matter) ambitions are often in need of regulation not by a despot but by a community of peers.

In his most intriguing study *Hierarchy in the Forest: The Evolution of Egalitarian Behavior*, anthropologist Christopher Boehm asks, "Are we by nature hierarchical or egalitarian?" Boehm studied primates with the goal of gaining insight into the origins of political egalitarianism. What interested him wasn't early America or ancient Greece but glimpses into our Paleolithic origins through our primate relatives of today. Boehm argues for a principle he calls "reverse dominance hierarchy," where a coalition of the weaker members of a community unite to thwart alpha types from dominating the group. The strong dominating the weak is, of course, most natural. The antidote to domination that Boehm witnessed: the weaker members joining forces to combat dominance by the few.

> Individuals who otherwise would be subordinated are clever
> enough to form a large and united coalition, and they do so
> for the express purpose of keeping the strong from dominating
> the weak. Because the united subordinates are constantly
> putting down the more assertive alpha types in their midst,
> egalitarianism is in effect a bizarre type of political hierarchy:
> the weak combine forces to actively dominate the strong.[2]

Egalitarianism has deep roots—a survival not necessarily of the fittest but of the united.

This balance of power can be seen as a three-tiered struggle of checks and balances. When the principle of reverse dominance hierarchy is present, intrinsic tendencies toward domination as exhibited by alpha types, altruistic moral and cultural codes known by all in the community, and the resentment of domination felt by the potentially subordinated combine to create a psychological tug-of-war that contributes to making societies egalitarian.[3] Boehm postulates the last five millennia—civilization—have witnessed a trend toward more and more hierarchy in human societies. Democracy, in a sense, has been the sophisticated political reaction by (mostly) the potentially subordinated in response to the dominance of monarchs, aristocrats, plutocrats, and despots. Equality and democracy are united in a fundamental struggle against hierarchy and coercion.[4]

Egalitarianism, defined, starts with equality; the French word *egal* (equal) is its root. But egalitarianism goes beyond *equality* to a deeper reality than simply equal quantities, measurements, or values. Egalitarianism—as Orwell and Boehm argue—emerges and comes to light from a situation of dominance-subordination, essentially *inequality*. It is political in nature:* a group or community engaged in the struggle of self-determination within the larger community or with a competing community seeks, attains, and maintains equality. Top-down hierarchy quite naturally comes first; egalitarianism is a political response to the context that a top-down hierarchy creates. The Animal Farm syndrome, where individuals or groups gravitate toward dominance, seems to be humanity's natural

---

* *Polis* (Greek) means "city" or "citizens," essentially "of the people."

inclination when left unchecked. Egalitarianism, in this context, can be seen as one of humanity's (and certain primates') greatest achievements.

The Canadian writer Margaret Atwood, in her nonfiction effort *Payback*, says that the concept of fairness is grasped early on by children. We've all seen four- and five-year-olds attempting to negotiate, verbally and otherwise, that which is fair in their mutual interactions. Fair is not the same as equal, she cautions. Simply put, the world is far too complex for "equalness"—be it material distribution or political power—to be considered as a viable option. Fairness, however, is a relative concept that has been and is a viable option for societal living. Fair distributions and shared power can be negotiated and practiced. Atwood cites a study of capuchin monkeys that illustrates how deeply the fairness concept is imbedded into primates and humans. In the study, by de Waal and Brosnan, the monkeys were taught to trade pebbles for slices of cucumber. Fair enough for the moment as they all learned the exchange and participated. When one monkey, however, was arbitrarily given a grape (of greater value to the monkeys than cucumbers) in exchange for a pebble, the transactions ceased. The monkeys who had received the now mis-prized cucumbers eventually refused to cooperate. While the trading part of the exercise had to be learned (pebbles for cucumbers), the anger they exhibited at the unfairness (only one of them getting grapes for pebbles) was quite natural and spontaneous.

Reciprocal altruism, or mutually beneficial behavior, is administered and allocated from a type of inner account book. Positive momentum enhances social cooperation. When a tornado hits Smalltown, those folks unaffected in surrounding communities will tend to help in recovery efforts. Related to reciprocal altruism is an inner sense of "cheater detection."[5] If a tornado then hits the previously unaffected communities and Smalltown doesn't help in the recovery efforts, then there is trouble. The inner ledgers monitoring altruism and cheating will sound their alarm. Egalitarianism is built from these ingrained qualities; the hierarchies that primates and humans gravitate toward (hunter-gatherer societies didn't practice slavery—to be further detailed in chapter 5) is held in check by practices such as reverse dominance hierarchy and egalitarianism.

In the introduction I discussed the importance of comprehending that arguments consist of more than their two polar extremes. Ample middle ground exists between being for something or against it. As concerns the concept egalitarianism, its use in this work doesn't relate to utopian (absolute equality) or communist (centralized decision making) societies. While socialist (common benefit before private profit) societies have rightful claim to the concept as I define it, I will argue that egalitarianism and democracy go hand in hand, to the point that *democracy needs egalitarianism in order to function at its best.* Even more so, the type of egalitarianism I advocate is distinctly American, in that it was forged from the experiences of those who left Europe, with its hierarchies and aristocracies, to found a new society.* Egalitarian democracy is a grand advancement over what existed before: monarchies, feudalism, aristocracies.

Egalitarianism Is Social Progress

Western philosophers through the ages—Isocrates, Plato, Aristotle, Cicero, Locke, Hume, Rousseau—and the father of modern economics, Adam Smith, all assented, in the words of political scientist Michael Thompson, to the idea that "extreme inequalities can only have a detrimental impact on society as a whole." Social dissention and fragmentation are the inevitable manifestations in a society that tolerates great disparities between the richest and poorest.[6]

The new country, America, would avoid (outside slavery) these excesses and extreme inequalities. This wasn't Europe: oligarchy, feudalism, and church authority would find no fertile ground for influence or function in the government of the new country. The Declaration of Independence proclaimed that "all men are created equal"; inherited wealth was held in suspicion, as were the vestiges of aristocracy and authoritarian officialdom. Voters had expectations of bringing the upper classes to heel—a modern-day reverse dominance hierarchy. This was what being part of a republic (*res publica,* "thing or affair of the people") entailed.[7]

America's egalitarian heritage is solidly based on the idea that the economic and political realms work together; one does not co-opt the other, but they are to work together in balanced tension for the common good. The ability to live without excessive want or dependency upon others—self-sufficiency—was essential to the human liberty the American republic bolstered. How was it possible for a person to know freedom if, for example, he depended upon another person for wages and those very wages forced him to live as a pauper while his superior profited handsomely from his labor? The owner class was not to live parasitically off the labor class.[8]

John Adams spoke of the importance of property ownership as the arbiter of equality. "The balance of power in a society," according to the second president of the union, "accompanies the balance of property in land. The only possible

---

* While distinctively American, this egalitarianism is not exclusively American. Also, the many imperfections of the new society, including slavery, racism, and genocide, will be discussed in upcoming chapters.

way, then, of preserving the balance of power on the side of equal liberty and public virtue, is to make the acquisition of land easy to every member of society." Property ownership was power; widespread power shared and diversified would help sustain the republican virtues of the people. Adams's successor to the highest office in the land, Thomas Jefferson, agreed: "A republic cannot invent too many devices for subdividing property."[9] Again, the example of Europe was (negatively) instructive: aristocrat elites, through Europe's long history, had gathered up vast stretches of land while throngs of poor remained landless.[10] With the new country having ample land to subdue and occupy, Europe's example would not be imitated.

Not only land was to be shared but also the fortunes of the well-to-do. Neither would primogeniture (the firstborn heir inheriting the entire estate), the law and custom of many European countries, be adopted in the new land. Vast concentrations of wealth were seen to threaten republican rule. Amassing great wealth from the labor of others was understood to be a corruption of republican understanding; *self-interest was to be subordinate to the common good and overall cohesion of society.*[11]

American egalitarianism was more than opportunity for available land and relative parity in wealth, earned and passed on; according to Thompson, it was about "political freedom and the absence of unequal power relations within every sphere of life." America was not to be a society of social hierarchies; voting by citizens would hedge against power plays by those in the republic with wealth. "Once certain individuals or segments of the community obtained unequal power over others, this would be the beginning of the end of any kind of democratic republicanism and therefore any real sense of political freedom."[12] The paramount goal was to continually uphold the conditions for non-dependence between citizens in the economic realm, which kept at bay subservience and other inequalities that would upset the balance of social power.

The distinctive character of American egalitarianism is that freedom is understood as the absence of inequality.[13] Starting with political equality based on the right to vote (albeit at this juncture only for white male property owners) and extending to economic affairs where exploitative or excessive gains were seen to unfairly empower the one garnering profits, American egalitarianism is entirely about sharing, not hording, power—political and economic.

Alexis de Tocqueville's oft-quoted descriptions of American egalitarianism in the 1830s are, as previously discussed, a fair analysis of life in the new republic outside Southern slave-holding plantations and Northern urban centers. The complex situation of the new country, egalitarian for many yet not for all, is an early indicator of the competing strains for and against egalitarianism that have always existed in American thought. Alexander Hamilton, the first secretary of the treasury, for example, held to the conviction—strongly present today—that economic liberty naturally would lead to financial inequalities. For Hamilton, wealth disparities were inescapable and even preferable.[14] At that time in the history of the republic, however, Hamilton's views were distinctly in the minority. Foreshadowing an eventual successor to the same post (Andrew Mellon), Hamilton would be accused of promoting policies that favored fellow wealthy elites.[15]*

These arguments and examples from the founding years of the new nation were, of course, antecedent to the momentous changes in manufacturing, labor, and ownership wrought by the industrial era. These two strains of thought—one that privileges power sharing to guard against inequality (identified with Jefferson) and the other that champions liberty over equality—would continue onward and beyond the industrial era with an uneven relationship. Egalitarianism still claimed precedence over its competing idea. The second strain, buoyed by the tenet that the state is not to control or interfere with markets, began to gather significant momentum and ultimately helped to develop the economic manifestation called modern industrial capitalism. Guided by mechanical and scientific gains, modern industrial capitalism transformed America from its previous status as a predominantly agrarian society and economy. The United States would now join Great Britain, France, and Germany as world leaders in the Second Industrial Revolution.

William Graham Sumner would provide, as if in a parallel universe, intellectual support for some of the economic accomplishments of the concluding thirty years of the nineteenth century. Teaching at Yale from 1872–1909, Sumner was one of the most influential American academics of his day. Arguments yet persist as to the influence of social Darwinism upon his thought and work; he was not an explicit apologist for what Michael Thompson calls the "industrialized aristocracy." Yet, his commentaries upon new, growing social divisions and inequalities exacerbated during the Gilded Age are decidedly survivalist. Liberty was emphasized over democracy, since it was obvious that all individuals were not equals as concerned abilities and competencies. To intervene on behalf of the unfortunate would be to inhibit the autonomy of the fortunate. Sumner aimed to show that the naïve aspiration of equality, either natural or manufactured, for

---

* In 1789, Hamilton called for the redeeming, at full face value, of US wartime debt certificates. Numerous speculators, some of them legislators, knowledgeable of the plan in advance, bought up the debt at rock bottom prices.

society was no more than nostalgia. Competition brought forth social progress as the creative and talented used their gifts and, in the end, everyone benefited.[16]

Sumner advocated "great rewards" for capitalistic leaders; his work helped legitimize the ideology of inequality that was then playing out in the lives of the affluent, the destitute, and all those in between during the Gilded Age. Sumner also helped set the stage for a deep-seated individualism that would come to fuller fruition in future generations.[17] As the century made its turn, the rivalry between egalitarianism and liberty found both at full force—the twentieth century in part would be defined by the pendulum swinging back and forth in both these directions.

"Great Compression" Egalitarianism

John Rawls, prominent Harvard political philosopher, proposed the following thought experiment: suppose a person could choose to be born into one of two societies—one where wealth was not distributed *equably*—that is, a lack of extreme variation or inequality—and significantly so, or the other where wealth was distributed equably, with some variance between richest and poorest. The final bit of information for the experiment is perhaps the most important factor: the person choosing between the two societies cannot choose her or his particular placement—whether higher or lower on the scale of personal wealth within either of the societies. Which would you choose?

Rawls argued that most people, upon reflection, would choose to be born into the society where wealth was distributed equably. Being placed lower or higher on the scale of personal wealth in that society does not carry extreme vulnerabilities one way or the other. Choosing to be born, on the other hand, into the society with wealth disparities is akin to playing the lottery. You could hit the jackpot, but the odds of doing so are quite small. Most people would choose the equable society so as to avoid the chance of living in the bottom sector of the unequal society.[18]

The 1920s, as previously discussed, was a moment in American history of great disparities between rich and poor. A few had hit the economic equivalent of the lotto, a good number were riding the cresting wave of prosperity, and a significant number were at the bottom of the swell. Rockefeller, at the time, was a widower and living in Florida. He was well into the ninth decade of life, and spent considerable time on the golf course. He and son John Jr. paid adamant attention to the stock market as their fortunes expanded through the decade;

when the market significantly went up or down, a personal messenger delivered the news, usually having to find the colossus on one of the fairways of the Ormond Beach Golf Club. He had achieved the ninetieth anniversary of his birth by the time the stock market began its inexorable slide in October of 1929. Both father and son were caught unawares when the crash came. Rockefeller's publicist Ivy Lee put together a press release that was encouraging and simple. In it Rockefeller mentioned the economic depressions that had come and gone in his ninety years of life; he was confident that prosperity would return once again to the good people of the nation. That Rockefeller bothered to speak up demonstrates the responsibility he still shouldered as the country's wealthiest citizen (and it speaks to self-interest as well). Both Rockefellers lost some 50 percent of their stock values in first five years of the Great Depression. Instead of giving out his trademark dimes to strangers and acquaintances, Rockefeller began to disburse nickels.[19]

Considering the excesses of the 1920s, the judgment can be made that the nation's leadership chose to make society less equable but with more opportunity for a few to strike it rich. We've already seen the consequences of those choices that led to the crash that started in 1929. With the challenges of the Depression, the nation consequently chose to make a society that was purposely more equable. While debates continue to this day as to the efficacy of President Franklin D. Roosevelt's New Deal, not debatable is the lasting egalitarian effect his tax policies had upon the country, continuing on some twenty years after his death. In his first term, Roosevelt shared his wariness about accumulated wealth, that "great and undesirable concentration of control in relatively few individuals over the employment and welfare of many, many others." And "whether it be wealth achieved through the cooperation of the entire community or riches gained by speculation—in either case the ownership of such wealth or riches represents a great public interest and ability to pay." Taxing corporations and the rich would redistribute wealth and diversify the power that they inherently held; "ability to pay," a phrase from the Progressive Era, spoke of the responsibility the fortunate were burdened with for the sake of the common good.[20]

Huey Long's Share Our Wealth clubs claimed seven million members in 1935. The clubs had a simple unifying credo: scale down big fortunes in America and share that wealth. Millions of Americans dealing with Depression-era poverty and fear responded fervently to Long's radio addresses and mass mailings. Long, a US senator from Louisiana, had his finger on the nation's pulse and his eye on Roosevelt's office. The president was not unaware of the political currents; taxes would be raised again on the wealthiest Americans in order to realize a more equable distribution of the nation's wealth. Long's assassination in Baton Rouge in September 1935 (by a family member of a political opponent) made

Roosevelt's reelection easier the following year, and taxes would not be raised again until the nation became involved in World War II.[21]

The country's entry into the war had a watershed effect upon the enforcement and collection of federal income tax that continues to the present day. At the start of the war, only 7.1 percent of Americans paid federal income tax; after the war 64.1 percent of Americans would be doing so. FDR wanted to keep war profiteering to a minimum, raise sufficient revenues for the war effort, and ensure that all Americans would contribute, as they were able, to the undertaking. Any personal income of more than $200,000 would be taxed at a rate of 93 percent.[22] Manufacturing soared, as did wages; the Allies won the war, and the dark days of the Depression were over.

Harry Truman continued the egalitarian tax codes of his predecessor. He was aided by a Democrat majority in both the House and the Senate after the 1948 elections, which saw Republicans lose majority control in both chambers. Truman painted the Republicans as the party that "helps the rich and sticks a knife in the back of the poor." Kevin Phillips opines that due to the whitewashing of the 1948 elections, Republicans, out of fear, did not challenge the federal income tax rates, at progressive heights, through all eight years (1953–1961) of Republican President Dwight Eisenhower's administration.[23]

Through the 1950s, the marginal tax rate on any personal income over $200,000 was stable at 91 percent. This high rate was essentially public policy— accepted by legislating politicians and citizens alike. Those who argued that the high taxes undermined initiative and investment were a small minority branded as ideological cranks. Profits were high, wages were climbing, the middle class was growing, and the American Dream was for many a tangible reality. Even in this period before civil rights legislation was enacted, paychecks of African American males averaged 67 percent of the paychecks of white males. Before World War II, it had been only 41 percent.[24]

Economists Claudia Goldin and Robert Margo have named this period in American history the Great Compression. A takeoff on the Great Depression, the Great Compression was characterized by a narrowing gap between the pretax incomes of the richest Americans and ordinary Americans (opposite of the 1920s). Favorable to the middle classes, compensation improvement was especially concentrated in the fiftieth to eighty-ninth percentiles of wage earners. A middle-class ethos dominated; the rich were less inclined to give offense by showing conspicuous consumption: fewer rich families had servants and some of their big houses were sold off and converted into orphanages or old-age homes.[25]

American society was evolving for the better; the child labor of the industrial era, the plutocracy of the Robber Barons, and the inequalities of the 1920s were all relics of bygone days. Society's egalitarian origins were not only alive but flourishing anew as never before.

Max Weber, the German social theorist, wrote his influential book *The Protestant Ethic and the Spirit of Capitalism* in 1904–05. His concept of the Protestant work ethic—that all work was a *calling*, not divine punishment for disobedience—described the ongoing fusion of labor and religion in capitalism, giving one's work a sense of religious moral obligation. The piety, frugality, discipline, and devotion nurtured in religious life regulated the adherent's life in the world, including work. Arrant moneymaking—which would have been akin to religious overenthusiasm—was contrary to the ethic. Self-restraint and delayed gratification, also part of the ethic, helped restrict consumption. Material accumulation, a possible outcome for the devoted and steady worker, was morally sanctioned as long as it did not invite self-indulgence.[26]

The combined effects of a national memory of suffering and want due to the Depression and the austerity placed upon the nation because of World War II brought forth from the 1940s–50s generation an especially vigorous manifestation of Weber's Protestant work ethic. The GI generation ("general issue" or "government issue") of the 1940s and '50s shared three important values: deferred gratification, group identity, and the assumption of sameness. (These values are further detailed below.) This generation lived during a time when there was also a shared skepticism of the rich; political proceedings and public policy were mostly devoid of the special favoritisms shown to the rich that had been common in the 1920s.

The characterizations that follow do not describe all Americans living in the middle part of the last century, but they do illustrate an atmosphere that dominated the era.

Deferred gratification included being responsible in the present moment (job, family, civic duties) and waiting for rewards related to those duties at a future time when rewards would be appropriate. One waited for marriage to have sexual relations, took one's place in line and moved upward in rank or social status slowly, and worked hard with intent and sacrifice up to the age of sixty-five—and then enjoyed retirement. Personal pleasure and gain could wait—the religious slant of deferred gratification meant living a pious life now in order to gain heaven in the world to come. Responsibilities were clear and determinable; individual desires were always subservient to the good of the group.

Group identity cherished "regular" ambitions and encouraged social cohesion; family members, townspeople, and all citizens were expected to be team players. The cultural lessons gleaned from their recent past taught people to band together. Individual tastes or preferences that deviated from the norm were understood to be eccentricities adverse to the larger group. Group identity,* closely related to the value of sameness, held that the individual was called upon to change and accommodate in order to support the needs of the whole group. Again, individual priority was subservient to the group.

The assumption of sameness encouraged uniformity. Looking at photographs from this era, especially family portraits, reveals that hairstyles, clothing, and eyewear offered scant variability. Everyone had the same type of telephone (black, heavy, rotary dial); churches of the same denomination, whether in Ohio, Wyoming, or Arizona, all used a standard hymnal; and A&W root beer and hamburgers were prepared to uniform specifications nationwide. Nicknames, which lend a sense of uniqueness, were common and useful during this time period, since the great majority shared the same handful of names: Jim, Bill, Tom, Richard, Jane, Mary, Diane. Conformity was the marker that determined social viability and relevance.[27]

Plutocracy, at that time, was a term that no longer carried a punch. Related terms *plutolatry* (worship of wealth), *plutology* (scientific study of wealth), and *plutomania* (excessive desire for wealth), never street language terms, were nonetheless deleted from American dictionaries as the 1950s forged ahead. The terms simply no longer applied to life in the United States.[28] The middle classes, their values prevailing, benefited from housing subsidies (to facilitate purchase) and small business loans. Disposable income was rising; the average family's real income climbed 30 percent during the 1950s. In 1950 America's wealthiest 1 percent owned 37 percent less of the nation's wealth than they did in 1929, just before the Crash. Also in 1950, America's highest paid CEO, General Motor's Charles Wilson, earned $626,300, equivalent to some six million of today's dollars.[29] It was a different age; wealth and political power were not as yoked as they had been previously. Numerous changes, however, were right around the corner. For better and for worse, the Great Compression's days were numbered. Gravity was calling the pendulum back for another ride to the other side.

---

* The shadow side to the value of group identity was especially culpable in the continued racism and prejudice exhibited by the white majority in the post-World War II era.

The Great Transformation—Citizens Become Consumers

Daniel Bell, the distinguished American author and sociologist, described with two words that which helped to end the egalitarian days of the 1940s and '50s: *instant credit*.

> The Protestant ethic was undermined not by modernism but by capitalism itself. The greatest single engine in the destruction of the Protestant ethic was the invention of the installment plan, or instant credit. Previously one had to save in order to buy. But with credit cards one could indulge in instant gratification. The system was transformed by mass production and mass consumption, by the creation of new wants and new means of gratifying those wants.[30]

Why wait when one could "buy now and pay later"? The Depression and war rationing were long over; who needed a layaway plan anymore? Slowly and surely, the three 1940s–50s values of deferred gratification, group identity, and the assumption of sameness were superseded by their exact opposites: instant gratification, individual orientation, and assumptions of difference.[31] Granted, a whole medley of societal changes occurred as the 1950s gave way to the 1960s. One thing did remain unchanged, however: the postwar economy continued its strong push. Robust economic production coupled with cultural shifts brought about new consumption habits.

Diners Club was the first national credit card (actually, charge card, as the bill needed to be paid in full when due), created in 1950. One of its cofounders, Frank McNamara, had been hosting a business dinner at a fancy New York City restaurant and realized, when the bill came, that he had forgotten his wallet. He worked his way out of his temporary predicament and came away with his great idea for diners and travelers alike—the charge card as an alternative to cash. In 1958 both American Express and BankAmericard (now Visa) cards were issued, the latter franchised to banks nationwide in 1966.[32]

MacDonald's offered food almost instantly—as compared to other restaurants of that day. In a battle of generational values, Bobby Dupea, Jack Nicholson's character in *Five Easy Pieces*, tries to order a side of toast for his omelet from an older waitress. She expects him to follow the rules and to not deviate from the printed menu as is; he, on the other hand, ventures to order precisely what he wants, no questions asked, whether listed on the menu or not. *Five Easy Pieces*, released in 1970, challenged the GI era's principles. Similarly, Burger King began to tell customers to "Have it your way." The younger generation—"Don't trust anyone over thirty"—started to make its own decisions without input from the older one. These are just a few of the value shifts representing the dethroning of the GI generation as it gave way to a new consumer generation. The language of responsibility and teamwork was now taking a backseat to the language of needs and wants, best summarized in the word *individualism*.[33] The GI generation and its values didn't simply dissipate, its position as dominant was usurped.

Thomas Merton, the respected Catholic monk and author, wrote about the new value system of personal consumption as it achieved ascendancy in the 1960s.

> Even though there's a certain freedom in our society, it's largely illusory. Again, it's the freedom to choose your product, but not the freedom to do without it. You have to be a consumer and your identity is to a large extent determined by your choices, which are very much determined by advertising. Identity is created by ads.[34]

Merton, born in 1915, had lived through the World War II era and through the changes the 1960s produced. As a religious committed to simplicity, he had a particularly poignant viewpoint on the shift that saw delayed gratification give way to instant gratification. Merton wrote *The Spring of Contemplation*, quoted above, just before his untimely death in 1968; his use of the word *consumer* recognizes a shift of emphasis in American society. No longer were Americans regarded first and foremost as *citizens*; the objectification of citizens as consumers has been our societal modus operandi ever since. Financial writer Yves Smith compared the uses of the words *citizen* and *consumer* in *New York Times* articles from 1965 and 2008. In 1965 *citizen* was mentioned in 1,131 stories and *consumer* was mentioned in 1,342 stories. By contrast, in 2008 *citizen* was mentioned in only 964 articles (this during a presidential election year) and *consumer* was mentioned in 3,203 articles, some two-and-a-half times as much as before. Smith quantifies the shift as one away from "membership in communities" to "actors in markets."[35] And speaking of markets, they were not seen to be virtuous in the 1950s and early 1960s, giving off a whiff of disrepute. Amateurs approaching the financial market felt a strong sense of caution; a portfolio heavily invested in stocks was seen to be pejoratively speculative. That attitude is distinctly antiquated in today's world. Yesterday's speculation has been transformed into today's walk in the park. E-Trade commercials, current at the time of this writing, feature mere children who are able to negotiate the stock market with dexterity and cunning. What's your excuse?

Comedian George Carlin always was a sharp social critic. In his 2005 HBO special *Life's Worth Losing*, he goes ballistic on American consumption and consumerism. He describes a land and a nation that used to be beautiful but is now covered in "mile after mile of mall after mall," a veritable "transcontinental commercial cesspool," where Americans "get to satisfy their two most prominent addictions at the same time: shopping and eating." Granted, Carlin was a comedian first; but especially in the last two decades of his life his outlook became quite acerbic, whether he commented on religion, politics, or society in general. A comedian is always looking for laughs, but as one of the country's most famous and successful comedians, Carlin didn't necessarily need the laughs. He prided himself considerably on his commentary, comedic and critical; he readily recognized American identity as consumers before citizens. Today's Americans "are efficient, professional, compulsive consumers." Consumption is the new American "civic duty . . . the new national pastime." "The only true, lasting American value that's left: buying things. Buying things—people spending money they don't have on things they don't need. So they can max out their credit cards and spend the rest of their lives paying 18 percent interest on something that cost $12.50. And they didn't like it when they got it home anyway."[36]

Having served as a pastor for more than twenty years, I've had opportunity to officiate at a number of weddings. Part of wedding planning is marriage preparation. For years I've used a communication assessment tool that gives couples feedback on various issues pertinent to the marital journey, including financial management. When I started out in the early 1990s, I usually asked the couple the following question when the time came to tackle financial management: Which of you two is the saver and which is the spender? Light laughter would typically ensue, and then the confession would come forth. It was always he or she, one or the other—rarely did I find that I was working with two savers or two spenders.

Nowadays I don't bother to ask the question as I once did. Now when I ask, nearly always both are spenders. One recent encounter revealed a young woman of twenty-two having already maxed out eight credit cards. Fortunately, she had cut them all up and was in the process of paying off and purging the accounts. Unfortunately, hers is not an isolated case. From 1975 to 2008, credit card debt in the United States increased sevenfold (adjusted for inflation), while the savings rate has approached zero and the national debt is equivalent to the size of the entire economy.[37]

As a 1980 high school graduate, I would have had a difficult time getting a credit card as I prepared to move on from high school to college. (I didn't even try to get a credit card.) By the time my oldest daughter was graduating from high school in 2005, the offers to open a credit card account reached her via the US mail on a weekly basis. Credit cards are great when one is in control of them. And on a deeper level, the good fortune to obtain and use credit is of special importance. Credit opens the way for opportunity.* My point is not to criticize the advent of credit cards; my point is to say, again, that some things are very good up to certain limits; but when those limits are crossed and excesses are indulged, then we all—individuals and society—are in trouble. Adults, of course, make their own decisions and deal with the consequences, good or bad. This society, however, as I will examine in chapter 5, has difficulty when it comes to overindulgence with credit and other things financial. And we're still paying the price for the role these issues played in the years leading up to the financial crisis of 2007–08.

The Two Strains

The 1950s weren't perfect—far from it. The paranoia of J. Edgar Hoover and his running of the federal law enforcement agency along with Senator Joe McCarthy's own brand of imbalances; the blatant racism, prejudice, and sexism that pervaded many parts of the country; the Cold War threat of nuclear fallout, replete with schoolchildren practicing the futile exercise of hiding under their desks in case of attack; all these prevented the decade from being touted as America's golden era. But because the progressive tax code, which consequently kept commercial wealth and political power at arm's length from each other, the 1950s were much better than this current day of corpocracy and loosely funded super PACs, where business and government elites are united in a virtual oligarchy. During the '50s, the two strains of American founding vision were balanced: liberty for making wealth and egalitarian principles to protect against the power of amassed wealth. When these two visions keep each other in check, like evenly matched basketball teams in a playoff series, the competition and interaction is worth watching. Since the mid-1970s, the game has not been competitive. It's been a blowout, for the most part, for unrestricted liberty; societal equalities have been marginalized and diminished. In some circles, terms like *common good* have been rendered to be anti-American.[38]

Egalitarianism—economic and political opportunity accessible to all—is a grand human-societal achievement. In the last five thousand years of civilization, purposeful egalitarianism, as we've seen, is the best hedge against the natural human tendency toward uncivil hierarchy that has produced slavery, monarchies,

---

* Muhammad Yunus claims that credit creates economic power, which in turn creates social power.

and plutocracies. Egalitarianism is not a naturally occurring reality. It needs advocates; we need to struggle for it and continually lift it up lest it disappear in our midst. Egalitarianism is what helped end slavery and definitively welcome American minorities and women to voting booths; egalitarianism generates social progress. We are constantly challenged by the first of Jefferson's self-evident truths in the preamble of the Constitution: "All men are created equal." We haven't fully reached our destiny; as a matter of fact, the farther we travel the more we see what is in need of amendment. The current struggle for egalitarianism has a formidable foe in the cohabitation, since the time of Rockefeller and the Gilded Age, of business and government. The struggle has seen advances for egalitarianism after extreme social crises, such as the age of Rockefeller and his cohorts and the combined traumas of the Depression and World War II. The battle is on for egalitarianism to advance once again after the 2007–08 economic swoon.

People learn to put up with difficulties and inequalities. To be able to withstand disparities and slights is part of survival. Prisoners of war who survived their ordeals have proven the ability of humans to adjust to situations of injustice and neglect. However, once another option—freedom or advancement—has presented itself, survivors will no longer tolerate the previous situation of bondage. The popular co-produced British/American PBS television series *Downton Abbey*, which portrays an aristocratic English family during the early part of the twentieth century, is attractive because of its fine scripts, acting, and production. A main protagonist in the show, the Earl of Grantham (played by Hugh Bonneville), shows considerable compassion toward his servants and subordinates, perhaps somewhat misrepresenting the majority practice of that day. It gives him, however, a sense of camaraderie with his American audience. Americans, having decidedly rejected the monarchy and aristocracy of its cousin society in 1776, look at the socially stratified relationships of aristocratic societies not only with suspicion but also with scorn. How is it that people in those societies put up with inequality and stratification? The egalitarian strain of American thought— which has fought against aristocracy and slavery—rightly questions traditional and systemic, structured inequalities.[39] Franklin Roosevelt in his second inaugural address stated the case for American egalitarianism, taking on the economically privileged and their accusations of class warfare. "The test of our progress is not whether we add more to the abundance of those who have too much; it is whether we provide enough for those who have too little."[40] If a prominent US politician today were to boldly declare her support for egalitarianism as did Roosevelt, she would be branded as "socialist" or "Marxist" by various media outlets and citizens alike.* Roosevelt's words, however, do not make the case for socialism

---

* See footnote on page 114 for further discussion of politically motivated name calling.

but for structured and purposeful equality in opportunity—egalitarianism. Many Americans do not know what egalitarianism is and are unaware of its prominence in their society's history; thus, they resort to name-calling using loaded words like "un-American" to vilify opponents. Egalitarianism is that which works to restrain oversized power; such an endeavor is categorically American as apple pie. Long live egalitarianism.

CHAPTER 4

THE UNDERPINNINGS OF AMERICA'S TRUE RELIGION

Twentieth-century Christian theologian Paul Tillich described religion as "ultimate concern."[1] Religion as ultimate concern is not the narrow or customary concern we typically think it to be: church, synagogue, mosque, temple. It certainly can be those things, but it also is much more. Religion, in this larger sense of the term, is the process into which human beings immerse themselves—striving, desiring, creating, wanting. Perhaps it's Donald Trump, three phones at once, assistants scampering, arranging and consummating a real estate deal; LeBron James, during game seven of the NBA finals, throwing down a dunk in the face of a defender; or Mitch McConnell working behind the scenes to advocate a desired bill for legislation. It can also be seen in groups: engaged parents watching their children perform in a middle school orchestra, expectant shoppers gathered at a mall awaiting a grand opening, exuberant music fans—chemical influences in force—crowding the stage at a rave.

Ultimate concerns—pursuit of money, care of family, allegiance to country—take on what can be called religious character. Religion, the search for ultimate meaning, calls forth and demands devotion. Goals, personal and societal, sought after and attained are what tend to give life its meaning. When a person puts all she has into achieving certain goals, her pursuit can be categorized as *religious*.

"Religion is the substance, the ground, and the depth of man's spiritual life. This is the religious aspect of the human spirit." Tillich says there is some part of us, individually and collectively, that strives for ultimate meaning.[2] There is no guarantee that we find it. The search for it—the process—is what categorizes it as religious. Not all participate; not all are religious, in this sense. Some opt out—either life is determined to be meaningless or the pursuit is not deemed worthwhile. Religion, in this larger sense of the word, implies action. It is the pursuit, conscious or not, of ultimate concern or meaning. It is both an individual and a societal endeavor. This is the *functional* understanding of religion; this is its original and classic understanding. Psychologist Erich Fromm agreed, calling religion that which "we are devoted to, and what we are devoted to is what motivates our conduct."[3]

What about pursuits destructive to self, other individuals, or society? These, by definition, are religious pursuits as well; they simply happen to be bad pursuits, or bad religion. A rapist, Nazism, and Bernie Madoff are some pertinent examples.

Thankfully and rightfully, customs and laws discourage such injurious strivings and protect individuals and society from them.

Another critique of this particular definition of religion would apply to its expansiveness. So many endeavors fit under the definition's umbrella. Don't we already have other words—like *passion* and *effort*—that describe these actions? If everything is religion, then the term loses its uniqueness and purpose. I agree. Consequently, the word *ultimate* is the crucial adjective for the definition to work. When actions do not involve that which is of ultimate concern—going to the grocery store, cleaning off one's desk—the action is not religious. When the actions are of utmost concern and importance—whatever that might be for a particular person, for better or worse—then I refer to them in this book as religious.

Two Understandings of Religious Conviction

There is another way to understand religion in our current day. The first, discussed above, is religion as action, function, or way of life. The second way is religion as creed, doctrine, and accepted beliefs. This latter understanding is fairly recent. Christian theologian Marcus Borg explains that *religion as belief* is an outgrowth of the Enlightenment. During that period science and accompanying scientific ways of knowing—facts and proofs—called into question the divine origin and the verifiable truth of many parts of the Hebrew and Christian scriptures. Consequently, certain parts of the Christian community undertook to fight the perceived assault of modernity upon the faith by shoring up particular vulnerabilities. In 1870 the Roman Catholic Church proclaimed the pope to be "infallible" in matters of faith; numerous conservative Protestant churches in the United States, with the publication of *The Fundamentals* from 1910–1915, adhered to the argument that certain *fundamentals* of the faith were nonnegotiable: the inerrancy of the Bible, the Virgin Birth; and the divinity, bodily resurrection, and second coming of Christ. Ardent believers in these doctrines were deemed true Christians, while those who didn't accept these foundational doctrines were not. The irony, according to Borg, is that these branches of the religion, by claiming certain unassailable "truths," were permitting the views of the Enlightenment too much influence in their ecclesiastical quarters. It was as if these parts of the religious system wanted their own incontrovertible facts too. "The Enlightenment identified truth with factuality: truth is that which can be verified as factual. Modern Western culture is the only culture in human history that has made this identification."[4] To claim that *the only truth* is that which can be demonstrated and verified scientifically—not allowing for any other types of truth (moral, ethical, mythical)—is itself a type of belief.

Neurologist Robert Burton makes the case that our *sense of knowing* resides deep in the limbic system of the brain, which includes the cortex and subcortex, the reptilian portion of the brain. "Clarity is an involuntary mental sensation, not an objective determination," Burton states in his book *On Being Certain.* "Certainty and similar states of 'knowing what we know' arise out of involuntary brain mechanisms that, like love or anger, function independently of reason." He challenges the concept of the autonomous rational mind, wherein a person can step back from his own thoughts with an ability to judge them with absolute and pure rationality, devoid of bias, and free of any constraints caused by the biological hardware that gave rise to the very thoughts in the first place. We typically assume most of our decisions and convictions are processed via the rational scrutiny provided by our advanced mammalian frontal cortex. Consider, however, the study Burton cites involving self-confessed political partisans: subjects were asked to process negative information about the candidate they supported in the 2004 US presidential election, George W. Bush or John Kerry. Brain mapping (utilizing fMRI) indicated that when considering negative information about their preferred candidate, the area of the brain that was engaged wasn't a subject's "rational" frontal cortex but the reptilian limbic system. The researcher concluded that political thinking by the subjects wasn't always rational but deeply emotional—almost unconscious. (This study also helps explain the dearth of rational political debate and the abundance of tribalistic verbal contentions between partisans.) Burton also cites the famous space shuttle *Challenger* study by Emory University professor and psychologist Ulric Neisser, in which he asked his students, the day after the unfortunate disintegration of the shuttle, to write down exactly how they heard the news of the explosion, where they were, and what they were doing at that time. Two and a half years later, he asked the same students the same questions, with the purpose of comparing their current answers with what they had written down previously. Half the participants had a fairly accurate recollection of the events when compared to their written responses, with only 10 percent of those having exact recall. Some 25 percent had recollections that were strikingly different than what they had recorded, with one respondent adamant: "That's my handwriting, but that's not what happened." His brain had reconstructed new memories and he believed these to be *right*, even though they were dead wrong (unless, of course, he lied when writing down his original responses).[5] Rationality is not always as crystal clear or infallible as its proclaimer may contend; those working from a supposed rational basis might be using more emotional and subjective sense than they want to admit.

The articulate British biologist, author, and avowed atheist Richard Dawkins exemplifies some of this type of rigid belief. His 2006 book *The God Delusion* takes on "God" generally and mainstream religions specifically. Dawkins tackles religious extremists and common practitioners alike, exposing, by anecdotal evidence, their shortcomings in living out their confessed faith.[6] This is critique of religion of its first understanding—religion as conduct; this is legitimate analysis that a number of confessed religious adherents welcome and would find much with which to agree! Where Dawkins (and fellow impassioned atheists, like comedian Bill Maher and philosopher Sam Harris) run into trouble, however, is when they attack religions as if they were systems *solely* of history and facts. This is critique of religion in its second understanding; that is, as system of belief. Religious systems can and do consist of history and certain authenticities, but these are not necessarily primary. Religion is myth, ritual, and practice. Religion is not science; it is not, primarily, history. To attack the belief system of a religion as if it were scientifically verifiable, provable, and dissectible is like raising cattle on corn. It can be done, but it's contrived. When Dawkins speaks about religious faith, he presents himself just as pejoratively fundamentalist as the religious types he pillories.* Atheism is a belief system just as much as any religion can be; they are essentially two sides of the same coin.[7] The existence of "God" cannot be proved; neither can it be disproved. Science cannot exhaustively critique religion, even though there are scientists, such as Dawkins, who will try to do so. Bryan Appleyard, the British writer, says it succinctly: "Science has shown itself unable to coexist with anything."[8]

Other types of truth outside modern science do exist; it is precisely (even more so in the post-Enlightenment world) the function of religious tradition and cultural myth to communicate and perpetuate these truths.** These are not scientific truths but are a type of truth nonetheless. They are, of course, open to critique. When Jehovah's Witnesses refuse blood transfusions for themselves and their children— especially in situations of imminent death—religious practice makes itself open to critique, and science is part of that debate. When certain Mormon sects practice polygamy, based in part upon Hebrew Bible or Old Testament examples, religious

---

* Theology can be complicated, heavy, and academic just like science. The "God" that Dawkins disproves in *The God Delusion* is an understanding of deity that isn't taken seriously in the higher levels of theological discourse. Liken it to limiting discourse of physics only to Newton—without considering relativity, quantum, or string theories.

** Enlightenment scientific values, in conjunction with dominant forms of Christianity, have relegated the word *myth* to mean something akin to "mistaken belief." Here I specifically use the traditional meaning, pre-Enlightenment, of the term: "metaphorical narratives about the relation of this world and the sacred." As with the word *religion*, the word *myth* has more than one meaning. See Borg, *Reading the Bible Again for the First Time: Taking the Bible Seriously But Not Literally,* Harper Collins, (2001), 71.

practice is open to cultural critique and certain states' laws. These two examples are specific to particular groups and their belief systems. These, and other similar manifestations of particular practice, are not what I consider to be included in the category of religious truths or myth.

What I do consider to be in the category of religious or cultural truth are those things that the various traditions have in common. The best example is creation myths. Jews, Christians, and Muslims (Buddhism is mostly unconcerned with creation narrative) share the creation myth of God making the earth and "all that exists" in six days and they also share certain aspects of the story of Adam and Eve. Some conservative religious adherents of each tradition will argue for the historicity of the creation accounts and for Adam and Eve's existence, as if the scriptural accounts are, first and foremost, history. These are, as stated above, attempts to infuse Enlightenment criteria into the ancient texts—akin to dubbing voiceovers into Charlie Chaplin's silent classic *City Lights* to make it "better," claiming all the while that Chaplin would have wanted it done this way. The religious truth of these shared creation myths is that there is an Existence from which all things emanate and of which we are a part; that we, the less, have derived from something greater and grander, the *More*. Science, chiefly antagonistic to religion in its opposing etiology that we humans are the more that has derived from the less,[9] can experiment and postulate all it wants, but it operates in a different realm than religious story. The argument boils down to this: is there *more* to the world than meets the eye? Religion can't prove it, especially according to Enlightenment criteria; but it can contemplate it and speak of it. Science, on the other hand, can't disprove it and can't even speak to it. The realm of the sacred is not, first and foremost, the endeavor and ambition of science. The sacred—the *More*—is the realm of religion.

The Greeks wrote down their mythical stories and painted them on vases; Carl Jung worked with the related ideas of the collective unconscious and archetypes; Joseph Campbell wrote and spoke of the monomyth. Thomas Mann, the German novelist, is said to have defined myth as "a story about the way things never were, but always are."[10] Some myths are universal in nature—creation, flood, afterlife—and other myths are specific to cherished values in certain societies, serving to perpetuate those values.

The children's story of the Little Red Hen serves those who value fairness and all foot soldiers of the Protestant work ethic; she did all the work and consequently got all the reward. Why do Santa Claus, the Easter Bunny, and the Tooth Fairy continue to proliferate as mythical figures in our society? The ritual enactments associated with these three figures can be employed in proliferating the spirit of "just a little bit more." Parents and grandparents—be warned about your next trip to Disney World for the young ones to see Mickey and Minnie: is the Magic Kingdom more about dreams coming true or about prolific consumption as the dominant way of life in this society? The Magic Kingdom is a fusion of both values: the great dream come true is that of voluminous acquisition of material goods and their consumption in today's America.

American Fame and Fortune and Its By-Product: Excess

American culture still claims a few mythical figures from days gone by—Paul Bunyan and his blue ox, Babe; Johnny Appleseed—but kids today would be hard pressed to recognize these stories. American society is no longer pioneering the land; these myths no longer serve today's reality. Cultural and religious historian Eric Michael Mazur argues that movies and film serve as the central transporter of cultural myths in the present day.

> Films often promulgate the myths at the center of modern culture. For example, American myths that espouse extreme forms of capitalism and excess are promoted in the "culture industry" in Hollywood, where the "stars" of film and television are subject to a cult of personality, coming to resemble the superhuman agents of traditional myth.[11]

Snow White and Cinderella exemplified the 1950s' ideal for a young woman to passively wait for a handsome and financially prosperous prince to make her day—and life. Nowadays, Elle Woods (of *Legally Blonde* fame) has evolved markedly beyond her Disney fairy tale predecessors; she is more independent and self-realized and can make it successfully on her own. Yet, she does tie the knot with a handsome guy—driving off not in a pumpkin carriage but in a candy blue Audi TT Roadster convertible. You'll need decent credit or $40,000 ready cash to ride in the same style that Elle does.

Frank Sinatra and Elvis Presley, singing sensations as never before, enhanced the myths of their personas through subsequent film careers. According to Mazur:

> Since fame is constituted mainly through the circulation of images and stories about someone, gods can be understood to have been among the first to have become famous in human societies. Tabloid celebrities, in America, like royalty elsewhere, border on the superhuman. Their extreme wealth and notoriety

allow them to do things other people cannot do—or at least this is the image that must be projected to maintain the myths about them. [12]

Myths must be remembered by the next generation for them to be maintained. Films have psychological potency because they are readily memorable (the modern adage says we remember much more of what we see than what we read or hear) and follow archetypal themes and patterns. Ol' Blue Eyes and Elvis—or at least their personas—helped forge the reality of the American success story in the mid-twentieth century. Being young, gifted, attractive, and white was a ticket to success. American egalitarianism, albeit severely hampered by racial and other prejudices, would give certain acceptable candidates a chance at fame in this time before the enactment of civil rights laws. Sinatra was scrutinized because he was of Italian descent; he was second generation American, the son of immigrants. Sinatra's popularity was enhanced because so many of those immigrants— Jewish, Irish, Polish and Italian—identified with him. To them, he represented opportunity.[13] Sinatra won the an Academy Award for best supporting actor in the production of *From Here to Eternity*, playing an ethnic, Angelo Maggio, a private in the US Army, son of Italian immigrants. *Oi sono Americano!*

Elvis, who borrowed heavily from black music and culture, confessed early in his career during a 1956 New York City interview that his greatest goal was to "go out to Hollywood and become the next James Dean."[14] That he did by starring in more than thirty movies; he sang in nearly all his films and, of course, always got the girl. His movies were essentially money-makers; at a rate of three per year through the mid-1960s, their poor quality is mostly unquestioned. His reputation consequently slid; at the same time, new groups like the Beatles and the Rolling Stones took rock 'n' roll to levels unachieved by Elvis. His status as America's preeminent entertainer, however, was not beyond redemption. His comeback in 1968, fueled by a recorded television special, marked the last moments of his supremacy as a mythical god in American culture. He was just thirty-three years old. Las Vegas beckoned, weight gain was soon to come, and erratic behavior became the norm after this moment of last apogee. In 1970 President Nixon received a letter from Elvis, who wanted to become a "Federal Agent at Large" in service of the country to fight the "hippie drug culture." Nixon had never met Elvis, but he obliged—perhaps thinking it could help his decidedly uncool perception with voting American youth; Elvis and his entourage were awarded agent badges from the Bureau of Narcotics and Dangerous Drugs. The irony of Elvis's star-crossed later life, of course, is that his excesses did him in. He was cross-addicted to amphetamines and various prescription drugs and had lost his ability to perform sexually.[15] Elvis Aron Presley, dead at forty-two in 1977, did death by excess like no other public American figure before him. Rockefeller and Carnegie were beyond rich, but they lived out an impassioned responsibility with their riches. Elvis, not as rich as either of the Gilded Age demigods, nevertheless wasted money in profuse fashion. "T. C. B." was the motto of Elvis and entourage; and when it came to money, drugs, superfluous possessions, and debt, they "took care of business" like no others.

Michael Jackson, the incredibly talented singer and performer, took up where Elvis left off. Born in 1958, the original "MJ" (sorry, Michael Jordan) was a child prodigy alongside his older brothers in the Jackson 5. Coming of age during the civil rights era, the Jackson 5 enjoyed a large following in and beyond the black community. Six years after Elvis's death, Michael, by then a solo artist, produced the best-selling album of all time, *Thriller*. And while his movie career was barely mentionable, a new venue, music videos, established his cult of personality. (His music video *Thriller* would be added to the Library of Congress's National Film Registry in 2009.)[16] He had taken Elvis's throne as the next popular mythic god of American entertainment culture. Jackson's subsequent and bizarre physical transformations (only in part related to his vitiligo, or depigmentation of the skin), revelations of an extremely strained relationship with his father, and the construction of his own personal Disneyland, dubbed Neverland Ranch, enhanced his incongruity with normal life. That he married Elvis's daughter, Lisa Marie Presley, in 1994 simultaneously seemed strange and fitting. Jackson, like his deceased father-in-law, was addicted to prescription drugs and increasingly had financial difficulties.[17] And just like the King, the King of Pop suffered a premature death, brought on by excesses and prescription drugs. His posthumous release toward the end of 2011 was, not surprisingly, entitled *Immortal*.

Theories and funny pictures abound on the Internet that assert, yes, both kings are still alive. They faked their deaths, so it goes, to get away from all the excesses that were killing them: the drugs, the overattention, the overadoration. Death at a younger age, of course, always enhances mythical status for the famous. There are Elvis and Michael sightings today, but never of Sinatra, who lived to see eighty-two years. In 1992 the US Postal Service asked the American public to choose between two images—youthful or mature—of Elvis for a commemorative stamp. It was no surprise that the younger Elvis overwhelmingly won the vote; to date Elvis's is the best-selling commemorative stamp of all time.[18] Our societal gods of today are young, virile, and phoenix-like. MJ is still touring; Elvis is still in the building.

Early American society, with its egalitarian and democratic foundations and in a time when youthfulness and instantaneousness were not yet deified, was led by wise and experienced leaders. At least, that's how we want to remember it. George Washington, Thomas Jefferson, Ben Franklin, Abraham Lincoln: we prefer to look at images of them in their maturity. We don't want to see an image of the young Lincoln who couldn't win election to political office and didn't yet have a beard. That Lincoln wasn't the Lincoln who saved the nation from rupture and demise. It is the wise and aged Lincoln—well into his sixth decade—whom we revere.

The Gilded Age titans Rockefeller, Carnegie, and Morgan are also best remembered in their maturity, by their respective photographs and portraits. To look at their images from their youth is done out of curiosity, to see the titans-to-be in their embryonic stages. At the beginning of the twentieth century a slight shift begins to take place—societal attention and admiration being diverted from political leaders (Teddy Roosevelt and Franklin Roosevelt being exceptions) to business leaders, the creators of wealth and capital. They weren't venerated by all—as we've seen—but there was something irresistible about their abilities that demanded attention. Incredible wealth imparted to them a power that previously was reserved only for political or military (sometimes one and the same) leaders. Mark Twain was arguably the most famous American in his day outside the realm of business and politics; with his death in 1910, the days of America celebrating a writer in the fashion that Twain had been were numbered. Ernest Hemingway approached a kind of celebrity status in the 1930s and '40s, but his status was more of literary genius than worshiped idol. Joe DiMaggio, Jesse Owens, Humphrey Bogart, and Bing Crosby all achieved fame—but it didn't compare to what was to come.

When Elvis came along—simultaneous with the advent of the credit card (instant gratification) and television—the shift was complete. Societal popularity, previously retained for political leaders and business titans, now claimed an entertainer, first and foremost. This popularity had a level of enthusiasm never before known; it welled up from American youth. The cult of Elvis wasn't like a yo-yo or bobby-sock craze—this was genuine and divine celebrity on a brand new scale, televised. A few years later Americans would vote into office the youngest US president ever, John F. Kennedy.* It was as if the egalitarianism practiced in the 1950s reached down and touched even the youngest generation. For the first time, youth had their own voice in the affairs of the society. The cult of youth was gathering momentum; the great influx of baby boomers entering their teenage years was paralleled by a welcome change in the nation's capital.

---

* CBS's Walter Cronkite, in preparation for the 1952 national political conventions, offered a first-time "school" to teach politicians the art of TV makeup, dress, and diction. Congressman John F. Kennedy was one of the attendees. Douglas Brinkley, *Cronkite*, HarperCollins (2012), 161–62.

President Kennedy and the First Lady, Jackie, brought their two young children into the White House. Fifty years had passed since the pitter-patter of small feet—from the six children of Teddy and Edith Roosevelt—had been heard in the White House.

Films glorified the cult of youth. James Dean, dead from a car crash at the age of twenty-four in 1955, was emulated not only by Elvis but also by throngs of American youth. Fueled by the younger generation's convictions and idealism, the protests of the mid-1960s then took center stage. *The Who*, singing "My Generation" in 1965, wasn't fooled by their elders' values of patience preached and reward held over: "Hope I die before I get old." In 1969 singer and actress Judy Garland, a former child prodigy, overdosed on barbiturates. She was forty-seven years old. Her demise was tragic; her excesses—booze and pills—foreshadowed what was to come for Elvis and MJ. The beautiful colors of her rainbow had faded significantly over the years of her difficult adulthood, her yellow brick road tarnished beyond recognition. But no matter; her innocence, youth, and charm—all-powerful and immortalized in the celluloid of *The Wizard of Oz*—overcome the bumbling and aging charlatan, the supposed great Oz, every single time.

Bound Together under a Thin Coating

Myth represents that which people want to believe and do accept. Myth helps conceptualize those things or beings in which people put their faith. It's both reality and something beyond reality, for better or for worse. Myths define a culture and give a sense of what carries ultimate importance in a society. Myths tie into a culture's functional religion and its accepted or sought after standards.

Religion is not just belief; religion is also how a person lives her life. Religion is how she carries out her business—with passion, resolve, and purpose. She lives her life according to her abilities, needs, and wants. This is not simply an individual endeavor; the many individual strivings constitute a collective whole. The root meaning of the word *religion* (Latin) is "to rebind" or "reconnect." Human beings are derived and propagate themselves from bonding; traditional religions make purposeful connections among humans in society, between the divine and individuals and society.[19] Thus, for those involved in decidedly shared societal endeavors and driven by ultimate concerns, their affairs are *religious*, whether they make it to a temple to worship or not.

I work as a pastor of a congregation. I've done so for more than twenty years. I don't work as a pastor to "save souls" and help populate heaven. That type of thinking hit its high-water mark (within recent context) for American Christianity in the 1950s and is no longer persuasive in the twenty-first century.[20] The reason I work as a pastor is to promote the common good.* I'm of the conviction that we humans are absolutely capable of killing each other—as seen throughout human history—and destroying other forms of life on the planet. Traditional religion, that which *binds us* together, keeps us in check by accountability within a wider community, giving us purpose, goals, and hope. This is "God's work" much more than what Lloyd Blankfein, CEO of Goldman Sachs, claimed it to be in 2009, when he inferred that the unrestrained creation of capital was divine vocation. Blankfein was pilloried for his comments (he claimed later to have been kidding); Goldman Sachs paid out $16.2 billion in compensation in 2009.[21] Blankfein and many of his colleagues certainly may work and get compensated *religiously*; his comments lend credence to the idea that consumption and materialism are part of the true religion (that which binds us together around an ultimate concern) of the land. When "just a little bit more" turns into multiple billions—for a company (Goldman Sachs) that has just over 30,000 employees[22]—it makes it look as if the divinity has turned green, not with envy but with the color of money. This god is to be differentiated from the *Sacred More* that is beyond the reach of modern science, and for that matter, economics. The Rockefeller credo—make as much as you can (with God's help)—is yet alive, kicking without restraint, and breathing; it's inhaling much more than its fair share of available oxygen.

Sociologist Daniel Bell, borrowing from historic Western religion and the literary expressions of Joseph Conrad, describes the angst of humanity's plight with similar gravitas: "Civilization is a thin coating of protection against the anarchic impulses and atavistic roots of life which lurk just below the surface of existence and which constantly press to burst out." [23] As the tragically bloody twentieth century has shown, we humans are capable of multifarious death and destruction. It's right there, under the surface, waiting to emerge when things get out of control. Civilization is what keeps darkness from dominating. Purposeful and meaningful work (from basic survival to creating art) helps keep us civilized; trust or fidelity is what keeps society in a state of functional grace. Society is a construct; arbitrary (agreed upon) sets of rules and regulations help keep the thin crust of protection in place so that we are not overwhelmed by our own capacity for chaos. There are necessary limits to our freedoms; balance between the extremes keeps the pendulum swinging at a measured and functional pace. In the administration of society, the overreach of regulations is potentially just as tyrannical as the absence of rules and regulations. The common good depends upon their proper balance; how much freedom can we handle, and when is too much of a good thing detrimental to our shared existence?

---

* Using overt theological language, I define my call this way: bringing the reality of God's realm to the life of the world; "your will be done on earth as it is in heaven."

Progress: For Better and for Worse

Paul Tillich, mentioned above, was a theology and philosophy professor who was run out of his native Germany before World War II. He had previously served as a chaplain in the German Army during World War I. It was a traumatic experience—the cruelty and terror of war—that influenced his thought and writing for the rest of his life. He was dismissed from his position at the University of Frankfurt in 1933, shortly after Hitler assumed power, because of his conflicts with the Nazi movement. He accepted an invitation from Reinhold Niebuhr to teach at Union Seminary in New York City. Tillich became an American citizen; after more than twenty years of teaching at Union, he also taught at Harvard and the University of Chicago.[24]

In his book *Theology of Culture,* Tillich sharpens an argument that has existed ever since the biblical story was told about Cain killing Abel. This second story in the book of Genesis—after creation—is about fratricide, brother killing brother. It's most telling that this type of story, a sibling rivalry gone dreadfully awry, has such an early and therefore significant billing. This is myth at its best: explaining in story form the angst that lies deep within the human psyche, in this case manifested in murder. Brother upon brother, friend upon friend, rival upon rival. Are human beings stuck with or enslaved to evil and hurtful desires? Or are humans capable of overcoming their urges toward destruction; are humans able to freely do what is right, loving, and beneficial?

Tillich alludes to two strands of thought on these questions: on the one hand, the freedom to choose to do good; and on the other hand, compulsion toward doing evil—to steal, lie, cheat, and murder. There certainly is ample anecdotal evidence throughout human history for both answers to have legitimacy. Many good and loving deeds happen on a daily basis, known (and unknown) to those who are positively affected by such actions. Yet also—consult the newsfeed of your choice—darker deeds are daily manifested and known to many, beyond the circle of their direct effect. When push comes to shove, so to speak, which of the two strands—good or evil—wins out? Which of the two is more prevalent?

Humanity's conquest of nature as realized during the industrial era afforded a new understanding of the human being in relation to the universe and the deity. The ability *to create* was now seen to be characteristic not of the deity alone but of humans as well. Whitney's cotton gin, Watt's steam engine, the completion of the transcontinental railroad (with the incredible feat of laying bridges and track through the Sierra Nevada Mountains in California), and Bell's telephone are just a few of the inventions and remarkable achievements that helped make possible this shift in understanding. Human destiny was not only to be fulfilled, it was also to surge forward. Creative powers, no longer pertaining only to the gods, would give humans the potential to overcome their own shortcomings.[25] For those understanding the world naturalistically without the existence of a deity, this was a time of yearned for emancipation. The greater that derived from the lesser could aspire to magnified, and perhaps, unlimited greatness. The present day and future were full of possibilities like never before, including heightened demands for production and consumption.

For those understanding the world to be of divine origin and direction, the Social Gospel movement—mirroring the Progressive movement of the late nineteenth and early twentieth centuries—also necessarily depended upon this shift in societal consciousness. The hungry could be fed and the illiterate taught to read; social evils could be eradicated by human effort. The lesser that derived from the greater could also lift itself up, with God's help. Present day and future hopes, including the full coming of God's kingdom on earth, reflected an optimism previously unattained.

Both understandings, though disagreeing about the existence of a deity, were cut from the same cloth. The human family had the opportunity to improve itself; effort, resolve, education, and principled approach were some of the ingredients necessary to bring about the desired results. Humanity was improving, progressing, and evolving—impediments to this progress were the enemy. Unbelief, laziness, and excessive regulations on business practices and money lending were the impediments that threatened to keep humanity's newly realized creative powers in check.

But then came World War I—the war in which Tillich served as a chaplain. World War I was not only one of the deadliest conflicts in human history (with close to thirty million military and civilian deaths), but it also brought a significant halt to movements, humanist or religious in nature, that took for granted the progress of the species. [26] Reinhold Niebuhr, Tillich's host in his new country, remarked, "There is therefore progress in human history; but it is progress of all human potencies, both for good and evil."[27] Again, the double-sided question looms: Are humans capable of self-improvement, with minimal regulation needed to guide them toward their achievements; or are humans in need of vigilant laws and exhortations in order to coexist without disorder?

This question, which cuts to the heart of human nature, is not best served by an either-or answer; again, there exists ample evidence for positive response on both sides of the query. Humans have achieved incredible feats and have committed horrific deeds. As Niebuhr proclaimed, our capacity for both good and evil seems boundless. Perhaps the question, more refined, is whether or not our creativity—seen in remarkable inventiveness, achievements, and efficiencies— has made us freer in spirit and brought us closer to a sense of self-actualization (individually and communally) in this world. We've become more prosperous in the industrial and postindustrial ages, but all things considered, do we surpass our ancestors in advancing the common good?

Tillich claimed that a counterforce has met our advancements in creativity and achievement, ironically brought about by the same system of production and consumption that has made the world so thoroughly different than it was before the industrial age.

> Man is supposed to be the master of the world and of himself. But actually he has become a part of the reality that he has created, an object among objects, a thing among things, a cog within a universal machine in which he must adapt himself to in order not to be smashed by it.[28]

The ante has been upped; certain things have improved (the availability of clean water, harnessing of power, access to technology), but who and what is in charge of shared society? Is the postindustrial economic reality the dominant force in today's world? In other words, are we at the beck and call of a power that serves mostly its own appetite?

The construct of the two extremes of human potential—the tendency toward good and the compulsion toward evil—leaves plenty of ground in the wide middle for their commingling and various combinations. A person's understanding of human nature will dictate whether he will treat greed—especially excessive greed—either as a mild social ill or as a serious social and moral corruption.

For those who tend to see humanity as having the ability to naturally self-correct and choose the good, the spirit of "just a little bit more" is essentially healthy and part of humanity's potential to achieve greatness. The creative powers that the industrial age brought—with the ability to overcome human shortcomings— opened the door for colossi like Rockefeller and Carnegie. If humanity can be given the freedom to do what it can do, free of binding regulations and controls from wherever they might emanate, the potential for achievement is practically unlimited. And since humans have the natural ability to choose the good, what harm can there be in unlimited growth, acquisition, and accumulation? The surplus goods and wealth can be used, if the individuals possessing them choose to do so, for advancing the common good. This was essentially the script followed by Rockefeller and Carnegie; it relies upon an optimistic view of human nature.

On the other hand, for those having a pessimistic or sober view of human nature, the spirit of "just a little bit more" gone overboard is definitely hazardous and part of humanity's potential not to achieve greatness but mobocracy. The creative powers harnessed in the nineteenth century, combined with the new permission of the colossi to accumulate and possess amounts of money previously unimagined, led to inequalities also previously unimagined. Humans tend toward self-survival, especially in competitive situations, and away from charity. Most all the religions and cultures of the world judge inequalities to be unhealthy and unjust. Consequently, human behavior is in need of positive guidance in the form of regulation and restriction. Unrestrained freedoms and unlimited growth are essentially illusions; they are idols constructed upon the religious altar of that which is of ultimate importance: getting "just a little bit more." The desire to accumulate, when overdone, becomes a god in and of itself. Long before the Industrial Revolution, French writer Michel de Montaigne commented upon humanity's propensity to create. "Man cannot make a worm, yet he will make gods by the dozen."[29] These words in their original context critique established religion; today these words can be used to critique a new religion: commerce-based money worship.

Money: The Common Denominator of Commerce, Materialism, and Consumerism

Theologian Philip Goodchild, in his intriguing work *Theology of Money*, argues that in today's world money has replaced God as supreme being and object of ultimate importance.[30] How many of us living in today's postindustrial society aren't afflicted with this recurring thought: If I just struck it rich—lottery, inheritance, or inventing the next gizmo—all my worries would go away. If I were to come into significant money, everything in my life would then be changed for the better. I could retire, I could pay off my bills, I could travel; I could be free to do what I want! This is today's American Dream. Whereas the original focused on opportunity to work and earn, the new American Dream is all about accumulation and acquisition—as Mark Twain said—by the easiest means possible. The original American Dream made a comeback of sorts in the 1950s; the new one, refashioned from its Gilded Age progenitor, has been ascendant since the late 1970s.

"They who are of the opinion that money will do everything, may very well be suspected to do everything for money."[31] This is religious pursuit—precisely—

according to the definition being using in this work. The power of money is akin to the power attributed to deities—the ability to influence human behavior and destinies. Who wouldn't do all they could do to acquire (more) money and its accompanying power? The pursuit of wealth is the one thing that, pragmatically speaking, unites the majority of the world's people. This is where money gets its power. Its power is not intrinsic; its power is derived from political and economic supports, granted by the near unanimous backing, participation, and desire of the world's citizens.

Goodchild states that money is a promise of value, an embodied social power. The power of a promise is in its ability to deliver. And worldwide, nothing else quite delivers (or promises to, at least) like money. Your family might promise you something, as might your employer or your government—but all these could let you down, reneging on the promise. Money, on the other hand, is distinctive: it can always deliver (according to our faith in it). If a person has money, she can do anything she wants. The demand for money seems unlimited, and it becomes the supreme social source of credibility. "Money posits itself as the universal, supreme value and the means of access to all other values."[32] Money talks and bullshit walks.

To be clear, money is not a bad thing; critique does not mean outright rejection. Money, like many things in this world, has its beneficial and utilitarian side. Money *does* help accomplish feats of justice, love, and good; money and its accompanying power contribute to the common good in many and various ways, especially in the form of credit. But once again, when certain limits are transgressed and money and its power take on the form of divinity and supremacy, it becomes gravely problematic. Goodchild draws an apt comparison:

> Where God promises eternity, money promises the world. Where God offers a delayed reward, money offers a reward in advance. Where God offers himself as grace, money offers itself as a loan. Where God offers spiritual benefits, money offers tangible benefits. Where God accepts all repentant sinners who truly believe, money may be accepted by all who are willing to trust in its value. Where God requires conversion of the soul, money empowers the existing desires and plans of the soul. Money has the advantages of immediacy, universality, tangibility, and utility. Money promises freedom and gives a down payment on the promise of prosperity.[33]

Heaven can wait as long as there is money to be made, acquired, and enjoyed.

Goodchild says that money, like God, can be in more than two places at once. Your money can be deposited at the bank, and I might be using it because the bank gave me a loan—your money and mine (and the bank's) at one and the same time. Money determines value—or so we allow it to. Money is the ultimate judge: it combines the promise of prosperity and the threat of poverty, the promise of freedom and the threat of exclusion. Money, and the power with which we ordain it, is able to erode the authority of other social formations. How many of us have lost a friendship, including extended family, because of a disagreement about money owed, borrowed, or loaned? Money has the ability to replace the divine as ultimate source and judge of truth, value, and power. [34]

And now that the divine presence has been replaced or rendered unnecessary, money will, in turn, take on the two other main societal protagonists, the state and the corporation. As mentioned above, the state can let you down and disappoint. Perhaps it will overly tax your income; or after returning home with post-traumatic stress disorder from fighting in one of its wars, not provide for your care properly as you attempt to reacclimate to society. A corporation that employs you might bypass you for a promotion based upon your gender or ethnicity, or (as has happened too often in recent years) simply eliminate your pension. Money, on the other hand, offers much more than these two entities. Corporations would be hollow without money and the meaning it gives; money makes the corporation. And nothing promised by the state can match what money promises to offer.[35] In the previous discussion of the battle for societal control that ensued as the Progressive Era encroached upon the Gilded Age, we noticed that corporate big business and government were two fairly equal antagonists.

Big business had its profits; government had its new power and mandate to tax. With ample give and take, the two opponents shared the same space—like equally matched Japanese sumo wrestlers—for some twenty years. The difference today, one hundred years later, is that government and big business—with Wall Street allied—are now almost wholly united. What has brought about such transformation from the previous age, and a harmony between the two adversaries heretofore unrealized, is the power of money. And since the market, represented by Wall Street, is more closely related to money and its powers than is government (which is related more to organization of society and policy), it's no surprise that significant momentum exists for market power to surpass once and for all that of government. Many argue that usurpation has already happened—*money is the market's lifeblood* and nothing shall stands in its way.

But alas, money is not infallible. At dreadful moments of hyperinflation in various places over the last two hundred years, money has been pushed around in wheelbarrows; its temporary owners invulnerable to stray gusts of wind that might take a loose bill or two, hoping to barter the airy load for a loaf of bread or small sack of potatoes. Money's promise is sometimes falsely puffed up and shown to be decumbent. Instead of bringing promised peace and prosperity, money has brought numerous lottery winners unforeseen misfortune. The promise of money is double-faced: value and freedom are offered, but for many, money delivers greatly reduced senses of value and freedom compared to what they had anticipated.[36] What would be the effects of your income increasing by 25, 50 or 200 percent in the coming year? A new security system for your home? Sudden attention from extended family and friends who heard that you came into money? Better access to antianxiety medications, as you now question the motives of those who seek your company? Those of lower socioeconomic status, as shown in numerous studies, generally have a greater orientation to the welfare of others than do those of higher socioeconomic status. The former—even with fewer resources, greater exposure to threat, and a reduced sense of personal control— have greater commitment to egalitarian values and feelings of compassion than the latter. When you have an empathetic sense of what other people are living with and going through and then act upon it, somehow that makes your own journey, if difficult, less onerous.[37] Money, in this case, seems to be less troublesome to those who are not under its spell.

Goodchild likens the days of yore, when religious offerings were given by the faithful or by the compelled (in state-run churches), to our current day of consumption:

> The physical expression of worship and devotion has mutated from the offering, through the tithe and tax, to the interest payment. One offers one's life and death for the sake of money— whether the chance to one day possess it or to guarantee its continued authority. The modern age is by no means impious. It has a political theology of money.[38]

We are, without doubt, a religious people. To make our offerings—principal and interest payments—most of us are required to work. Our work and accompanying materialistic consumption, imbued with the belief that the market will provide all we need, is our true religion. Politics and economy, entities previously kept at arm's length one from the other in our society's history, are now united in the service of this ultimate concern. We have come to believe that money promises to provide us with all that we might imagine we need and want—materially, socially, spiritually. Goodchild states it clearly: "Money is the supreme political authority in modernity."[39]

CHAPTER 5

AMERICA'S TRUE RELIGION:
COMMERCE, MATERIALISM, AND CONSUMERISM

Dawn Hughey routinely put in seventy-hour workweeks as a retail store manager, making about $35,000 a year as a salaried employee. Abel Lopez had the same type of job, worked the same long hours, and brought home an equivalent amount of pay. Hughey managed a Dollar General store in Detroit and Lopez a Family Dollar store in El Paso; they both performed the same tasks as did the sales associates under their supervision: unloading trucks, stocking shelves, cleaning toilets, running cash registers, doing inventory, moving boxes. Since Hughey and Lopez were categorized as managers, they were exempted from receiving overtime pay. When one does the math, both made a little less than ten dollars an hour. Until they were fired, that is.

The 1938 Fair Labor and Standards Act put in place the forty-hour workweek, mandated a minimum wage, established overtime pay at a rate of time and a half, and further regimented child labor law. This federal statute—still enforced today by the Department of Labor—also exempts "executive" and "administrative" salaried employees from receiving overtime pay, as long as they make more than $455 a week. The statute specifies that executive and administrative employees are to manage the work environment, to direct other workers under their supervision, and not to engage in manual labor. This last provision serves a double purpose: to distinguish managerial work from manual labor and to ensure that manual laborers are not taken advantage of. In the growing economy of the mid-twentieth century, the line of demarcation between managers and laborers was clear. In today's stagnant service economy, workers like Hughey and Lopez perform the tasks of traditional management while also doing anything else needed, because they don't have the budget to staff more workers. Putting in more hours—many more—is sometimes the only difference between supervisors and their subordinates.

"All these dollar stores, their company structure is the same. Their largest controllable expense is their labor budget," says Lance Gould, an Alabama attorney whose firm represents frustrated managers like Hughey and Lopez. "It's corporate theft." Dollar General, Family Dollar, and Dollar Tree jointly have more than 25,000 stores and employ more than 220,000 people, mostly part-timers. All three companies, publically traded, have seen their stock prices soar since the economic collapse of 2007–08. Traditionally the destination of the poor, the dollar stores with their rock-bottom prices now also attract middle-class shoppers. The dollar stores have filled the tight niche between Walmart and weekend garage sales. Razor-thin margins on merchandise, lower rents because the stores inhabit less desirous locales, and a thin yet replaceable labor force squeezed for time combine to make up the basement of American capitalism, also known as the *dollar store economy*.

After two strenuous years as store manager, Hughey was fired after having been injured on the job. She was told her termination was due to productivity problems previous to her injury. She sued and eventually reached a settlement with Dollar General. Lopez was fired after having worked seven years for Family Dollar—he was told his store lacked proper upkeep. Lopez now leads an El Paso labor organization that advocates a fifty-two hour maximum workweek for store managers.[1]

Americans have always worked hard. A grand generalization to say so, yes; its validity, however, is not discredited by confined cases of dependents and slackers who have bucked the societal norm. The norm was cast early on by Pilgrim and Puritan journeyers who crossed the Atlantic as indentured servants, working off the price of their passage, typically in five years. In 1648 the Puritans of Massachusetts made legislation proclaiming idleness to be a punishable crime.[2] European immigrants busting their backs, shoulders, and fingers in factories, foundries, and meatpacking plants in New York City, Philadelphia, Chicago and other urban areas reinforced that same ethos. Their living conditions were sometimes as deplorable as their working conditions. The norm was also established by homesteaders in the Upper Plains bearing their first Dakota winters without a potbellied stove and accessible firewood. Having broken and plowed the virgin prairie the previous fall—no easy task—they hoped to survive the winter in order to sow the spring grain that would flourish in the summer, thereby enhancing their odds for survival the following winter. Colonist families in Texas, seeking river bottomlands for planting and ranching, sparred with Comanche, Tonkawa, and other Indian tribes.* Snakes, scorpions, summer sun, and drought also plagued the first Texans. African slaves labored in cotton fields in Texas

---

* Texas *empresario* (Spanish for entrepreneur) Stephen F. Austin had a telling encounter with the one of the chiefs, Carita, of the Tonkawas. Austin attempted to convert the Tonkawa from their traditional ways of hunting and gathering (or stealing, according to the empresario). Austin presented the chief with farming implements and seed corn, in the process securing Carita's promise that they would clear land to settle and farm it. Not surprisingly, after Austin left, the Tonkawa simply ate the corn. When Austin later returned to check on the tribe's progress, Carita informed him that the Great Spirit had enlightened the Tonkawa: they were to keep to their traditional ways—hunting and gathering—and not become "sedentary" like white men. Greg Cantrell, *Stephen F. Austin: Empresario of Texas*, Yale University Press (1999), 140.

and other southern territories, sacrificing much more than simply wages in the process. Like the slaves, other "unofficial" Americans—illegal immigrants,* or undocumented workers (depending on one's point of view), and seasonal workers and their families—followed the harvests, all working hard for minimal pay. The wages they accepted, of course; part of foundational American egalitarianism says that anyone can work their way up. Kings, queens, and other silver-spoon types are not the only ones who can know privilege. The land of opportunity is also the land of production and consumption; traditionally, work has been the means to achieve privilege and advantage. People have come to America— legally and otherwise—for more than three centuries for the express purpose of working and making a living, or simply making money.

Today American workers labor more hours than workers in most other industrialized nations. South Korean workers lead the way in total hours worked per year; American workers have less vacation and fewer holidays than all other workers in the Western world. As for average number of weeks worked per year, only Australian workers at 47.6 bested the American figure of 45.9, the two highest figures among industrialized Western nations. This was not always the case; American ascendency in hours worked, resulting in a decline in leisure time, began in the 1970s.[3] It marked the end of a trend of decline of hours worked. As the industrial era progressed, the hours in the typical workweek declined from roughly seventy in 1850, to sixty in 1900, to fifty in 1920, to forty by the middle part of the last century. At the end of the post–World War II economic surge, many commentators, confident of increased gains in productivity and innovation, foresaw a shorter workweek as the United States advanced toward the last few decades of the century. Those predictions fell completely flat. Americans worked, on the average, 160 hours more a year in 2000 than in 1970. Contributing to the increase in hours worked were the increasing numbers of women entering the work force. As of 2009, for the first time ever recorded, more women than men were on American payrolls. In part, this is further confirmation that as a culture, Americans have chosen money and possessions over leisure time.[4]

America, historically associated with the opportunity to work, now seems to be associated with the domination of work. Consumption, of course, has brought about work's ability to rule.

---

* As of 2010, immigration, legal and illegal, has slowed considerably from Mexico into the United States. The main culprit is the economic downturn since 2008. Mexicans come to the United States to work, and when there is less work to be had, migration slows. More favorable economic conditions in Mexico along with a declining Mexican birthrate are additional factors. Juan Castillo, "Study: Net immigration slows to near standstill," *Austin American-Statesman*, April 24, 2012, A1.

Early Work

Anthropologist Marshall Sahlins described our ancient hunter-gatherer ancestors as the "original affluent society." When he proposed this contrarian idea in 1966, he meant that many of these tribes in favorable settings spent less time working— gathering sustenance—than have many peoples and societies since. The common notion, challenged by Sahlins, was that hunter-gatherer tribes nearly always worked hard to survive on bare sustenance levels, and were fortunate at that. Quite possibly, according to Sahlins, they had significantly more leisure time than many of their descendants, especially their industrial era and postindustrial era descendants.[5]

Hunter-gatherers did not practice slaveholding. Settlement or civilization— private ownership of land, development of commodity production and markets, and scarcity of communal labor—brought slavery into the human story. Wars and the capturing of the conquered increased slaving activities as well. Ancient Babylon and Egypt practiced slavery, as did ancient Greece and the Roman Empire. The esteemed Greek philosophers in their writings covered considerable territory; they wrote extensively about human nature, political society, education, and the acquisition of knowledge. Yet they didn't have much to say about slavery, except to justify it. Slavery was a thoroughly accepted and unchallenged reality of their day. The paradox of nascent democracy and political freedoms arising from an Athens that was rife with slavery is obvious.[6] The same can be said for the Christian scriptures' ambivalence toward slavery. A compilation of struggles, history shows itself in grand progress, continuing ambiguities, and certain mysteries.

In the practice and theory of the Abrahamic religions, manual labor, which was the curse laid upon Adam and Eve for their disobedience,* has been reviled and redeemed. In the Middle Ages, to be a soldier, warrior, or crusader mattered. Peasants, however, worked with their hands, devoid of significant liberties, tending their lord's land, mines, forests, and roads. Monasteries, convents, and abbeys required of their inhabitants the same manual labor; because in these settings the work was religious in nature, it tended to be categorized as dignified. Thus, the bane and blessing that is manual labor. Depending on place and status, one person abhors manual labor, another is liberated by it. Chinese of the merchant and ruling classes would grow out their fingernails, protecting them with elaborate casings, to show that they did not have to do manual labor.[7] Slavery and serfdom kept the hands, and fingernails, of the powerful free from the dirt of the earth and accompanying self-degradation.

---

* Genesis 3:17–19.

Work Grows Up

Working with one's hands, and getting them dirty in the process, would eventually change the world as the industrial era dawned. Worker guilds flourished in the later Middle Ages, with the purpose of carefully passing on the skill of a particular trade from one generation to the next. The original trade cartels, guilds helped regulate production and maintain proficient technique. They also helped resist market forces that might erode the proper workmanship of their products with inferior, cheaper, and simpler products. The guilds jealously guarded their "mystery," or skill; the self-governed guilds not only preserved their own production quality but they also had a great part in transforming European society, which was centered on religious and military activity, to one increasingly defined by economic activity.[8]

Work historian and commentator Richard Donkin credits the hands and ingenuity of the English Quaker Abraham Darby with helping bring about the steady job as we know it today. Darby, who lived only thirty-eight years, was the first of three generations of Darbys with the same name. He held a 1707 patent for casting iron pots. Darby's principal innovation was to use coke (derived from coal) instead of coal itself for the smelting process of iron ore; the higher burning temperatures resulted in higher quality iron, produced faster and cheaper than what had been accomplished previously. Darby's cast-iron pots were stronger and not as brittle, yet with thinner walls—a cutting-edge advancement. Darby didn't work alone; he had regular workers who lived, as did Darby and his family, in cottages in the vicinity of the forge. Darby's son, just six years old at the time of his father's death, eventually took on leadership of the work. His innovation was wrought iron—the carbon beat out of the hot metal—which was stronger and more workable than its predecessor. Wrought iron, with its enhanced workability (and cheaper price than that of brass), brought forth affordable and reliable iron rails, locomotive wheels, and improved steam engines. Soon enough however, it was made obsolete by its successor, steel. With regular workers and shares of the company owned and exchanged, the Darby business transformed the way of life in Coalbrookdale, its home base. Money circulated among those employed, and their bartering, unlike before, involved more than simply the exchange of small produce. The Darby family's enterprise—four generations' worth—helped transform a job from a specific task with no promise of continuity to a reliable source of continuing employment.[9]

Long before the Darby clan changed the world with their innovations, windmills and watermills did the work of multiple laborers. The mills primarily crushed grain. Their utility later expanded to run saws, spin cotton, manufacture textiles, make paper, and produce other goods. Milling ("to grind") is among the oldest of the world's vocations. Miller is one of the most common surnames in the English-speaking world; Mueller for Germans, Molinari for Italians, Moulin for the French. Slaves and hired workers manned mills; as the industrial era gained momentum, more sophisticated mills made some worker tasks obsolete and the terms associated with the word *mill* acquired a negative reputation. The Luddite movement in early nineteenth-century England is the archetypical example of reactive protest against the changes brought about by new technology. A miller was a processing agent or middle man that added value to grain or cotton or wood. That value could be added to the final product while fewer workers were required to make it was a new and counterintuitive concept. The modern world was emerging.

Mill, as a general term, was so dominant that other factories adopted the same name (cotton and wool mills, steel mills), even though their work did not include grinding grain or other materials. And while certain worker tasks were eliminated as mills evolved, other tasks were added. The Luddites, in a sense, represented the end of the line for the golden age of guilds and their influences. The Luddites dismantled, destroyed, or burned new power looms and stocking frames (for mechanized knitting) installed by owners who simultaneously decreased worker wages. The new machines' ability to achieve magical and prodigious production led to the dismissal of certain skilled male laborers. They were no longer needed. Women and children were able to do the work needed; they were paid less and their hands were smaller (to better work the looms) and more dexterous than men's. The Luddite unrest (1811–12) was not able to withstand the oncoming revolution created by the new machinery. Weavers working by hand in England had numbered close to a quarter million in 1820; a generation later, with the advent of mechanization, there were only twenty-three thousand.[10]

Numerous children were taken from poorhouses to work in the mills. Compulsory public education in England and the United States was not widespread until the last decade of the nineteenth century. Historian Stephen Nissenbaum relates how, until that time, children were seen as miniature adults who occupied the bottom rung of hierarchy in the family along with servants. Unless extremely privileged and therefore privately educated, common children apprenticed at a skill, were dedicated to religious life in a monastery or convent, or otherwise worked to help out the household. His engaging history *The Battle for Christmas* shows the development of the revered holiday from that of the tradition of "misrule," common in European societies and colonial America, to what we know it to be today, where in secular observance children are the center of attention and charity. The practice of misrule allowed servants, common workers, and lower social status individuals to become kings and queens for a day or short season.

During the whole year long, those of lower socioeconomic status lived in deference to the rich and resourceful. During December in the Northern Hemisphere, when the harvest was in, beer and wine maturing, and animals slaughtered for fresh meat, people took time to rest and enjoy the fruits of the year's labors. It was also time for the tables of fortune to be turned, if only for a moment. According to Nissenbaum, misrule was "the time when peasants, servants, and apprentices exercised the right to demand that their wealthier neighbors and patrons treat them as if *they* were the wealthy and powerful." Servants pounded on the door of their patrons and came in for a feast, expecting fresh meat and fresh brew.[11] The colonial Puritans of Massachusetts did outlaw the celebration of Christmas for a spell in the late 1600s; it wasn't the legendary December birth of Jesus they had trouble with, it was misrule with its tendency to get out of hand. If you've ever received a Christmas bonus at a job where you felt you were underpaid, you can see that misrule, for better or worse, is still with us. It's part of the misrule bargain: accept the once a year bonus and do not grumble about your low pay for the balance of the year, a gift given in exchange for goodwill. The holiday season bonus—and misrule—come just once a year.

The great Chicago crooner Mel Tormé was right: "Christmas was made for children." However, it didn't happen until the mid–nineteenth century. Modern Christmas came into being at that time, celebrated privately in homes with immediate family. Children, not peasants and servants, became the focus of the season's charity and display of social inversion. Misrule was now domesticated.[12] Children gradually came to be seen as we see them today: minors who need to be protected, educated, and developed in order to become properly functioning adults. Only after this modern understanding of children became established did employing children take on its offensive character. Before the 1850s, there were concerns about child labor, but these were in the minority; in general, society was indifferent about child labor.[13]

In the sixteenth century, house chimneys burning wood became commonplace in English homes. In the subsequent centuries, coal replaced wood as the fuel of choice, as wood became scarce. Coal necessitated a narrower flue to make for a better draw on the fire. The smaller flues, however, created a problem for their maintenance and cleaning. The prevailing solution of the day was to use children for the job, boys and girls as young as five years old. Some children were sold by their families, others were stolen. To get the children to do the job of cleaning the inside of the chimney, any number of persuasions was used: the promise of plum pudding when they reached the top, setting straw on fire below them, or pricking their feet with a sharp object. What was called chimney sweep apprenticing back then, we could today call human trafficking. In nineteenth-century England, duping or forcing children of insecure status into sweeping, albeit beyond public view, was fairly common practice. Ironically, at this same time slavery was being abolished in England. The young sweeps suffered from "chimney sweeps' cancer" (scrotal cancer)—the first occupational cancer—and other ailments.[14] The practice of using children to clean chimneys was finally abolished in 1875; the unfortunate death of a twelve-year-old boy, George Brewster, who got stuck in a flue and was smothered by ash, provided appropriate outrage for British Parliament to pass new legislation. Master chimney sweeps, opposed to any regulation of their vocation, decisively lost the battle on regulation that had been ongoing for close to a century. They would be strictly monitored by police for permission to work—a late nineteenth-century form of a work permit.[15] Donkin comments, "This was not the first time, nor the last, that society and legislators would respond either slowly or inadequately to the social upheavals resulting from technological change."[16] Coal seemed to be an improvement over wood for burning in fireplaces, but the other associated costs, unforeseen by many, tarnished and sooted progress. The words of Niebuhr again ring true: progress for better *and* for worse.

The regular job, as seen with Darby's ironworks in the early 1700s, steadily became more commonplace as the industrial era made headway. Mill and factory workers, meatpackers, railroad workers, refinery workers, miners, and various types of machinists combined to make America the world's industrial leader as the nineteenth century came to a close.[17] The masses came, and they came to labor. Work was becoming ascendant, it was what Americans did. The English economist and historian R. W. Tawney made the claim that Puritanism—with its emphasis on thrift, frugality, and industry—was indispensable in making America the economic colossus it became. As Rockefeller and Carnegie made their hundreds of millions and the masses labored, the *Protestant work ethic became secularized.* The history of civilization has witnessed to various times and places where people sought out fortunes. These, however, had always been a miniscule minority. As the Gilded Age reached its apogee, seeking one's fortune was extended to a much larger congregation. This was good news: many were fed, clothed, sheltered, and blessed by economic growth. But the dark side of economic ascendancy was always there. In the words of Tawney, that dark side was "the uncritical worship of economic power." He further described it as "the assumption, accepted by most reformers with hardly less *naivete* than by the defenders of the established order, that the attainment of material riches is the supreme object of human endeavor and the final criterion of human success."[18] The secularization of the Protestant work ethic meant that salvation, once found by a prudent and pious lifestyle, was now found in secular work. Performed with devotion and dedication, work would bring money, which was the means of salvation in the new secular order.

Brave New World of Work

"Work was a divine gift and those who refused it were sinners." Thus Richard Donkin describes the secularized Puritan philosophy that was a guiding principle for Chicagoan George Pullman.[19] His worker town in the 1890s for his railway sleeping car company was ambitious and well planned; ultimately, however, it was manipulative, paternalistic, and doomed. Pullman's sense of religious business philosophy was based upon the writings of early English Puritans John Dod and Henry Cleaver, who held that the duty of vocation opposed the sin of idleness, and that the poor were at times responsible for their own poverty. True enough in certain circumstances, but in the possession of Pullman these ideas made for a worker town that was ruled autocratically. Pullman notoriously profited on almost every transaction conducted in the community, from water and gas usage to rent—homeownership was not permitted. In Pullman's defense, he realized that a direct correlation existed between worker contentment and rising productivity in the workplace. The town of Pullman boasted parks, schools, a boathouse, recreational access to Lake Calumet, and indoor toilets in all the company homes. His worker town was not the slum settlement that nearby Packingtown was, which housed the proletarians working the Chicago stockyards; by comparison it was paradisiacal. With the economic downturn of 1893, Pullman slashed worker wages without reducing housing rents, which led to a strike. The experiment was over, and Pullman was denounced. Hundreds left the worker town and its end was ensured. Pullman, who lived in a lakeshore mansion, died in 1897. Upon interment, his coffin was encased in thick concrete lest any of his legion detractors were to desecrate his grave.[20] His experimental city was eventually annexed by the city of Chicago.

Henry Ford's assembly line changed work and the world. Ford had a vision, and he followed through on it with alacrity. He wanted common folks to be able to own automobiles. Like Edison and the light bulb, Ford was not the inventor of the car, but he was the one who made it popular by making it affordable. His enterprising assembly line enabled increased production, reduced price, and increased wages for his employees. In 1909, before assembly line construction, Ford's Model T cost $950. In 1914, the first year of assembly line construction, the cost decreased to $490, with production at 230,788 cars. In 1916 the Model T sold for $360 with 585,388 produced. Ford adapted a line process used by Chicago meatpackers to disassemble carcasses. His workers, previously generalists, now became specialists, concentrating on one or two tasks of the assembly process. Profits were excellent; Ford was able to pay line employees an unheard of five dollars per day for their eight-hour shift (six days a week), doubling their previous wage. This was at a time when most industrial employees were garnering eleven dollars a week for a nine-hour daily shift.[21] One winter during the 1920s on a visit to Ormond Beach, Florida, Ford met a fellow business titan, from the previous generation. It was the aged Rockefeller himself, the two grasping hands in immediate mutual admiration.[22] Can we guess at their initial exchange? Thank you, Mr. Ford. No, thank you, Mr. Rockefeller.

In any discussion of Ford's assembly line, Frederick Taylor's influence must be acknowledged. An American born in 1856, Taylor is regarded as the father of scientific management; he specialized in studying worker movements, with the express goal of attaining greater efficiency. Taylor benefited from the recent refinement of an earlier nineteenth-century invention: the stopwatch.* In 1881, at Midvale Steel Works in Philadelphia, Taylor made his first stopwatch timings to evaluate worker efficiency. Taylor was employed at the mill, having started in 1878 as a laborer and machinist. Within a decade, after working as a factory supervisor and carrying out further evaluations, Taylor became one of the first of a new breed, the management consultant.[23] His work was extremely influential and the term *Taylorism* was coined to describe his philosophy and recommendations— the goal of increased worker efficiency attained by repetitive movements and enhanced managerial control. His 1903 publication *Shop Management* sold well and helped establish his reputation. However, not everyone was taken in by the new "science." Historian Charles Morris describes Taylor as a narrow-minded, obsessive, and hard-driving plant manager who was better at tool design than he was at management. He also portrays Taylor's publication as a "splendid example of sham science and spurious specificity run riot."[24] Taylor's penchant for lacing his prose with formulaic explanations might have looked impressive in the early 1900s, but it has not stood the test of time. Taylor did contribute to worker and industrial efficiency, but he also helped further worker alienation and degradation. Most any worker was capable of an instituted repeatable physical movement; the monotony of the assembly line challenged workers to use their brains in inventive ways to combat the novel drudgery.

No Ford assembly line would have been concocted in 1914 without the influence of Taylorism. Donkin makes a striking and controversial assertion:

> Taylorism and Fordism transformed factory working so completely that the systems together must be viewed as perhaps the most enduring societal change of the twentieth century,

---

* Days, nights, and seasons have rhythmically paced humanity's sense of time. The mechanized clock of the industrial era, by accurately dividing time into units, has made possible the coordinated activity of workers and accompanying commercialization. Whybrow, 158, 238.

arguably more influential and wider ranging than the competing ideologies of fascism and communism, although the destructive impact of these political ideologies is seared far more deeply on the collective memory of the human race.[25]

What the assembly lines produced was and is unquestionably staggering. Ford transformed the twentieth century, purposely making a vehicle that his own employees could purchase affordably and use. Mass production of the automobile further hastened the age of consumer consumption that has defined this society from the 1870s onward. Because of the automobile, people had more choices. Train travel was available, of course, but car travel was new and specific to one's liking; it gave an individual or a family fresh experiences. Car owners could purchase necessities from different locales now within driving distance, they could go to a different church, they could visit different areas of the state and country where people did things in their own peculiar ways. Places about which people previously had only read and heard now could be seen with their own eyes. Their cars took them farther away from home than did their horse carriages, if they had even owned one. Also, people did things in cars that perhaps they weren't free to do at home—drinking and other types of indulgence. The world got bigger and smaller and racier thanks to the assembly line.

The assembly line, for all the good changes it brought about, didn't maintain its innocence all that long. It was challenged and judged by popular and literary culture in the 1930s. Aldous Huxley's *Brave New World* and Charlie Chaplin's *Modern Times* attacked the monotony and tediousness of the assembly line along with its overall dehumanizing aspects. Huxley was especially unrelenting with his various premise and plot arrangements. The Gregorian calendar year in his novel is realigned according to the year Ford started selling the Model T; the year AD 2540 is renumbered 632; anno Domini is replaced with "the year of Ford." Ford is venerated as a deity; short reflexive prayers are offered: "Thank Ford." What were once Christian crosses have been modified; without its top vertical rise the Latin cross resembles a T. Huxley's dystopia recognizes the changes that the Model T's assembly line ushered in: mass production, consumption, homogeneity, and predictability are revered values. Constant consumption is the bedrock of society; "Ending is better than mending" encourages people to throw out the old and buy new! The Bureaux of Propaganda and world controllers, like His Fordship Mustapha Mond, make sure that things continue to move forward according to function and expectation. The stratified and controlled society is akin to a grand assembly line; the kingdom of scientifically controlled work has risen in the brave new world. Keep at your task, and if it gets monotonous, just take some soma.[26]

Chaplin's famous character the Little Tramp works an assembly-line job in the 1936 release *Modern Times*. As if the assembly line job is not enough, the Tramp's boss has him serve as the first-time subject of an automated feeding machine, designed to make lunchtime more efficient. The machine turns out to be an abject bust. The combined experiences drive the Tramp over the edge. He enters the assembly line conveyer belt apparatus, eventually ending up in the hefty gears of the factory's machinery. This, the most famous scene of the film, metaphorically portrays the plight of the modern worker in the early twentieth century assembly-line world: chewed up by the changes and spit back out.* The plant manager's surveillance cameras reveal everything the workers do on company time, but they fail to disclose their sense of despair. But the Tramp, as always, survives and perseveres. The assembly line is ascendant, but the spirit of the worker is not to be subdued.

The assembly line fostered mistrust and resistance among workers toward management—in the search for industrial efficiency work began to lose its meaning.[27] Chaplin aptly portrayed these realities in *Modern Times*; some one hundred years after Ford's assembly line, that reality continues throughout the world wherever workers serve the doctrine of maximized profits at the cost of their own dignity and safety.

One Hundred Years of Déjà Vu

Naomi Klein's book *No Logo* depicts, among other things, the plight of workers in the so-called Third World, not working assembly lines but working in sweatshops. Though she wrote in the late 1990s, not much has changed about Third World sweatshops, except for their venues. An astute critique of this particular part of international commerce, most of what she wrote about the sweatshop industry still applies. Many sweatshops, like the Chicago meatpacking industry at the turn of the twentieth century, consist of deplorable working and living conditions. Klein helped expose the shameful conditions of some of the sweatshops that supplied the apparel and shoe industries. A typical arrangement included most if not all of the following descriptions: A manufacturer arranges with a country to set up shop, usually tax-free for the first number of years of the agreement. Local workers, strictly nonunion, are hired, fulfilling the promise of new jobs created. Workers are housed, by requirement, in company-owned housing, where they pay room and board back to the employer. These workers are often young

---

* Echoing Upton Sinclair's assessment of the plight of meatpackers of the early 1900s in *The Jungle*.

women, typically more timid and pliable than young men. If the host country advocates worker rights too forcefully or withdraws certain concessions, like tax breaks, the manufacturer-employer threatens to up and leave the country—moving equipment and starting the same process in another country. An important realization is that the big companies—Reebok, Apple, Nike, Polo—do not own these manufacturing companies. They contract with them; in effect, releasing some sense of responsibility in cases of worker abuse or violations. The manufacturers, however, follow the big companies' production instructions precisely. They are not producing solely for the open market. Indonesia, Honduras, China, Mexico, Vietnam, Bangladesh, and the Philippines have been primary locations for *exporting process zones*, where many manufacturers house together various production capabilities. Klein documents the Cavite Exporting Processing Zone in Rosario, Philippines, a 682-acre walled-off industrial zone home to 207 factories that focused exclusively on export production. Her visit occurred in 1997. As in Chicago's Packingtown, workers lived just outside the production zone. The fly-by-night workshops, closely crammed together and made of cheap plastic and aluminum siding, were windowless; entry to the production zone was monitored by armed guards, who checked worker IDs. The hustle and bustle typical of a Philippines town (in 1997, Rosario had a population of sixty thousand) was not permitted inside the production zone, as buses and taxis, upon entry, were required to slow down and refrain from using their horns—in the developing world a taxi without a horn is like a pig without a squeal. Cavite, Klein says, felt like a different country. The tax-free economy, isolated from the local governments of the town and its province, was like a "miniature military state inside a democracy." First World consumers, buying golf shirts, sneakers, and iPads made in the aforementioned work zones, typically feel justified in their purchasing decisions, believing that workers in developing countries have the opportunity to work and participate in the worldwide market: production and consumerism as the two sides of the same coin of salvation. If, however, the working and living conditions of today's export zones are just as deplorable as those denounced by Sinclair, Pulitzer, Riis, and Steffens one hundred years ago during the Second Industrial Revolution, the same problem simply and sadly has been exported and perpetuated. Klein reported that work days in the various production zones were long, ranging from twelve to sixteen hours a day; child labor was a constant problem, and unsurprisingly, wages were low.[28]

In the fifteen years since Klein wrote, not much has changed. Foxconn, the Taiwanese multinational electronics contract manufacturer, makes Apple products and video game and computer components. Foxconn has numerous facilities in China. Low wages, worker dormitory suicides, and poor working conditions have hounded Foxconn for years.[29] In Bangladesh, a garment factory building of eight stories collapsed in April 2013 killing more than one thousand workers.[30] Not much changed? Maybe things are actually getting worse.

Many manufacturing jobs that used to be in the United States have been moved to these and other foreign locations because of the savings from lower worker wages and the dearth of benefits. Large-scale, worldwide competition has demanded the shift. Manufacturing jobs in the United States peaked in 1979 at just under twenty million; that total has been in slow decline ever since, decreasing to less than twelve million by 2011.[31] The minimum wage in the United States, as of 2012, was $7.25 an hour. Meatpacking is one manufacturing job that has had a long history in America. A number of meatpacking jobs pay better than minimum wage, but as it has been for well over one hundred years, the jobs inside the plants are dangerous and undesirable. As has been typical in the history of commercial meatpacking, the jobs have been filled by immigrants. For the last thirty years or so, packing jobs in the United States have been performed principally by Mexicans and Central Americans, documented and undocumented.

In the early 1980s, coincidental with numerous civil wars and conflicts in Latin America, nonunionized Latinos began to dominate worker rolls in the meatpacking industry. Innovations in the industry during the previous twenty years allowed plants to hire workers who were less skilled due to experience and language abilities. The guiding principle of the innovations was to make the job tasks less dependent upon skill. Sometimes worker tasks were created that required only a single cut made thousands of times during a shift. It was Taylorism ramped up all over again. The packing industry left Chicago and other major markets where unionism was strongest to relocate in rural spots in Iowa, Nebraska, and Colorado, closer to farms and animal populations.[32] The pendulum was swinging back against unions; the percentage of unionized workers in the United States has steadily declined since the mid-1980s (from 20.1 percent in 1983 to 11.8 percent in 2011).[33] Meatpacking had been a job that supported middle class families in previous decades when unions were stronger; now it has become an exclusive partnership between mostly powerless immigrants and leveraging proprietors. With diminished union representation, wages were low (40 percent lower in some cases), and health insurance and paid vacation were offered only after a probation period of six months to a year. Turnover rates were extremely high (100 percent yearly rates not uncommon), but employers didn't mind, because not having to pay insurance and other benefits made their businesses—on paper—more profitable. In addition, a workforce with a high turnover rate is much less likely to unionize, and, as with the younger and mostly female workforce in export zones, more likely to be reticent. This has been the state of affairs in the meatpacking industry since the early 1980s. High turnover rates are bad for the workers and their families because of the instability it creates, but the high rates are also bad for the communities they live in, due to increased medical costs that are transferred to the community when workers lack insurance coverage. Transient populations are more susceptible to drug use and crime. Established taxpayers in those meatpacking communities rightly protest the misuse of their tax dollars; but their ire should be directed at owner-employers (often unaffected nonlocals) who are essentially using public funds to subsidize what they should be paying their workers in wages and benefits.[34]

One thing that hasn't changed since commercial meatpacking started is the danger of the jobs inside the slaughterhouses. We Americans like a cheap Whopper or McRib, and meatpackers subsidize it for us with their arms, legs, fingers, and sometimes brains. It is America's most dangerous job. One would think that from the time (1906) of Sinclair's exposé, things would have become much safer for meatpackers now due to technological advances in tools and equipment and the implementation of modern safety measures. Not so—the main reason is profit margins expressly related to *speed*, the speed of the disassembly line. Annually 25 percent of meatpackers in the United States suffer injury or illness requiring more than minor medical attention. As the line speeds up, so does the injury rate.[35]

At a Hormel subsidiary slaughterhouse in Austin, Minnesota, one of the line tasks performed was hog brain harvesting. High pressure hoses forced the brains out of pig heads at the rate of one every three seconds—almost 1,300 heads per hour. Ten years earlier, in 1996, the same plant processed 900 heads per hour. (The pink slurry was shipped to Asia where it was used as a thickener in stir-fry.) Some of the workers manning the pressure hose developed a neurological disease that exhibited itself in headaches, dizziness, loss of motor control, and in extreme cases, temporary paralysis. An eventual diagnosis from the Mayo Clinic neurology department determined workers were suffering from a form of neuropathy. Porcine and human neurological cells are quite similar. When inhaled by workers, aerosolized pig brain cells caused the production of human antibodies, which in turn destroyed some of the nerve cells of slaughterhouse workers. This explanation seemed to make sense, but the employer countered that the disease had not existed in the ten previous years of brain hosing. As it turned out, the culprit was line speed. The disease symptoms had not been noticed until the speed of the line pushed toward 1,300 heads per hour. A worker who was permanently injured, no longer employable at the plant, received a one-time settlement of $38,600—mere pennies on the hog head. Ultimately, the slaughterhouse ceased pig brain harvesting. Whether that decision was made for financial or humanitarian considerations was not disclosed.[36] Maybe the buyers of the pig brain slush started to use corn starch to thicken their stir-fry.

The Secularization of Puritan Thought

Slaves, immigrants, and migrants busting their tails as workers: it's not exclusive to American history, but it's foundational. Africans picking cotton, Chinese laying railroad track, Mexicans picking fruit and vegetables, following the harvests; these are just a few examples of people coming to this land to work, some by their own volition and others by coercion. This is the land of opportunity; work is the true religion of the land. The benefits of work—a sense of accomplishment and community building, pay, and utilization of one's physical strength and dexterity and intellectual ability—are the promises met for the one(s) adhering to the religion. These are good promises and worthwhile goals and they have served the republic well. If you work hard, you can advance and prosper. But as we well know, there are always those who are not true believers, those who do not adhere to accepted practice and opinion. They've been described with various monikers—as lazy, unproductive, and on the dole; as sinners, welfare mommas, deadbeats, and slackers. The Puritans set the framework for this understanding, dating from days prior to the American Revolution. The Puritan solution to poverty, based upon their idolization of industriousness, was diligent labor. The poor had caused their own poverty as a result of their own idleness and propensity toward other vices. Idleness was chief of all vices in the Puritan worldview. Consequently, charity toward the poor was seen to be sinful, because it enabled the poor to continue in their debased idleness.[37] This idea, having its roots in the Protestant work ethic, has been secularized in today's American society. Drive by any major intersection of a prominent American city where someone is soliciting assistance—food or money—and the following is what you'll notice: A few drivers, stopped by the red light at the intersection, might be helping out the solicitor with food or money; the overwhelming majority of drivers will be staring straight ahead (or at their phones) as if the solicitors are not there. I'm not judging, per se; I often practice the latter of the two options I've described. My point: if commerce is our collective object of greatest importance, then those who are not participating—homeless or shifty beggars—are either ignored or despised as a result of their nonconformity. In a religious understanding of work and commerce, those who are not active participants—welfare recipients, slackers—are the unredeemed on the road to condemnation. Because of the choices they have made that contribute to their current state of nonproductivity (idleness), they are therefore getting what they deserve. For those who are true believers, that is, active participants and working conformists in the system, the act of helping the poor is enablement, as it was for the Puritans. This mindset—based on a specific Christian interpretation—is alive and well in the United States today, having been dominant for some thirty years. Originally religious, the conviction has been thoroughly secularized: if you work and play by the rules, then you eat. On the other hand, if you don't work and play by the rules, tough luck for you and your family. You are consequently banished to hell on earth (as long as you refrain from working).

This secularization of early Puritan thought has certain beneficial and practical truth. The hedge against idleness didn't start with the Puritans, but has been around for a long, long time. It's basic common sense combined with the principle of survival of the fittest, or survival of the least idle. The Christian New Testament records the authoritative figure the apostle Paul: "We were not idle when we were with you . . . Anyone unwilling to work should not eat."* The best interpretation of any text—religious or otherwise—pays close attention to the context from which it was written; the apostle was referring to a small, nascent community that needed everyone's best effort and cooperation to ensure survival and growth. No one was allowed to lie around idle while there was work to be done! The Little Red Hen agreed with this sentiment; her folk tale is Russian in origin. With its deep connection to the collective human story, the value of personal initiative is one that Americans have passed on to the next generations from the beginning of colonial life. This value, also expressed as "Idleness is the devil's workshop," is laden with religious innuendo; its importance is woven into American identity and purpose. There is profound and pragmatic goodness in this shared societal value; like the idea of good and evil *yetzer*, two related issues—work and hunger—combine forces to play off each other and serve the common good. Americans embrace work because it keeps us from going hungry. My neighbor also needs to work to keep from going hungry. Everyone needs to do their part, and all participants will consequently share in the bounty. Those who don't do their part suffer their own consequences. It's an integral part of our social contract.

As with most values, the "work or don't eat" value has a balancing principle. Just as plants need rain and sunshine in the right balance, one without its counterbalancing principle leads to overkill. The balancing principle for "work or don't eat" is *compassion*. Compassion is able to see that some people, including

---

* 2 Thessalonians 3:7, 10.

children, don't eat (or don't eat well) because of decided circumstances, some of those outside of their own control: famine, disease, corrupt governing bodies, poverty, injustice, family dysfunction. The two principles of self-reliance and compassion keep each other in check; when they work together a broad and flexible balance can be maintained. When one or the other dominates, inequalities result and societal stability is threatened.

Another factor that mitigates the value of work or don't eat is its susceptibility to racism. A majority of white Americans, shunning idleness, have prized the virtues of self-reliance and frugality for generations since the early days of the (white) Puritans. They could do so since, for the most part, playing by the rules has paid off for them. These virtues have worked for a majority of white people in this society. Blacks, Latinos, and other minorities have not always had the same positive experience, and there is ample anecdotal evidence in support of this claim.[38] Alternative perspectives are acknowledged in a democratic society; the legitimacy of one perspective to dominate all others is perilous. Interplay and interchange between different angles and various perspectives is much more organic and true to the way the world is now and always has been—ideological wrangling is more akin to the marketing ploy that one size fits all. Those who are able must work to eat and prosper; there are, however, multiple mitigating and correcting factors to that general rule. Reality, the further one delves into it, tends toward complexity more than monochromatic ideology or simplicity.

The balance between self-reliance and compassion has been skewed for more than thirty years in the United States, since the late 1970s. The United States dominated the world economy after World War I; much of Europe was decimated and the United States, with gold reserves bulging, didn't have much competition as the supplier and convener of reconstruction. The US economy was also dominant after World War II; the Marshall Plan helped to officially promote American economic supremacy in a world market where American manufacturers and suppliers lacked stiff competition. This lack of competition led to healthy corporate profit margins, which were taxed significantly in the 1950s and among other things, helped build the US interstate highway system and broaden the social safety net. New Deal influences still held sway. The economic playing field, however, eventually leveled out during the 1960s as Europe and Japan started to catch up.[39] At this same time, the United States was implementing, with great growing pains, civil rights enactments and was being torn apart socially because of its involvement in the Vietnam War. President Lyndon Johnson's War on Poverty, which continued New Deal objectives, shows the last gasps of an era that espoused some sense of social egalitarianism (indirectly related to economic egalitarianism). In the 1960s a figurative war on poverty was yet permissible. In the decades to follow, however, the tables would be turned and attacks would be waged on those living in poverty, along the lines of the secularized Puritan ideal of work as salvation and idleness as condemnation.

The increased competition in global economic conditions led to decreased profit margins in the United States. This was only natural; for American corporations to treat the post-World War II years as if they were the norm was unrealistic. The ongoing desire to maintain that previously attained profit margin, however, along with other factors, contributed to a reworking of the American social contract: *less emphasis on social policy and greater emphasis on fiscal policy.*[40] Two important factors buttress this claim: from 1980 on, homelessness in the United States has increased significantly and worker wages, adjusted for inflation, have essentially remained flat. (Disposable income for nonsupervisory workers in the United States peaked in the late 1960s).[41] The reasons behind the first factor of increased homelessness are many and varied, from deinstitutionalization of mental health systems to the failure of large public housing projects, to veterans of the Vietnam War and other subsequent military conflicts falling through widening safety-net cracks. The reasons for stagnated wages, the second factor, are based in an increased stratification of American workers, globalization's pursuit of low-wage earners, and in the United States, the thirty-year drift away from egalitarianism as a social value. As American society has given more emphasis to profit making, its rich have gotten richer, its common workers have gotten poorer, and more people, including children, live on the streets. Presidents Reagan, Clinton, and Bush (II) all oversaw welfare reform during their administrations. Reform is usually a good thing in a world of changing context and reality. Each reform in its own way moved American society farther away from its New Deal aspirations of the 1940s, '50s, and early '60s. In fairness to those three presidents and their supporters, however, welfare reform was seen to be a necessary moderator to welfare dependency. The pendulum does swing both ways.

In 1959 the US government published its first national poverty rate. It was 22.4 percent. This rate was a significant improvement over the rates estimated for earlier decades, according to researchers. Estimated poverty rates for the 1870s hovered over 60 percent; for the first decade of the 1900s they were on either side of 40 percent; and during the Great Depression they approached the higher 1870s' rates. Great Compression–era economic egalitarianism was beneficial to a majority of Americans: from 1939 to 1959 poverty decreased to the point where 60 percent of American families earned enough income to be lifted out of poverty. (This marker peaked at 68 percent in 1969 and has been falling ever since.) That first published poverty rate of 22.4 percent represented colossal progress for the twenty years that had passed since the Great Depression. Most minority families were left out of that progress, however. Consequently, Johnson's War on Poverty was egalitarian in that minorities (and poor whites) were to be lifted up economically through greater educational opportunity and health care. The legislation was effective: the US poverty rate hit its lowest all-time mark of 11.1 percent in 1973. This was amazing progress not only for the one-hundred-year period leading up to 1973 but especially for the thirty or so years coming out of the Depression. But then social policy took a backseat to fiscal policy. The memory and reach of the Depression's dark imprint was waning; compassion's half-arc swing on the pendulum had maxed out. The poverty rate jumped up to 15.2 percent by 1983.[42]

The unification of big commerce—represented by Wall Street—and government is the specific manifestation seen in the shift from social to fiscal priority that began in the early 1980s. We already saw what happened in the 1920s when the third wealthiest American at the time, banker Andrew Mellon, served as treasury secretary. In the spirit of Alexander Hamilton, Mellon subscribed wholeheartedly to the ideal of profit generation as society's primary priority, accepting social and economic inequalities as a necessary by-product. This is a legitimate strain in the history of this society; it is, however, extremely vulnerable to abuse, especially when its counterbalancing principle of egalitarianism is diminished. Mellon was unable to tune out profit's siren call. Undoubtedly with someone like Mellon in mind, *The Nation* magazine, in 1933, intoned: "If you steal $25, you're a thief. If you steal $25,000, you're an embezzler. If you steal $2,500,000, you're a financier."[43] I say again, 1929 sounds a lot like 2008.

Keynes versus Friedman

The pendulum does naturally swing; the New Deal era—generated partly in response to the excesses of Mellon and the 1920s—wouldn't last forever. The context from which it was born was transformed and left behind; new influences would offer perspectives for a new context and day. The dominant economic system coming out of the post-World War II era was based on the ideas of British economist John Maynard Keynes. Keynesian economics, formulated previous to the Depression but also forged through the experiences of the Depression, held that the economic future, based upon the interactions of erratic human beings having limited knowledge, was fundamentally uncertain. Prior to Keynes, classic and neoclassical economic theories were more optimistic about human behavior, translated as it was via market control of prices through supply and demand. (Mercantilism—which was heavily tariffed, crown or state run, and the cause of numerous wars—shaped the economic ideas formulated by Adam Smith, the father of classical economics.) The market economy was understood to be self-righting if left to its own devices. The *market*, the new guiding authority, was a better option than self-interested monarchies and countries. As the nineteenth century and its ambitious progress churned forward, this new understanding and practice of economics was superior to what had existed previously. The impressive wealth of the Gilded Age was the culmination (and for some, the continued promise) of what open markets could accomplish. The Depression, however, significantly challenged that construct; Keynes's theory, with its built-in suspicion of unfettered market economies, became ascendant. Government has the responsibility to spur economic growth when markets fail and, if necessary, keep markets from becoming predatory. (The Bush bailouts of 2008 and those of Obama that followed, along with stimulus measures, for the most part represent Keynesian thought.)

Keynesianism is a reformation of sorts of classical and neoclassical economic theory and practice. Keynesianism is realistic about collective human endeavor and its potential toward societal harm. The long-term effects of the Depression, although invidious, are Keynesianism's validation. As the lingering fallout of the Depression waned, however, Keynesianism as the sole legitimate understanding of economic reality also weakened. Its accompanying counterreformation soon followed, and this countervision was much more optimistic—or less worried, at least—about human interactions in the economic realm. Milton Friedman, the 1976 Nobel Prize winner in economics, was an advisor to presidential candidate Ronald Reagan in 1980. At that time, Friedman had recently retired from a thirty-plus year teaching career at Rockefeller's institution, the University of Chicago. Friedman was the high priest who resurrected neoclassical thought; he dogmatically advocated rolling back regulations, cutting taxes of the wealthy and corporations, and privatizing public enterprises. Just as Keynesianism is still influential in our day, so are the thoughts of Friedman. The battle between the two visions helps define the conflict between those who support neoliberalism, largely based on Friedman's theories, and those who don't.[44]

Neoliberalism, for our purposes here, is defined as the political-economic proposal and practice that emphasizes free trade, privatization, deregulation (or minimal government interference toward commerce), low tax rates, and reduced or minimal publicly funded social services. Friedman's ideas were entirely crucial to the development of the neoliberal vision. These ideas have been put into practice since the mid-1970s; proponents include Ronald Reagan in the United States, Margaret Thatcher in the United Kingdom, and Augusto Pinochet in Chile. Liberalism itself refers to the market theories advocated by Adam Smith in 1776 that signaled the transition away from mercantilism. Neoliberalism is therefore the new understanding and manifestation of classic market theories, updated for the postindustrial age. There is, however, one important addition: the political component. Harkening back to the days of the Gilded Age when government and big business sparred for control of the country's soul, neoliberalism joins that historic struggle on the side of big business. Though typically aligned with the Republican Party in US politics (Friedman was an ardent Republican supporter), Wall Street and big business have been just as friendly with the Democratic Party since 1980. Presidents Bush, Clinton, and Obama have not done much of anything to dampen the cozy relationship between the White House and Wall Street that gained renewed traction during the Reagan years.

Alan Greenspan, US Federal Reserve Board Chairman from 1987 to 2006, served by appointment under both Democratic and Republican presidential administrations. While a sense of bipartisanship might be construed from his continued appointments (five) by presidents of both parties, another view needs to be considered: mutual allegiance to an agreed-upon goal of ultimate importance—making money. Greenspan's philosophical apprenticeship at the feet of ideologist and free market fundamentalist Ayn Rand is well documented; Greenspan parlayed her philosophical dogma into an economic one. Markets are to be left to their own devices; this philosophy was deemed best not only for general economic growth but also—and still to our day—undeniably best for financial elites to grow their already substantial holdings. Friedman is classified as a strict monetarist (the supply of money being the determining factor of economic variables within a system). Focusing on money supply, Friedman advocated a laissez-faire approach to and within the market. Greenspan appreciated Friedman's monetarism and shared his faith in an unfettered market, but he chose also to mediate the market in a way with which Friedman would not have been comfortable: Greenspan was interventionist regarding control of interest rates. For the better part of his chairmanship, he was an effective leader who was able to raise or lower interest rates (the benchmark federal funds rate) as needed to keep inflation in check while encouraging the economy's growth. Greenspan was universally praised for his leadership. Perhaps he began reading the accolades and favorable headlines too much, however. In the last five years of his leadership, he did all he could do to keep the economy chugging along at its fervent pace by keeping interest rates at record low rates, thus making money cheap and available. He was the "Maestro" after all, who was held in such high regard by companies like Enron. The dot-com bubble had burst in 2000, yet housing sales kept the economy percolating along. But it turned out to be another bubble. During the first six years of the new century, house prices in the United States rose faster than any other time in modern history.[45] In hindsight, we now know that this aspect of growth was distorted and manipulated. The economy that looked so great in the early 2000s was, in part, a sham. Greenspan shares a large part of the blame for this sham interval in the economy. Another part of the Greenspan legacy is that during his watch, the financial industry lost its original and proper role of being the servant of commerce.[46] Greenspan was part of the usurpation the financial industry has wreaked upon other sectors of general commerce. From 1996 to 2005, the financial industry's (including insurance) share percentage of gross domestic product (GDP) was 7.5. This represented an increase of more than 25 percent from the previous decade.[47] The 1920s saw a similar buildup prior to the Great Depression, when the share percentage hit just under 6.0, a near 100 percent increase from the late 1910s. Business booms from railroads to automobiles to housing to pharmaceuticals naturally increase the financial industry's share of GDP. But, again, how much is enough? Even after the 2007–08 crash, the financial industry continues to carve out an ever-increasing chunk of the economy. As of 2010, the industry achieved an all-time high of 8.4 percent of GDP, employing some 6.5 million people.[48]

What Phil Gramm and Mr. Krabs Have in Common

Democrats and Republicans differ in a number of ways, but they are essentially united when it comes to uncritical acceptance of the ways of Wall Street. Yes, some tea party Republicans and left-leaning Democrats speak out against Wall Street excesses, but the large majority of both parties in Congress offer few protests or legislation designed to keep Wall Street from being its own master. The Dodd-Frank Reform Act of 2010 hasn't made too many people happy, from those who wanted the act to have more bite to the majority of Republicans in Congress who didn't support its passage. As we saw during the Gilded Age, when a large number of congressional members are themselves wealthy or beholden to those with wealth, significant challenge to the status quo is unlikely. Whereas 1 percent of Americans were millionaires as of 2010, almost 50 percent of US representatives and US senators were millionaires.[49] That in itself is not an indictment; but to imagine that one's wealth does not affect the way one votes, especially concerning issues involving personal financial interests is naïve. As an old Russian proverb says, "When money talks, the truth is silent."

My son and I went to see the *SpongeBob SquarePants Movie* when it came out in 2004. He was twelve years old; the movie had something for both generations, as the theater was evenly populated by kids and their parents. SpongeBob is the main character in one of the most popular animated cartoons of the first decade of the 2000s. The series features a number of lead characters (all sea creatures); a handful of Internet bloggers revel in the alleged representation of the seven deadly sins in seven recurring characters of the show. Restaurant owner Mr. Krabs (who is, yes, a crab) is especially fond of money, both its procurement and its retention. In the movie, Mr. Krabs decides to open a second restaurant adjacent to his original one. At its grand opening, he confesses his love for money with an interviewer, as he is asked what inspired him to duplicate his efforts. He answers the question instinctively with one word: "Money." Sometimes it's the jolt that comes from a change of scenery—in this case a cartoon—that helps one to hear the truth loud and clear. The implied mocking of Mr. Krabs's greed drew one of the largest laughs in the theater that day; even children are able to recognize that the inordinate love of money skews a person's—or a crab's—perspective.

As with Andrew Mellon in the 1920s, the 1980s marked another time (continuing to the present) where Wall Street types or financiers served as secretary of the treasury in the US government. Donald Regan (secretary of the treasury, 1981–1985) had previously worked for Merrill Lynch, Robert Rubin (1995–1999) had been co-COO for Goldman Sachs, Henry Paulson (2006–2009) had been CEO of Goldman. Larry Summers (1999–2001) is described as having been mentored by Rubin; Timothy Geithner (2009–2013) has close ties with Summers and Rubin. Greenspan, Rubin, and Summers famously "saved the world—so far" according to a *Time* magazine cover article in 1999. The repeal of the landmark 1933 Glass-Steagall Act (separating the activities of commercial banks and securities firms; lessons learned from the crash of 1929) was highly promoted by the three saviors. The repeal, the 1999 Gramm-Leach-Bliley Act, once again allowed for commercial banks to engage in securities transactions and for securities firms to "become" bank holding companies. Cosponsor Phil Gramm (Republican senator, Texas) echoed Friedman-like ideology upon its signing into law by President Clinton: "We have learned that government is not the answer. We have learned that freedom and competition are the answers. We have learned that we promote economic growth and we promote stability by having competition and freedom." History, some ten years later, wasn't kind to Gramm's pontifications. Many commentators include the repeal of Glass-Steagall as another major contributing factor to the economic troubles that began in 2007.[50] Gramm seemed to have spoken eloquently at the bill signing, using words like *competition* and *freedom*. Truth be told, Gramm is not much different than Mr. Krabs—what he seems to be saying is that he too really likes *money*.*

* So does his wife, Wendy Gramm, who holds a PhD in economics (as does Gramm himself). Mrs. Gramm chaired the US Commodity Futures Trading Commission from 1988 to 1993. After helping to push through a ruling of the commission to exempt energy futures contracts from regulation—*an Enron request*—she promptly resigned her chair with the CFTC. Five weeks later she was appointed to Enron's board of directors. Her Enron pay and perks totaled somewhere between $1 and $2 million

According to Yale University economics professor emeritus Charles Lindblom, a major flaw in American democracy is that market elites have special access to political elites. It takes money, today more than ever, to win political election. Consequently, political elites give ample attention to market and business elites (and their political contributions); there is a definite symbiotic relationship between the two. Presidents-elect, whether Democrat or Republican, now meet with corporate leaders before taking office; this practice is not something accorded other groups. It is an obvious affront to political egalitarianism. Is the trade-off worth it? Jobs and the predominance of industry are in the balance. Democracy is downgraded, in a sense, in order that the market be its most robust. The battle of control between commerce and government, waged in earnest since the days of Rockefeller, has squarely sided with big commerce for more than a generation. And to speak of the market and democracy as if they go hand in hand is disingenuous. In that market systems produce inequalities of income and wealth, Lindblom warns, they can obstruct democracy.[51]

The market system is more than an economic system, according to Lindblom. It's a system that serves as a method of controlling and coordinating people's behaviors. More complex than Adam Smith's earlier conception of the market as consisting of individual actors following their own self-interest, Lindblom describes the market as people "tied together" through myriad social and commercial interactions. The market gives freedom, but it also constrains and constricts.[52] The next time you go to the grocery store and try to decide which crackers to purchase from a selection that might run up to forty-one brands and 139 varieties,* you'll understand that both Smith and Lindblom are describing market realities. Was it the feeling of freedom or constriction that made you walk out of the store with not one, but three or four varieties of crackers?

The market system is simply the best and most detailed organizer of social cooperation that has existed in the history of the world. More than two billion people worldwide cooperate as people drink their morning coffee made from Colombian beans, have a technical support call for their laptop computer serviced from the Philippines, or go out to enjoy nightlife dressed in Italian leather shoes. This organization or grouping of participants is the world's largest, besting the Roman Catholic Church or the nation of China. Only the two gender groups within the human family are larger. Yet, Lindblom cautions, the market system is not an autonomous entity. Government aid and support thoroughly prop up

---

from 1993 to 2001. Her official duties on the Enron board of directors included service, sadly amusing after the fact, on the audit committee. David Corn, "Foreclosure Phil," July/August 2008, *Mother Jones* website, www.motherjones.com/politics/2008/05/foreclosure-phil, retrieved May 15, 2012.

* This total comes from my own count at a local grocery store in Austin, Texas, on June 7, 2012.

the market system. "If the market system is a dance, the state provides the dance floor and the orchestra." Sociologist Barrington Moore generalizes that up until the nineteenth century or so, the best way for ambitious types to pursue power and riches was through force and violence. Alexander, Caesar, and Genghis Kahn come to mind. In these last 250 years of world history, ambitious types have achieved great power and greater riches through the market system of economic exchange. The former method was generally violent, the latter—on the surface—generally peaceful.[53]

But as the saying goes: all good things in moderation. Rockefeller, Carnegie, and Morgan made their hundreds of millions thanks to the market economy, but their business practices were eventually challenged by antitrust measures. A healthy democracy allows for balance so that disproportionate powers are not able to dominate to the point where competition no longer exists. Big corporations, because of the power they wield politically and socially (the ability to offer jobs), have the potential to sabotage or bring an end to democracy. This is not a far-fetched assertion. Big corporations—even though publically held and vulnerable to downward market swings—can be understood to be authoritarian systems operating within democracies. According to Lindblom, many big corporations "exercise powers inconsistent with democracy . . . and play the role of an oversized, greatly powered citizen." Popular control of corporate (and other) elites—through the vote and the establishment of laws—is a defining characteristic of democracy. Democracy or "reverse dominance hierarchy," which we saw earlier with primates who practice a form of egalitarianism, needs to be defended in this current day, not against communism or other types of economic organization but against corpocracy. Lindblom states it succinctly: "It is the large enterprises that pose obstructions to political democracy. Through their spending and their relations with government officials they exercise much more power than do citizens. Their power swamps the power of all but a few enormously wealthy citizens."[54]

We've heard it said "that government is best which governs least." There's a lot of good sense in that statement—nobody needs overbureaucratized intrusions or expectations put upon their lives. But it's a tough balancing act in this post-9/11 world, the best (or worst) example being airport security lines; we want safe airline travel, but we resent the extra waiting in line and the body and luggage checks. When Henry David Thoreau penned the above quote in 1849 (not original to him), the American nation was in many ways still in its formative stages. Built upon a foundation of antimonarchism, American society was more socially egalitarian in theory than in practice. Thoreau was particularly agitated by two things: slavery and the Mexican-American War. Because it resulted in additional land for the United States and increased the number of southern and slaveholding states, the war was a contributing factor in bringing about the Civil War a little more than a decade later. *Civil Disobedience* was Thoreau's commentary of disgust for his own government that was expansionistic and suppressive. If Thoreau were alive today, would he have more repugnance for government or corporate overbearance? One imagines the early environmentalist would be more disgusted with the corporate malfeasance that has been rampant since the 1980s. And more than that, one imagines his rebellion would be squarely directed toward corporate entities motivated by one thing: profit.

Since the mid-1970s, Phil Gramm and many other free market types have been explicit in their embrace of neoliberalism's concepts, throwing in Thoreau's line (creating a new context for it), whereby *freedom* becomes code for *making money*. The government, co-opted and subdued, does best to stay out of the way. Regulations, impinging upon the freedom to make money, are as undesirable as a short sale on a rising stock. Yes, profit is to be sought, but when it's the utmost goal of an individual or corporation, trouble is never too far removed. Historically, the profit motive has stood against regulations on child labor, excessive work hours, occupational work hazards, and unequal gender pay for equal work.[55] Yes, governmental regulations sometimes inhibit profit making. But in a democracy, you and I do not have to live in subjugation to a corporate power that places profit making over other objectives. Government doesn't need to get out of the way so that corporations can reap maximum profits above all other considerations; government puts a brake on unmitigated greed and keeps the playing field balanced. But government has a hard time doing that when it is beholden to Wall Street. Phil Gramm calls Wall Street a "holy place."[56] Goodness only knows: Would Jesus ring the opening bell on Wall Street? Or, perhaps, the final bell?

Sandy Weill, the former CEO of Citigroup, was the most visible corporate proponent for the repeal of Glass-Steagall. The 1999 signing of the Gramm-Leach-Bliley Act saw President Clinton hand Phil Gramm the pen he used to sign the bill into law. Four others received commemorative pens from the signing, one of them being Sandy Weill. The pen, a small accoutrement, wasn't enough, however, to commemorate Weill's efforts. Weill also prominently displayed in his office a four-foot wooden plaque featuring his portrait with the descriptive title "Shatterer of Glass-Steagall."[57]

In 1998 Weill, fresh off the merger and acquisition of his own Smith Barney Shearson with Travelers Insurance Company, was ready for further growth through consolidation. Even though Glass-Steagall legally separated insurance, commercial banking, and investment banking at that time, Weill had Citicorp

Bank in his sights. Citicorp, headed by CEO John Reed, was one of the biggest banks in the world. A merger between the two equivalently valued companies was desired by both CEOs; Glass-Steagall, however, stood in the way. Weill set up a back door meeting with Alan Greenspan, the Federal Reserve chair, who certainly would have had the power to deter the proposed merger. He didn't. As a matter of fact, Greenspan was downright unconcerned about the brazen move, commenting to Weill, "It doesn't bother me at all." We've heard of so-called activist judges who try and change the law from the bench via their rulings; this was a case of an activist Federal Reserve chair essentially bypassing Congress concerning a law that had been on the books for more than sixty years.[58]

Many in the financial industry saw Glass-Steagall as a dinosaur of sorts. European banks were already offering multiple services (saving, investing, and trading); the American financial industry was at risk of falling behind the competition. This viewpoint was assiduously shared in the halls of political power in Washington, DC. Phil Gramm wasn't alone—Chuck Schumer (Democratic senator, New York), Tim Johnson (Democratic senator, South Dakota), and Al D'Amato (Republican senator, New York) all stumped for the repeal of Glass-Steagall. President Clinton already supported the repeal; he had been informed in April 1998 by to-be Citigroup co-CEOs Weill and Reed of the inevitability that Travelers and Citicorp would merge. *How kind of them to inform the president*—a classic case of the tail wagging the dog. Robert Rubin, Clinton's treasury secretary, was also on board with the proposed merger and the sidestepping of Glass-Steagall. It is clearly seen that big commerce—Wall Street's financial industry— and government were no longer joined at the hip, they were fused into one entity. Greenspan's Fed, on October 8, 1998, gave Weill and Reed two years in which to operate legally as they waited for the repeal of Glass-Steagall. Reed says that they were assured (by the Fed) that repeal would happen, without any doubt. In October 1999, as the maneuverings for Glass-Steagall's repeal were being worked out, Citigroup made a splashy hire: Robert Rubin. Just a few months removed from service as US Treasury Secretary, his new role was "office of the chairman" and go-between for the two new co-CEOs.[59] Rubin was paid CEO money (more than $100 million during an eleven-year span), and he outlasted Reed and Weill.[60] He didn't see the crash of 2007–08 coming, however; perhaps all those shards of broken Glass-Steagall, representing the death of superfluous regulation, blinded him as they reflected the sacred light emanating from the icons of *freedom* and *competition*.

Weill didn't make his money the old-fashioned way by business innovation or new products or entrepreneurial skill. He made it by growth through consolidation (and cutting jobs) in the financial industry. Size was his great advantage, and consequently, he had more control of wages, costs, and prices. Weill helped bring about the era of "too big to fail." In 1999, when the Citigroup merger was completed, the biggest ten banks in the country controlled 45 percent of all banking assets as compared to only 26 percent ten years earlier. For those in the largest of companies who were so motivated, pursuing short-term profits was a no-brainer. There were no constraints, except moral ones, to make as much money as unethically possible. Rockefeller and Carnegie would have approved.

Reed and Weill shared CEO duties at Citigroup for only a year and a half.* During that time, Weill introduced Reed to a new culture he wasn't entirely comfortable with: get as rich as possible. Part of Weill's previous pitch to Reed—when advocating the potential merger—was "we could be so rich." Before the merger of Citicorp and Travelers, Reed's largest year-end bonus was $3 million. After the merger, his year-end bonus was $15 million. He admits it was excessive; he was the same guy doing the same work that he had done before. He now deserved a year-end bonus five times what he previously had received? According to Reed, this was the culture "developed by Wall Street."[61] "Just a little bit more"—literally—since Reed's total compensation that year was $290 million. Weill's was $225 million; they were the two highest compensated CEOs in the country.[62]

In the Market We Trust

Religious fundamentalists—Jewish, Christian, Muslim, and others—have in common, first and foremost, an adherence to a system of thought and practice that in their point of view emanates from the sole source of objective truth. This in turn leads to a dogmatic conviction of correctness; they refuse to have their ideas challenged, examined, or criticized. Atheists can also be fundamentalist in the convictions that define their rejection of deity; and as we've seen previously, scientists can be fundamentalist also. One other group needs to be added to the category: market fundamentalists. These believe that the Market will provide all that we need and that the Market, served by its main deputy, unfettered free enterprise, is all-knowing, all-seeing, and wholly (phonetic pun intended) worthy of worship and praise. American historian of culture Thomas Frank calls this conviction market populism. Market populism is the idea that markets express popular will better than democratic elections and that they are accessible to

---

* Weill has since seen another type of light: he recently advocated breaking up the big banks as a way of restoring confidence and profitability in the banking system. "Wall Street Legend Sandy Weill: Break Up the Big Banks," July 25, 2012, CNBC website, http://www.cnbc.com/id/48315170, retrieved September 14, 2013.

all, regardless of gender, ethnicity, or social status. Market populism is also the devotion to see the market as more than the natural product of human endeavor or a phenomenal tool by which to shape society—the Market as a religious ideology.[63]

An important component to this article of faith is the idea that markets and democracy go hand in hand, as if they were a match made in economic heaven. Not so fast, according to Frank, Lindblom, and others. Political scientist Benjamin Barber has a long history of being able to differentiate between the two. "Democracies prefer markets but markets do not prefer democracies. Having created the conditions that make markets possible, democracy must also do all the things that markets undo or cannot do."[64] Markets are mostly interested in profits; left unchecked, they produce the parallel results of the Gilded Age, the 1920s, and 1990s and 2000s. Democracy and those that participate in democracy have the responsibility to keep the darker sides of the market—the siphoning upward of wealth and the power it can create for elites—in check. The Progressives at the turn of the twentieth century did so, as did the egalitarian spirit of the 1940s and '50s. To the contrary, few people are willing to stand up to the darker edges of the market today. Again, critique does not mean rejection. But when market fundamentalists come across a correcting or antagonistic word toward the Market, defenses are marshaled and the name-calling commences: "socialist," "anticapitalist," and the like.* As with a religious fundamentalist, a market fundamentalist doesn't need to debate or converse; the conformist value from the 1950s (for older Americans) combined with the fall of the Berlin Wall in 1989—the emblematic demise of communist USSR—still lingers and has fostered an environment where sober examination of market forces is unbecoming. Victory over communism has meant that, for some, the debate is over. Similarly, after both world wars when the United States lacked economic competitors, we see that temporary superiority doesn't necessarily mean continued hegemony. Lindblom agrees: "The steady and indiscriminate overendorsement of these [certain] virtues is supplemented in every period by additional messages relevant to the culture of

---

* Rush Limbaugh, a prominent dogmatist of market fundamentalism, went so far as to call the teachings of Pope Francis "pure Marxism" in November 2013. The newly appointed Pope, in *Evangelii Gaudium*, criticized the "crude and naïve trust in the goodness of those wielding economic power and in the sacralized workings of the prevailing economic system." The Pope was simply espousing long-held church teaching. Limbaugh purposely uses loaded terms like "Marxism" and "socialism" to sway opinion. He, and many others who loosely and pejoratively use the terms, often confuse the terms with egalitarianism. Rush Limbaugh radio archive website, http://www.rushlimbaugh.com/daily/2013/11/27/it_s_sad_how_wrong_pope_francis_is_unless_it_s_a_deliberate_mistranslation_by_leftists retrieved December 8, 2013; Vatican Press document, http://www.vatican.va/holy_father/francesco/apost_exhortations/documents/papa-francesco_esortazione-ap_20131124_evangelii-gaudium_en.pdf, retrieved December 8, 2013.

the time. At one time they taught the divine right of kings; in our time they teach the doctrinal correctness of capitalism."[65]

With its market forces, capitalism is the economic system that is currently ascendant. It has benefited the peoples of the world over and again with the creation of wealth, the advancement and proliferation of foodstuffs, and the exchange of products. Undoubtedly, capitalism is the best economic system produced thus far in the history of the world; but, it does have a dark side. Veblen named "conspicuous consumption" god during the Gilded Age; it's fairly easy to argue that since the 1970s the god has made a comeback that has not abated. Maxed-out credit cards, an overheated economy based on borrowing and spending, and a culture of propaganda and advertising that encourages continual consumption are defining characteristics of the current era. But buyer beware: in the United States we might have more people addicted to shopping than to drugs and alcohol. Free market proponents prefer to let individuals in a market society make their own mistakes—as opposed to a government or centrally controlled economy deciding what might be best for individuals. Persons inevitably will make bad choices; they can learn from these poor choices, and what is equally important, in the process their personal liberties are upheld. The market chooses winners and losers, all done within the context of "freedom." But the concept of freedom needs to be questioned. How free is someone who is addicted—to cocaine or shopping for shoes? When a person consumes because the pursuit of material possessions is desirable to the point of obsession—purchasing being the lynchpin of the continuous cycle—how much freedom exists therein? And for those who are not addicted to shopping or acquisition but live in consumer society—how do they determine whether their purchases are free of constrained motives?[66]

Marketing is mainly about creating desire for consumption. William Cavanaugh, professor at the University of St. Thomas in St. Paul, maintains that what primarily defines consumerism in the United States is not consumption but the pursuit or desire for consumption. As with an addict obtaining a drug of choice, the act of purchasing doesn't ultimately satisfy. When I buy a new widescreen TV, I might have a week or two of excitement because of the purchase, but that feeling will pass. The cycle soon starts again, and the pursuit calls. Besides that, we live in an increasingly throwaway society. Yes, many of us recycle paper, plastics, aluminum, and tin cans. But in our brave new world economy, we'll also buy a new DVD player because fixing the old one costs as much or more than buying a new one. Living in a consumerist, throwaway society is a great place to learn how to continually acquire and toss out more and more and more stuff. Huxley was prophetic: "Ending is better than mending." Consumerism is a type of spirituality in American society; it is for some a primary way of achieving meaning and identity.[67] We are the hungry ghosts, and because we continually want just a little bit more, we are hooked.

Homo Economicus: Worker-Believer-Consumer

As I have argued, the combination of commerce, materialism, and consumption is our bread and butter religion in the United States. It's a good religion for the most part; it has defined who we are as a people and society. This religion has fed us, clothed us, sheltered us; it's our ingrained sense of purpose. It has modernized the world and lifted millions out of poverty. Its development coincided with the beginning of the industrial age; work and America have had a great partnership for some 250 years, and even longer, going back to the colonial days. That which conveys a sense of ultimate importance is one's religion; work does that for Americans, because it is our means of materialistic consumption. Like any religion, however, this one has had its dark sides and difficulties: slavery, child labor, unfair and abusive labor practices, gender and racial discrimination. Answering the challenges of these injustices, it has adapted and modernized. Schools serve its purpose by educating continual new waves of workers; Americans, newly meeting one another, will ask each other the basic question, What do you do? Most of us know what the question is getting at; work is arguably the main form of self-identity in American society.* And as we saw before, if you can't answer the question forthrightly, woe be upon you. Work is the basis of our religion and our identity, the latter enhanced and defined by what we purchase and consume.

Social ethicist David Loy describes, in ways similar to Tillich, religion in functional terms. A religious system, understood functionally, can center adherents by teaching what the world is and what their role in the world is to be. The value system of consumption—delayed gratification long ago usurped—dominates because we understand the world, postindustrial era, to be exploitable. Take a three-hour car trip, for example, with a group of young adolescents who have money in their pockets, stop an hour into the trip at a roadside quick mart, and see if they are able to suppress the urge—nay, compulsion—to buy soda or candy. I'll bet you a bag of Sour Patch Jelly Beans that the majority of them can't! Loy calls our present economic system our de facto religion, binding disparate peoples together with a common worldview and a set of values grounded in consumption. Consumption is of course a secular activity—yet we carry it out with religious

---

* As further support for the argument, consider the well-documented sense of malaise and loss of identity and sense of purpose that oftentimes affects American men upon retirement.

devotion. Loy calls consumption the most successful religion of all time, winning more converts more quickly than any other previous belief system or value system in the history of the world. Work and consumption go together; the "theological" system that explains their workings is economics.[68]

Loy and others tell how economists (with support in the business world) in the last four decades have striven to make economics more scientific in its explanations. A cursory study of the development of economics in this time frame reveals its scientific aspirations (echoes of Taylor) as *ergodicity* (consistency in a system over time), *natural rate theory* (no permanent correlation between employment and inflation), and *econometrics* have come to be assumed concepts. In practical terms, that there is a full employment rate, that value is always adequately indicated by prices, and that the market is ultimately fair are some concepts that recent economic theorizing assumes to be actualities. To make for a more scientific understanding of economics, certain variables of human behavior such as swindling, corruption, and overconfidence—Keynes's "animal spirits"—have been deemphasized. Neoclassic economists (Friedman is the best representative) have made the case that since we now have a better ("scientific") understanding of economics, we are safer from the ravages of downturns and negative cycles.[69] This type of thinking took a significant blow from the economic difficulties that started in 2007–08. It takes a quixotic faith to believe that all participants in the market, as claimed by neoclassicists, are making rational decisions based on purely economic motives. Humans certainly have the capacity to make rational decisions based purely upon economic motives; but as Niebuhr implied, humans also, without question, have the capacity for irrationality and malfeasance (not to mention indifference) in economic and other decisions. Economics will always be confined to the realm of social science; enlightened and studied, yes, but a blend of fact and *opinion*.* A Nobel Prize is offered in economics—bettering philosophy, religion, sociology, political science, and psychology—yet, to treat economic understandings as if they are "scientific" and unassailable is an act of faith.

Does our understanding and practice of economics—neoclassic style—fulfill a religious function? Loy answers in the affirmative with the following assertion:

> The global victory of market capitalism is something other
> than the simple attainment of economic freedom: rather, it is
> the ascendancy of one particular way of understanding and
> valuing the world that *need not be taken for granted.* Far from
> being inevitable, this economic system is one historically

---

* Economist Ha-Joon Chang says economics is a "political exercise." Chang, 10.

conditioned way of organizing/reorganizing the world; it is a worldview, with ontology and ethics, in competition with other understandings of what the world is and how we should live in it.[70] (Italics mine.)

Economists George Akerlof (2001 Nobel Prize in economics) and Robert Schiller also answer affirmatively that our economic understandings and practices are quasi-religious:

> This New Classical view of how the economy behaves was passed from the economists to the think tankers, policy elites, and public intellectuals, and finally to the mass media. It became a political mantra: "I am a believer in free markets." The belief that government should not interfere with people in pursuit of their own self-interest has influenced national policies across the globe. In England it took the form of Thatcherism. In America it took the form of Reaganism. And from these two Anglo-Saxon countries it has spread.

Akerlof and Schiller make it clear that this belief is a type of religion with pitfalls intact. "Yes, capitalism is good. But, yes, it does have its excesses. And it must be watched."[71] As a people, we've learned that governments, even democratic ones, are not to be trusted entirely: Watergate. Politicians must be watched; as a consequence, we participate in public life as citizens, protest if necessary, and vote. But to believe that markets are unblemished and infallible, or more realistically, that markets, blemished and fallible, are not to be interfered with, is to have made peace with the modern spirit of profit motive before all other things.

Karl Polanyi, the Hungarian political economist, lived through the same societal experiences as did Paul Tillich: both were Continent born in 1886 and profoundly shaped by the events of two world wars. Polanyi's main work, *The Great Transformation*, was published in 1944. It describes the economic and social transformations in the nineteenth century that were brought about by industrialism and the prevailing market economy. Although the work has been legitimately criticized over the years for an overly romanticized view of past cultures, its staying power has been its critique, by contrasting description, of modern market economies. "Instead of economy being embedded in social relations, social relations are embedded in the economic system."[72] The profit motive of modern society has the potential to disrupt social relations. Again: how many of us have had a disagreement of a serious nature about money—loaned or owed—with a family member? These disagreements and disruptions have been around for as long as there have been families, to be sure. In our modern society money and economic status continually define relational values on their own terms. Ancient Israel, as we saw previously, used a system of jubilee laws to protect the whole community against inner-tribal exploitation. Whether they carried it out (mostly they didn't) is not the issue; the expectation was put in place so that *social relationships would be based on things other than economic status and wealth*. Polanyi rightly argued that capitalist society has an overt tendency to define relationships, individual and communal, on its self-imposed foundation of economic gain. *Homo economicus* has evolved and so has her religion: if we so believe, we can all be rich. Is any other pursuit truly legitimate in this life?

The Unlimitedness Delusion

A delusion is alive and well in America; it is the supreme myth no less of modern capitalism: economic growth is unlimited. And because growth is unlimited, everyone has a chance to attain riches. Social critic and author Barbara Ehrenreich spent part of a year as an unskilled worker, somewhat undercover, and in the process wrote *Nickel and Dimed*, her best seller that examined American prosperity from the underside. She worked as a restaurant server, hotel maid, cleaning-service employee, nursing home aide, and Walmart clerk. Sometimes she held two jobs at once to get by. When terminating her job with the cleaning service (where the cleaning crew labored in the homes of the well-to-do), she comes out to her fellow employees, explaining her motive for the book project. In her confession, she asks her co-workers their opinions about the disparities between the wealthy, who have so much, and regular workers like themselves, struggling to get by. She was surprised by similar answers from two co-workers: for different reasons, both respondents were okay with the disparities. One, younger, said she was motivated to continue to work so that "someday" she could "have this stuff" too. The other respondent, older, said she wasn't motivated to have the possessions of the well-to-do that they saw in the houses they cleaned. All she wanted was a "day off now and then . . . if I had to . . . and still be able to buy groceries the next day."[73] If classifying this second respondent as somewhat agnostic toward our proposed religion—commerce, money, and the pursuit of possessions—seems fair, there shouldn't be much protest against calling the first respondent a true believer. Grand disparities are tolerated because there is no perceived limit to the continually expansive nature of wealth available in capitalism; all, consequently, have the opportunity to pursue and attain it. A late 1990s (contemporaneous with Ehrenreich's book) *U.S. News and World Report* article on wealth disparity stated it succinctly: "Americans don't always love the rich, but they harbor the abiding hope that anybody can become prosperous." It's practically sacrilegious to opine that the American Dream of limitless opportunity is flawed.[74]

Where this myth most fervently thrives is on Wall Street, where money mostly serves itself. Because potential growth (as the myth proclaims) is unlimited, Wall Street types using money to make more money, with a lack of social purpose, is tolerated. There's something American about someone being able to make a fortune while the rest of us stay out of that someone's way. Rockefeller and Carnegie did it this way; and who's to say that the rest of us can't do likewise? As long as we aren't inhibited by unnecessary regulations, restrictions, and redistributions, we can achieve even beyond our imaginations. This mentality helps explain how middle-class Americans come to tolerate and support what happens on Wall Street. The average American sees the evidence of government regulations in many matters of everyday life. Taxes are paid daily on transactions, at times quarterly and yearly to the IRS; permits or licenses are needed to drive a vehicle, construct a deck on the back of a house, fish, hunt, or buy a gun. Most of these regulations are tolerated, but then an overbearing regulation confronts us by making a mockery of common sense: to put up a lawnmower shed in my backyard, for example, I'll need to pay fifty dollars to secure a permit from a paper pusher in the county office. In such a particular case, and in those similar to it, governmental ubiquity is glaringly cumbersome. While we understand that tax dollars help build roads and bridges, educate our children, and care for the elderly, we're also susceptible (in this post-Reagan era) to the idea that regulation and taxation, sponsored by the government, sometimes go too far and are somehow inherently evil, even anti-American. Consequently, this same line of reasoning is applied to Wall Street and how it operates. We think the local dynamic (overbearing regulation) we sometimes experience must operate the same way at a place like Wall Street. The worst case scenario is that government regulator wonks—who don't understand all the intricacies of Wall Street—get in the way, with their regulating control and intervention, of Wall Street machinations. If that happens, then that which could be unlimited is unnecessarily limited. Money to be created and made is squandered.[75] The American Dream is compromised by curtailing opportunity. So goes at least the rationalization of American unlimitedness writ large for Wall Street and other points beyond. To hinder money making at its center core—Wall Street—is to defy it elsewhere.

Social Immobility

Social mobility refers to the movement of individual or group social position from generation to generation related to changes in income. It is also called economic mobility. America, the society that was forged to be different than aristocratic and stratified Europe, historically has had a high level of social, or economic, mobility. From the descriptions of egalitarianism and opportunity by Alexis de Tocqueville to the rags-to-riches stories of Horatio Alger to the rise of the young Rockefeller (whose father was rarely supportive and mostly absent), America has been defined by greater social mobility than other societies the world over—until now.[76]

Data from various sources increasingly show that economic mobility in the United States is lagging behind that of similar developed countries. More so today than a generation or two ago, your chances of being well off are good if your father was well off; similarly, you most likely won't be well off if your father was not well off. It is three times more likely today as compared to the 1960s, '70s, and '80s, that your father's income level, for richer or for poorer, will determine your own income level. Five Western European countries and Canada, all having less income inequality than the United States, boast much greater economic mobility than the United States. The land of opportunity is increasingly becoming a blessing for those well born and a curse for those who are not.[77]

According to a 2009 *Pew Economic Mobility Project* report, men in their thirties earned some 12 percent less than their fathers did at a similar age. The factors to explain these numbers vary from the decline of unions to increases in immigration. Simply put, rising income disparity and decreasing social mobility are becoming more entrenched in the United States. Even after the 2007–08 crash, one survey proclaimed that 71 percent of Americans believe that hard work and personal skill are the two main components for economic success.[78] True enough for some, but not for all. Individual stories (politician Marco Rubio is fond of telling the story of his own family's rise) illustrate that belief in the ideal continues. Multiple stories (represented in many of Barbara Ehrenreich's co-workers in *Nickel and Dimed*) counter its reality, but they are oftentimes dismissed by the rhetoric—yet alive today—put into law by the Massachusetts Puritans so long ago: the poor can change their lot by working harder. True in a certain sense, but it's simply much easier to be well-off, and maintain that status, if one is born into that status. The myth of unlimited growth availing riches to all (who work hard enough) is a one size fits all legend. It is true and has been true for many; but for just as many, if not more, the legend is no more than false hope. Those who didn't have the foresight to be born rich are increasingly out of luck in today's America of social immobility. Some realities are more complex than the myths that attempt to explain them and give them meaning.

The exaltation of unlimited growth and social mobility is a chimera that, in American society of the last forty years, truly has been "the opiate of the masses." Karl Marx claimed such despised status for religion, of course; the American fixation upon the ability of all to attain wealth is a value that has become—in this day of social immobility—bad religion. Capitalism, in a larger sense, is more than an economic system; it is a culture or way of life. It has its grand advantages and benefits, socially and economically, for so many. But it does not have unlimited powers; it is not transcendent.[79] Whereas all religions and cultures teach and attest to the limited nature of human beings and things material, the religion of the Market claims otherwise: *There is never enough.*[80] The religion of the Market offers heaven on earth; work hard enough and it all can be yours. If you choose, however, to slack off and not work hard enough, you get what you deserve: hell on earth. To quote Tawney again, "A society which reverences the attainment of riches as the supreme felicity will naturally be disposed to regard the poor as damned in the next world, if only to justify making their life a hell in this."[81]

The Mall as Holy Place

If our true national religion is the confluence of commerce, materialism, and consumption (all market components), what then are our modern day places of worship for this religion, places that call people together and reinforce the belief system? One modern day abode of gathering, analogous to churches and synagogues, is undoubtedly the shopping center and mall. The three components of the religion—commerce, materialism, and consumption—define precisely what happens at shopping locales, malls being the archetype. Sports stadiums and manufacturing plants (some in the category of cathedrals) are also included as places of gathering and worship. In the words of sports savant Frank Deford, stadiums were places of "essential democracy . . . the arena made for a grand public convocation, a 20th-century village green where we could all come together in common excitement."[82] A resolution of winners and losers—a subtheme of the national religion—drew in the faithful (and still does). In the stadiums of yesteryear, corporate executives and blue-collar workers sat in proximity one to another, waited in the same lines to purchase the same beer and the same hotdogs; unwelcome rainstorms dampened richer and poorer alike. Those idyllic days are long gone; the Dallas Cowboys installed luxury suites in Texas Stadium in the 1970s—beginning a new trend—and life inside and outside sports arenas reflected the same reality: the privileged elite began to separate itself from the rest of the crowd.[83] Consequently, stadiums, as alluded to by Deford, have lost their identity as the best representatives of the national religion. Even though sports stadiums hold a special allure—recognizable to a large part of the general public because of television—they increasingly restrict the public's access as ticket prices (and related costs like parking) have escalated greatly in the last few decades. And besides, not all Americans are enamored with sports. Manufacturing plants are further removed than sports stadiums as the best representatives of the national religious gathering: they are significantly less recognizable to the general public, mostly inaccessible, and subject to relocations—stateside and abroad. Shopping centers, malls, and big box stores (Walmart, Home Depot, Best Buy, IKEA) are, on the other hand, accessible to the majority of Americans, nationally (if not globally) recognizable as chain retailers and open for business in most cases 365 days a year. In the last forty years, American real estate allocated for shopping has increased twelvefold, with a total tally of more than (2009 figures) 105,000 shopping malls, or centers, or strip malls. This is not to say that shopping, a necessary and beneficial activity for all Americans, is an evil enterprise. Shopping is what we do; rich or poor, the masses make the pilgrimage many times a month (some many times a week) to these temples and lay their money down. More than ten million people are employed at America's shopping centers, with more than two-thirds of the population served at shopping centers each month.[84] By vote or by dollar, that's a solid American majority. Shopping centers and malls, therefore, are the societal temples that gather the faithful.

The Mall of America is one of the largest malls in North America. Located in Bloomington, Minnesota, it is part of the Minneapolis-St. Paul metroplex, the sixteenth largest metropolitan area in the country. Fully enclosed, it boasts stores (mostly large national retailers), restaurants and bars, an aquarium, movie theaters, a roller coaster, a mirror-maze fun house, miniature golf, a comedy club, and other attractions. It claims close to forty million visits per year—more than the Grand Canyon, Graceland, and Disney World combined.[85] Historian James Farrell traces the first modern (completely indoor, climate-controlled) mall to the nearby Twin Cities suburb of Edina. Shopping malls previous to Edina's Southdale were extraverted, with storefront windows facing the parking lots and connecting pedestrian walkways. Opened in 1956, Southdale was entirely different: it offered stores on two levels, all under one roof, with a communal area inviting shoppers and guests to gather at the middle heart of the complex. It was designed by Austrian-born architect Victor Gruen and developed by the Dayton Company (now the Target Corporation). Trees, fishponds, exotic colored caged birds, gardens under a bright skylight—Southdale was described at its grand opening as a "pleasure-dome-with-parking" by *Time* magazine. The Jewish Gruen, a fervent socialist who escaped Vienna when Hitler's Germany annexed Austria in 1938, worked on forming contacts in America and quickly made a name for himself, working first in New York City and then opening his own architecture firm in Los Angeles in 1951. Gruen's vision was pioneering; he believed that the more time people spent in a particular commercial environment, the more money they would spend there. Thrift, frugality, and prudence were challenged in Gruen's commercial world; splashing fountains, spiraling sculptures, and escalators enticed and seduced consumers to spend both time and money. A Gruen biographer, Jeffrey Hardwick, says that because of Gruen, shopping "has become a distracting and fulfilling experience, a national pastime."[86]

Gruen designed more than malls; his passion was urban revitalization and he understood his mall designs, even though most were created for suburbs, to be subjugated to civic renewal. He envisioned a combination of commercial and civic participation through his designs that eventually directly impacted more than two hundred American cities and suburbs. White flight from large cities to new suburbs was prevalent in the 1950s; Gruen sought to create community with his malls, injecting commercial and civic gathering places into otherwise fledgling, monolithic suburban constructs. He had larger plans for Southdale that did not come to fruition. Apartment dwellings, schools, medical facilities, and public parks were also part of the original Southdale design; the intent was to recreate what had been lost as people, largely whites, abandoned the cities. Historian Lizabeth Cohen, in her book *A Consumers' Republic*, reveals a photograph of presidential candidate John F. Kennedy in 1960 addressing an all-white crowd at the relatively new Bergen Mall in suburban Paramus, New Jersey. This is what Gruen had in mind—he wanted to unite Americans, giving opportunity for richer public life, and to aggrandize retail profits. Both could coexist in his visioning.[87] And for some time, he was correct. A *U.S. News and World Report* survey in the early 1970s discovered that Americans spent more time at malls than anywhere else, besides work and home.[88] Work and related consumption—with time at home to recuperate and recharge—defines America's true functional religion.

Gruen's "shopping towns," attempting to bring the best qualities of urban life to the suburbs while leaving out undesired aspects of downtown life, reflected the socioeconomic and racial exclusion inherent to the mostly white suburbs. While downtown urban commercial districts were accessible for local pedestrians, those commuting by car found that parking was problematic (with delivery trucks, for example, competing for precious space); for both pedestrians and commuters chaos reigned, security was dubious, and supply varied. A suburban mall, with centralized administration and mandatory tenant cooperation, ample parking and hired security guards, and specified truck delivery areas, *by its very design* became restricted (and efficient) public space. Downtown regulars, like vagrants, prostitutes, racial minorities, and the poor, were excluded from suburban malls. While this type of exclusion was beneficial to business—racial exclusion being culturally acceptable in the 1950s—a certain caste was set that has hindered some malls ever since. Highland Mall was the first regional mall built in Austin, Texas, and is emblematic of this problem. Constructed in 1971 on the city's north side, Highland Mall began to experience economic decline in the early 2000s. In the decades since it opened the demographics of the surrounding neighborhoods have changed, and today Highland Mall is frequented more often, but not exclusively, by Austin's African American community. Every spring the University of Texas at Austin hosts the Texas Relays, one of the premier track and field events in the country. Due to the large number of African American event participants, the relays are also a social gathering and destination event for African Americans in general. Highland Mall, due to its proximity to the university, had become a local gathering area for young African Americans during the relays. In 2009, after two consecutive Texas Relay weekends of tension between mall tenants and visitors (in 2007 and 2008), Highland Mall officials determined that the mall would close early on the weekend of the event, effectively barring young African Americans from congregating there. Predictably, many sectors within the Austin community, not least its African American community, decried the decision. Highland Mall, previously in decline, has consequently experienced further decline since the 2009 strife.[89] Highland Mall's Texas Relays controversy is not directly attributable to Gruen, yet, at the same time, its manifestation is not surprising. It was fueled, in part, by a model and design that had been forged before civil rights era sensibilities were widespread. Malls have been intended, from their beginnings, for a certain clientele. Upper- and middle-class whites, with their children, were first on that list.

Would there have been a more apropos place than the mall for Santa to inhabit?* Santa, the very embodiment of consumption's blessings for the youngest members of society, has for three generations gathered the faithful at America's malls in the Christmas season. Why not reinforce the value of consumption at the place it can be fulfilled? The domestication of misrule moves forward, as the bearded and bellied commercial icon par excellence looks into the eyes of a child and all but promises her that her material dreams will be fulfilled. Her parents, doing their part to fulfill her dreams by shopping at the mall's stores, reinforce the image of Santa as the most appropriate icon for an affluent society.[90]

---

* Santa's first appearance in the Macy's Thanksgiving Day Parade was in 1924.

Farrell describes our malls as "cathedrals of consumption" and Santa as our national patron saint. The American Santa, unlike his European predecessors, does not have any religious associations—no religious robe, mitre, or staff. His belly is evidence of his self-indulgence; Farrell calls him a "symbol of material abundance and hedonistic pleasures." Yet, he does have a religious aura; divinely supernatural and omniscient, he knows about all our activities (if we've been good or bad) and gives pleasing gifts to the deserving. And, he is *chill*; he'll laugh off our indiscretions and with a twinkle in his eye, give his divine-like blessing on our American Christmas. Santa was present in the department stores for the Christmas season in the pre-mall era, but truly hit his stride in the post-World War II consumerist age. The Christmas holiday season, presided over by Santa, is the high holy season for the market. More Americans exchange gifts during the season than make religious observance; it's common knowledge that many retailers make the bulk of their profits during the winter holiday season. Malls serve as the official sponsors of the American Christmas.[91]

At two years of age American children are able to name certain products. At four years of age, they begin to evaluate products for their relative worth, and at six years of age, they are able to internalize the idea that better brands cost more. In comparison with other kids throughout the world, American kids aren't as good as they used to be in math and science. But fear not and don't fret: American kids are really good at *consumption*. Farrell is insightful: "Kids learn the pleasures of consumption before they learn any of its costs." Christmas, the preeminent public ritual of consumption in American life, serves as a type of home schooling for American youth in the arts and ways of consumption. In his tenth year of living, a typical American kid will make 270 store visits. He is being educated in the ways of consumer culture, for better and for worse. When he becomes a teenager, he understands advertising to be popular culture. Getting an iPad for Christmas is truly "getting lost in the things we love" (quoting the iPad TV commercial), because adolescents do understand that receiving and having an iPad is a status and ego enhancer.

The mall, besides being the place to be during the Christmas season, is the place to be during the rest of the year as well. As we saw before, malls are not welcome territory for beggars, drug dealers, or gang members (real or alleged). For parents of youth a mall, by design, is an oasis of security. A parent can feel relatively safe about her child going to the mall. It's an enclosed area, and no prohibitive activities are sponsored at the mall. Like churches, malls offer interpretations of the good life.[92] The architecture inside the mall is uplifting, the lights are bright, and the material items presented for consumption are desirable. This is the good life, and the mall offers an edenic vision for those who believe. If you have enough credit or ready cash, the mall, like a church, can be understood to be a place that points to a type of salvation.

But, alas, modern malls are aging. The proliferation of mall construction in the United States—coinciding with the advent of credit cards and the era of instant gratification—reached its apogee not long after it started. Growing bountifully in the 1950s and early 1960s and populated mostly by whites, like country clubs and a number of suburban churches, their day in the sun has faded. The International Council of Shopping Centers lists some 1,100 enclosed regional malls in the United States; a third are doing well, another third are dealing with difficulties, and the final third (those like Highland Mall) are in financial distress or in the process of closing.[93] While construction of new malls today in the United States is almost unheard of, numerous American-style malls are currently being constructed in China, India, Dubai, and other regions throughout the world.* Globalization includes exporting the American version of the consumerist religion. China boasts the two largest malls (by leasable space) in the world. The New South China Mall in Donggaun and Golden Resources Mall in Beijing—twice and one and a half times as big, respectively, as the Mall of America—are not experiencing the business activity that had been anticipated. The Donggaun mall is described as a ghost town at less than 20 percent occupation by retailers. The Beijing mall's developers might have overstepped with their advertising and propaganda: "The mall that will change your life."[94] Back in America, where the mall was created and established, many malls are being redone or updated if not being closed down and abandoned altogether. The Mall of America is now twenty years old; its luster is fading and its restoration and revitalization necessary if it is to remain a player in the American commercial scene. Seniors walking a mile or two in the malls' climate-controlled environs and leaving without spending money—Gruen didn't foresee this—won't keep J. C. Penney, Gap, Old Navy, and Finish Line in the black.

Shopping centers and big box stores, however, are saving the day and filling the void created as some malls are pushed aside. The Internet, also, has carved out its share of the commercial transaction pie, with ample expansion expected. The Internet is a virtual mall and then some. Its individualistic nature perfectly fits younger consumers who have been raised in the ethos and aura of individualism. What will the future hold? We are told that there will be no limit to the commercial expansion possible in a freely open-market system—the pie will only get larger. Heightened consumption, the storyline continues, is only natural in an ever-expanding and unlimited system. British theologian Peter Sedgwick

---

* The September 2013 attack on the Westgate Mall of Nairobi by the Somali terrorist group al-Shabaab can be seen as a clash of religions—jihadist Islam against Western consumerism.

hints at twenty-first century, post-mall Britain and America where, ironically, mall-style consumption upsets the social and ethnic stratification suburban malls helped solidify in the first place: "Identity in today's society . . . is no longer given by ethnicity, class, gender or social status. People find out who they are or want to be, by consumption."[95] Religion is function and belief; consumption, be it at big box stores, shopping centers, malls, or via the Internet, bridges the gap between function and belief. We've come to the place where we believe that we are what we buy.

Is It Worth It?

The good old American Dream—which in more egalitarian days spoke of *opportunity*—is manifested today as *consumption*: get a job (or inherit money or win the lottery) and start accumulating stuff, things, and whatnots. Due to decreased economic mobility, separate groupings exist for those chasing the dream. For those born into favorable economic conditions, *start* accumulating stuff is amended to *continue* accumulating stuff. For those not born into favorable circumstances—best of luck, because your journey (if pursued) toward greater wealth and accumulation continues to be hindered, as it has been for forty years now, by the ideology of excessive self-reliance at the cost of the ethic of compassion. Opportunities that had previously existed for many now exist only for a small minority. Democracy is potentially diminished by market systems that produce inequalities of income and wealth.[96] The market system as we know it, especially in its recent history, is not an entity best left to its own devices. As we've seen, the market system is fully able to incorporate racism, sexism, other prejudices, and blatant injustices. It will play favorites, and it can be manipulated for one's own unrighteous gain at the expense of others. These unfortunate realities are not always rooted out of the system as "inefficiencies"; as long as there are those who, because of greed or other self-serving reasons, advocate and strive for them, these injustices will be market realities.

In a recent worship service at the dual-language congregation I serve, during the message time we engaged in a conversation about the anxiety caused by living in an overtly consumerist society. (Anxiety and depression are recognized as the most common mental illnesses in the United States.)[97] Specifically, this conversation involved a number of first-generation immigrant Latinos who are adroitly able to make comparisons, economic and otherwise, between the societies they left behind in Latin America and the one they live in now. One of our members, originally from Guatemala, spoke of the weariness she experiences in trying to keep up, working two jobs, and helping to care for her family, now blessed with four grandchildren. "When I look in the mirror, and I see this person who is tired and aging, I ask myself: Is it worth it?" (my translation). Her husband immediately reassured her that her aging face was still beautiful, but her question struck a chord with all those present.

Work is a great opportunity in the United States. We're thankful for it even as it saps our energy and youthfulness. But, does work always deliver on its promise to take care of us? Whom does our work benefit—ourselves and our community, or are we unwittingly part of some larger design where our contributions are parasitically annexed for someone else's gain? Is the pace that we keep with our work one that gives freedom or creates bondage? Increasingly, our rates of consumption with their propensity toward excesses speak of bondage— exorbitantly so. Americans have 1.3 billion credit cards (four for every man, woman, and child) while our savings rate continues to plummet to nearly net zero.[98]

If hunter-gatherer societies experienced what we today call leisure, how far have we come since then? The postindustrial age promised leisure in abundance because of mechanical and technological advances: electricity, indoor plumbing, automobiles, washing machines, dryers, stoves and ovens, freezers, blenders, lamps, and so many other conveniences were to make our lives freer and easier. Somehow, the promise is not fulfilled. Yes, without question, most of us are better off than our ancestors. But the ailments and deficiencies of previous ages have been replaced by modern ones—many related to our frenzied belief that more is always better.

The true religion—ultimate concern—of American society is found and based in the confluence of commerce, materialism, and consumerism. It's been a good religion that has taken care of many of us very well; millions of lives have been lifted up from poverty and provided with food, shelter, clothing, and further material blessing. (It has simultaneously destroyed a good many as well.) There is great purpose in work, and oftentimes our toil, ingenuity, and perseverance in work have served the human family admirably. But this religion—especially in the last one hundred years of Rockefeller's new permission—has pushed to pierce the soul, individually and collectively, adulterating our spirits with its creed of more is better. Truth be told: more is not always better.

CHAPTER 6

EXCESS

We return to George Carlin for further description of present-day America: "Only a nation of unenlightened half-wits could have taken this beautiful place and turned it into what it is today: a shopping mall . . . That's all you got here, folks, mile after mile of mall after mall."[1] Hyperbolic, yes, but descriptive nonetheless. "Just a little bit more" has in this early part of the twenty-first century officially gone overboard into *excess*. After the attacks of September 11, 2001, President Bush consoled the country and called upon Americans not to fear but to continue with regular plans, like flying and doing "business around the country" and going "down to Disney World in Florida." (The alleged Bush quote about going shopping in response to the 9/11 attacks is erroneous; the president did encourage Americans to "go shopping more" during a news conference in December 2006, some five years after the attacks, in comments unrelated to 9/11. An offshoot of Neisser's *Challenger* experiment [chapter 4] lives on.)[2] As the president counseled, we did continue with regular activity for the most part. Many throughout the world grieved those who passed away in the attacks—representing sixty-two countries and nearly every ethnic group and significant religion practiced within the human family[3]—as US and British forces, with NATO support, entered Afghanistan to fight "the war on terror." Soldiers and their families sacrificed; the rest of us, however, continued on with our lives as we knew them. Credit was easy, homes were being bought, flipped, and sold; the consumerist binge—sans the airline industry—continued unabated. "Just a little bit more" gone to excess wasn't to be stopped by a band of religious extremists gone odious.

Racing to the Red Light

How many of us have traveled at an unsafe speed in crowded and treacherous conditions but were unwilling or unable to slow down because everyone else was racing right along? Nobody wakes up in the morning thinking, "I'm going to start my day off with a car accident on the way to work!" Yet it happens just about every morning in large cities across the country—tune into your local radio traffic report. During the morning rush hour on December 1, 2011, outside Nashville, in heavy fog and black ice, 176 cars were involved in a chain reaction of traffic accidents. One person perished, sixteen were injured, and fifty cars were left to be towed.[4] Sometimes we're driving a bit blind, moving forward at speeds that can't be maintained. Sometimes *slow is fast*: it can be faster to get to our destination by slowing down, and arriving alive, than it is to get there earlier, arriving bruised, beaten, or worse, on a gurney.

Do people love their jobs so much that they literally rush most every morning to arrive as fast as possible? Nobody wants to get stuck in traffic, but we rightly assume that the morning rush is not about the love of the job. The competitive urge naturally emerges when we are among many who are pursuing the same perceived goal. "Racing to the Red Light" is how musician James McMurtry describes our style of living, played out on rush-hour freeways and elsewhere, betraying the societal penchant to "cut your throat for your space in line . . . racing to the red light."[5]

I asked my local car mechanic, Raymond, a guy who's been in the business for almost thirty years, if drivers are using up brake pads on their cars faster than they used to. I wanted to get his perspective on whether people's driving habits have changed in the past few decades, racing to and then braking at all those red lights. In my own completely unscientific opinion, a bevy of American drivers has taken a page out of the manual of the charter bus driver who doesn't get paid until the bus arrives at its destination: ride either the accelerator or the brake pedal abusively, one or the other at all times until said destination is reached— passenger sickness bags at the ready. Raymond said that brake pads are better now than they used to be, and highway speed limits are considerably higher now than previously. Those two considerations balance each other out, in a sense. Whereas 36,000 miles is the lifespan recommended by the brake pad manufacturers today, Raymond said that he's seen instances where people get only 15,000 miles out of their car's brake pads. That's a lot of stop and go—and riding the brake. I recently got 85,000 miles out of my brake pads, but I am older and slower than I used to be—and drive that way, too. Don't get the wrong idea, though: awhile back I decided that it's much better to coast to the red light. Like I tell my friends, the *fourth* time I went to defensive driving classes, the slow is fast philosophy started to make sense.

Certain situations and conditions dictate how we drive, and there will always be limits on speed. (Even the famous German *Bundesautobahn* is regulated by speed limits for particular vehicles and for all vehicles at junctions, urban areas, and construction zones.) When the Middle East oil crisis hit in 1973, the US national speed limit was reduced to fifty-five miles per hour. It wasn't too popular; it was amended in 1987 to sixty-five miles per hour, and then abolished altogether in 1995, jurisdiction for highway speed limits returning to the states. That sped things up a bit, as most states opted for higher limits. The change wasn't a bit surprising, and it reflected similar changes happening in other areas of American life. "Just a little bit more" was the rule of thumb for Wall Street, as we've seen, for Main Street, and for many points between.

The Big Three—Fat, Sugar, and Salt

David Kessler, MD, served as commissioner of the US Food and Drug Administration under Presidents Bush (elder) and Clinton. He's a pediatrician who has witnessed firsthand America's struggle with obesity. He says the struggle went awry in the 1980s—"something changed." Not until the early 1990s, when researchers were evaluating data from the 1980s, was the drastic change noticed. Whereas just under half of the American population was overweight or obese through the 1970s, the rate increased steadily beginning in 1980. The increase continues more than thirty years later; close to two-thirds of all American adults are overweight or obese, with nearly one-third of children and adolescents in the same category (a threefold increase from 1980). Diabetes in America is rampant, increasing by 275 percent in the same time period. The most intriguing detail herein is that the heaviest people in the country were and are gaining disproportionally more weight than others—similar to the reality that the very richest of the economically rich have gotten significantly richer in America over the past thirty years.[6]

Kessler states the obvious, with scientific backing, that "weight gain is primarily due to overeating." He cites a number of contributing factors that have led to increased consumption: more chain restaurants, larger portion sizes being served, increases in available ready-to-eat food, a breakdown in meal structure at homes including the acceptance of eating alone, increases in snacking, and social settings supplemented by food.[7] The modern sedentary lifestyle, metabolism rates, and genetic factors are also outcome determinants, but none of these can explain the incredible epidemic of weight gain sweeping across developed countries, including the United States, Great Britain, Canada, and Greece. In these and other developed countries, for the first time in human history, the poor are obese and the rich are thin. Fat has become a class issue, and the poor are increasingly getting more of what they don't really need.[8]

A woman I know who suffers with obesity tells of a childhood where most of her meals came from fast-food restaurants. For the time period of the woman's childhood, she describes her mom as loving, busy with work inside and outside the home, but not especially enamored with their home kitchen. As a result,

McDonald's, Burger King, and Wendy's did most of the cooking. Today, the woman and her husband, who also has struggled with obesity, are homeowners and parents of two children. Their combined income places them sufficiently above the poverty line but under the median income mark for dual-earner households. Fortunately, the couple has altered their eating habits significantly and taken on, for the first time in their adult lives, purposeful physical exercise. They are becoming healthier, but it's a daily struggle—especially with diet choices—when the *big three,* fat, sugar, and salt, dominate so much of American food.

Kessler spotlights the three-pronged culprit of fat, sugar, and salt to explain the not-so-great gains since the early 1980s. *Palatability* refers to a food's ability to stimulate the appetite and prompt us to eat more of it—even after our caloric needs are satisfied. Palatability is based on how food enlists the full range of our senses. Like the anticipation of material consumption (Cavanaugh's pursuit or desire to consume), the *idea* of consuming certain foods—bacon comes to mind—is how the brain motivates the mouth and the stomach. The most palatable foods are those that employ a combination of two or all three of the fat, sugar, and salt triad. Again, bacon comes to mind, as does ice cream, grilled steak (salt seasoned, of course), chocolate, and chicken wings. Is it any wonder, as you think about it, that a Snickers bar satisfies your hunger much more than raw carrot sticks? Sugar and fat make the most pleasing combination—it's what people will eat the most of—and the right combination can turn palatable foods into "hyperpalatable" foods.[9]

Our brains are engaged, according to Kessler, and even changed by that unholy triad, just as a drug addict's brain chemistry is changed by excessive drug use. Neurons, the opioid circuitry, dopamine, and endorphins are all part of the brain's pleasure system, which can be activated by using drugs or eating high-sugar or high-fat foods. Depending on the person and her emotional relationship with food, the effects can be calming, relieving stress or pain. Careful, however, warns Kessler: "Foods high in sugar, fat, and salt are altering the biological circuitry of our brains." Comfort food can become a trap. As of 2010, restaurants and other out-of-the-home eateries took in almost 50 percent of American expenditure on food. (In 1970 total out-of-home eateries claimed only 30 percent.) The food industry is well aware of the allure of the big three, slathered and served on a hot plate at a restaurant near you at this very moment.[10]

Do you remember your last meal at a chain restaurant—Applebee's, Chili's, or Buffalo Wild Wings? Kessler points out that their entrees' palatability refers not only to their desirability but also to the ease and speed of their physical consumption. There are no bones to slow the ingestion process of chicken wings (now boneless), and much of the meat served is supplied to restaurants deboned, pretenderized, marinated, and frozen—with salt, sugar, and fat.* The tenderizing and marinating process breaks down the cellular structure of the meat, making it go down easy. Less chewing and more consumption faster—sugar on sugar and fat on fat. Pass the salt, please.[11]

It's interesting how food—basic for our survival—has become entertainment. Don't get me wrong, I'll savor a well-planned and prepared meal with family and friends just as much as the next foodie; paella, fish tacos, and homemade pizza are some of the specialties that come from our home kitchen. Yet, those of us living far from the poverty line in the bounteous United States take food for granted. It has transcended its status as a source of human fueling and a necessity for survival; it is consumable entertainment, and for some an addictive substance, whether they are visiting Dairy Queen, cruising on Carnival, or sitting in a car eating takeout.

Wanamaker, Woolworth, and Walton

Consumables: we have even more than we know for our eyes, hands, mouths, and imaginations. John Wanamaker, the Philadelphia originator of the department store (1876) we met earlier, is credited by author Ellen Ruppel Shell as the inventor of the price tag. Much of the world today still barters or haggles; Wanamaker, however, helped bring about its demise in the industrialized world with his conviction—egalitarian in nature—that all are "equal before price." Shell attributes Wanamaker's equitableness in price setting to his religious views; all being equal before God was extrapolated to "one price for all." Wanamaker eliminated price breaks or discounts for the connected, favored, and powerful. It didn't hurt his business; he did extremely well financially. Wanamaker was devoted to purchasing in bulk (for greater economies of scale), and he offered a wide array of items with low set prices. His critics decried him as a bottom-feeding monopolist and accused him of putting smaller merchants out of business.[12] Times were changing, but a mold was being cast.

The main reason Wanamaker could offer so much for so little was because of the newly burgeoning reality of mass production. As we've seen before, industrialization, with its consequent mass production, was a world changer like no other. Rockefeller was able to sell his lamps and kerosene and Carnegie

---

* KFC went nationwide with its Boneless Chicken in April 2013.

his steel beams because of the climate that prior industrialism had wrought. US population roughly doubled during the Gilded Age (40 million after the Civil War to 80 million after the turn of the century), and mass production was well matched for the great growth of US population.* Mass production, which helped bring about a decline in the status and power of craftsmen and craftsmanship, brought something else that suddenly dominated: the subjugation of value to price. In our current day, the high volume–low price strategy continues to dominate for better and for worse.[13]

Frank Woolworth and his brother Charles, the originators of the five and dime store, took Wanamaker's innovations steps farther. Whereas Wanamaker's many clerks would tend to customers, assisting them to make a sale, Woolworth understood that customers could more efficiently and conveniently sell to themselves. Wanamaker's clerks served mostly to show and display merchandise to customers, like a jewelry clerk in our day working with interested customers. Woolworth—selling goods exponentially less valuable than jewelry—put it all out on tables and let customers self-select. His floor workers were cashiers, mostly unmarried women; they were paid meager wages, two to three dollars a week, significantly less than a livable wage.[14] The foreshadowing of Third World sweatshop labor, and Sam Walton's Walmart, is unmistakable. Woolworth became a rich man; toward the end of his life his company boasted more than one thousand stores and he built, at that time, the tallest building in the world, the Woolworth Building in New York City. His fifty-six room mansion was constructed on Long Island in 1913, six years before he passed away. All this was possible by selling mass-produced items very cheaply and by paying the majority of his workers minimally. Sam Walton was not original with his business plan of low prices and low wages.

Walmart is the biggest company in the history of the world. Impressive are the following stats about Walmart: 140 million people (nearly half the US population) make purchases at one of the 4,400 stores each week, with 93 percent of the national population shopping there at least once a year; more than 2.1 million employees make it the biggest private employer in the world; it is the largest grocery chain in the country; and, 90 percent of Americans live within fifteen minutes of a Walmart. You're getting more than just low prices at Walmart, you're getting a large slice of Americana.[15]

---

* World population, which had crested one billion at the turn of the eighteenth to the nineteenth century, would not spike until after World War II.

Sam Walton was singular in his pursuit of lower prices when he opened his first store in Rogers, Arkansas, in 1962. Walton valued frugality, efficiency, and accountability; infused with gargantuan competitiveness, these values were the secrets to his success. His life and his work were inseparable. When Walton was declared the richest American in 1985 (net worth $4.5 billion), his personal vehicle was a run-down '75 Chevy, devoid of hubcaps, muddy and dirty, musty smelling from his frequent-companion bird dogs. When Walton died in 1992, at age seventy-four, he was still the richest American. Days before he died, he was reviewing store-level sales data from his hospital bed. "Sam was no genius. Sam was a workaholic," said a longtime employee in remembrance. "He wanted to be the best at whatever he did. He was not driven by money, but by competition."[16] Money, however, was competition's measuring stick, and Walton, like Rockefeller in his day, was lapping his competitors.

Goods priced cheaper were the backbone of Walmart's growth. Wherever inefficiencies resided—whether in small towns where a particular store owner overcharged because of a lack of competition or among a manufacturer's workforce unaccustomed to sweating—they dissipated in Sam Walton's presence. Efficiencies realized is how Walmart became the biggest retailer in the history of the world. Walton and his company are best described as game changers; they can also be described as culture changers. Sam Walton worked extremely hard; he rarely saw his wife and young children at home when he was starting out. Managers who worked directly under him—apprenticing in the early days— adopted the same work ethic. That hasn't changed over the years in Walmart culture; veteran managers do get three or four weeks of vacation a year, but they can take off only one week at a time.[17]

Penn State University economist Stephan Goetz analyzes economic development as it pertains to reducing long-term poverty. His 2006 study concludes that the presence of a Walmart store *increases the poverty rate* for the specific county in which it is located. The changes in the poverty rate—before and after the arrival of the Walmart store—were unmistakable. According to Goetz: "We find that the presence of Walmart unequivocally raised family poverty rates in US counties" where the stores were located. Other businesses are closed, of course, when a Walmart comes to town, because its lower prices attract consumer dollars. This is principally how the Walmart effect takes place: the less efficient are put out of business and local employees are reshuffled, with some (but not all) of the newly unemployed ending up at Walmart. New jobs are created and previous jobs are eliminated when a new Walmart comes to town and the end result is always the same: profits are siphoned away from local economies toward Bentonville, Arkansas.[18] Some might respond by saying, "So what? That's how things operate in a free market system. If a business can't supply goods more efficiently and inexpensively, let another business do it."

Walmart doesn't always act in accordance with the market expectations. In his book *The Wal-Mart Effect* journalist Charles Fishman highlights numerous examples of Walmart's *monopsony* (one buyer, many sellers), a term used to describe buying power like Walmart's that acts as a threat to the market. Walmart—in this case, the one buyer—is so big that it is able to control certain prices and markets. The classic example is Vlasic's gallon pickle jar. Vlasic at one time had a relationship with Walmart, which marketed Vlasic's product line of pickles and relishes in Walmart stores nationwide. The gallon jar of whole pickles—a niche product—was proposed as a possible showcase product (displayed prominently in the front of the stores). Vlasic and Walmart agreed it was worth a try. Their purposely chosen price was a splashy $2.97, hardly profitable for either of them; the year was 1998. Beyond its seller's dreams, the gallon jar of Vlasic pickles was a huge success—more than expected. For the supplier, Vlasic, it turned out to be, as described by Fishman, a "devastating success." Vlasic's employees saw customers, who previously bought the comparably less than one-third size liter jar, now buying the gallon jar (from Walmart) and just throwing away the remaining half jar when the contents got moldy. Who could have blamed them—they were paying less for more pickles. When Vlasic wanted to increase the price on its gallon jar, Walmart responded with a threat: increase the price, and we'll stop buying your other products. This went on for two and half years. Finally, Walmart let the $2.97 gallon price disappear into history. The price Walmart and Vlasic had created together was a lie, unrelated to either supply or demand. It was a fiction perpetrated, essentially, by Walmart higher-ups. In January 2001 when Walmart let Vlasic breathe after two and a half years, Vlasic filed for bankruptcy.[19] There were other reasons Vlasic filed for bankruptcy, but Walmart was one of them because of a monopsonistic low price, which was less than pennies above cost.

People love cheap stuff. As a matter of fact, a lot of us find it difficult not to buy something cheap that looks like a good deal. Securing transactions (for sellers) is simply a matter of getting the word out, as long as consumers are convinced that low price trumps all other considerations. For generations, advertising in the United States (and elsewhere) has predominantly focused on items that can be bought at extremely favorable prices rather than regularly priced stock items. We love our discount chains (like Walmart), and discount chains specialize in stocking items that turn over quickly. Where they come from doesn't matter; it's all about price. In 1965 the United States ran its first postwar trade deficit with Japan. At first glance, US workers and manufacturers weren't afraid of the low-end stuff coming from Japan. Americans like low prices. As the discount chains grew, however, department store jobs were lost and replaced with low-wage jobs at the discount stores (of forty-two US department-store chains in business in 1980 only twenty survived intact into 1990). We've seen this phenomenon before: many low-wage earners making up a bottom tier that supports a few loftier management and owner positions above them. Former CEO of Walmart Lee Scott made more in his biweekly paycheck than the average Walmart employee would make in a lifetime at Walmart.[20] Carnegie's maxim for the owner to make only twenty times more than a regular employee in his own company would be giggled at in the boardrooms of America's largest companies today.

Shouldn't a person who makes cheap stuff readily available be compensated accordingly? It's fair to say that America has become a nation of people who value their expenditures just as much as anything else. Historian Charles McGovern, in his book *Sold American*, opines, "Market replaced polis in a new communal public life characterized not by geography, religion, or politics, but by spending."[21] The other day my wife and I were bicycling with a good friend in his immediate neighborhood. As we approached an upcoming turn, we noticed a group of people gathering at a neighborhood house. We were impressed; with some twenty people gathered early on a Saturday morning, it must have been an important neighborhood meeting. We slowed down as we got closer—the parked cars were numerous—and our friend expressed regret that he hadn't been informed of the meeting. It turned out that our hopes and fears of a communal meeting were unfounded: it was an estate sale. Estate and yard sales help recycle valuable goods and raise funds for families. Bicycle riders best approach such sales with caution, however, wary of consumers in cars racing to the next sale.

The prosperous post–World War II years, when egalitarianism had some life and real median family income doubled in America, are remembered nostalgically by many. The baby boomer generation came of age at a time when business growth and social mobility were assumed to be permanent attributes in an ever-increasing economy. We're glad to have bid adieu to some antiquities of that age, like overt racism and sexism, but it's sad to realize that social mobility is a thing of the past. Look at what has replaced egalitarianism and worker gains that many of the previous generations knew well: the façade of social equality without an equable distribution of wealth. The support that holds the façade upright is the low prices of so much stuff and its availability. Low prices—and credit cards—give us the idea that we are getting some of what we need, if not everything. And we dutifully work and trudge along, not complaining, because the bargain is too good: we're getting all this stuff at good prices. What more could we want—except more stuff? And who knows—if we hang in there, we might get rich someday down the road, and then we too can attain more stuff—like a second or third house, a Maserati, or diamond manicure.[22] The generation coming of age in this day assumes that the abundance of consumer goods is the best marker of the good life: *the goods life.*

Many Americans shop at Walmart not to get luxuries but to buy the basics. Buying them cheaper—toilet paper, laundry detergent, and underwear—can be done at Walmart more so than at other places. What's wrong with that? It all depends; when a family or individual is in dire economic straits, they might not have much choice. Yet, the hidden costs of excessive cheapness, for those who are able to count that cost, do add up. The prices are low because the wages of the workers are low, their benefits are minimal, and their treatment by management has been, at times, exploitative. Also, there is the relentless pressure on certain suppliers and the abysmal wages of those laborers (many foreign) who produce so much of the merchandise on Walmart's shelves.[23] All these factor into Walmart's low prices.

Walmart is not some greedy behemoth, riddled with upper management graft and corruption. Its ratio of total profit to employee hours worked is pretty thin. Maintaining their low prices and paying significantly higher wages to regular employees is not mathematically possible. Yet, scales of economy are a many-splendored thing; they have made the Waltons the richest clan in America. Their net worth of more than $150 billion is greater than Bill Gates (richest individual) and Warren Buffett (second richest individual) combined. Is it a good thing that the richest family in the country has achieved that status on the backs of cheap labor the world over? Rockefeller supplied kerosene to many parts of the world, transforming it from item of luxury to utility. It can be argued that Rockefeller's distribution of kerosene has had a positive effect on the common good. Sam Walton started out with a good mission—low-priced goods to southern climes—that his own company has simply outgrown in the last two decades. The ideological commitment to low prices has negatively affected suppliers, factory workers, communities, and Walmart's own workers; the effect upon the common good is debatable. And the Waltons as a clan are, like Rockefeller, excessively successful in the financial realm.[24]

Shopping for a Better Life

According to psychologist Dan Ariely, shopping is not a rational exercise but an emotional process full of guilt, jubilation, and uncertainty. When firing up her computer, going into a store, or shopping by phone, a consumer has to extrapolate future needs in contrast to current realities. When she is just getting a gallon of milk—and she has a teenage boy at home—her shopping task is quite easy. If she's going to buy a car and not sure what she can afford, then the task is somewhat sterner. In this day and age of discounted goods and unconcealed consumption, we all seek bargains, whether indicated by price, brand name, or circumstances. Ariely says that humans can deal fairly well with a significantly delayed reward. For example, if you are a smoker and I tell you that I will give you five hundred dollars to stop smoking next month (with the stipulation that it last six months), you might not have that much trouble agreeing to do so. If I give you the same challenge, but tell you that you have to stop smoking today—as a matter of fact, right now—you most likely won't be ready to agree to it. The first deal looks good: five hundred dollars to stop smoking at a certain *manageable* point in the future. The second deal puts you between a rock and a hard place because it exudes impulsiveness; resolutions, just like shopping for future needs, can be easy to make. It's much more difficult to make a good or realistic decision about a shopping need when you are confronted *unbeknownst* with a sale opportunity. *In the next fifteen minutes, make up your mind quickly. I can set you up with a 16G iPad3 for $299—are you interested? You have to let me know within fifteen minutes!* We're rational about the future, but we're *emotional* about the present. Those who sell us stuff know the difference between the two, whether or not they can articulate the psychology behind it.[25]

The nucleus accumbens, a tiny part of the brain located beneath the eyes, plays an important role in addiction, reward, laughter, pleasure, fear, and aggression. Part of the limbic system, the nucleus accumbens operates just under our conscious control. It works with well-known neurotransmitters dopamine (promoting desire) and serotonin (promoting inhibition). It also helps and hinders things like shopping. Stanford neuroscientist Brian Knutson ran an experiment where subjects were viewed under fMRI; they were given a specific amount of money to spend and options of items to purchase, specified by price. If they did not spend their money on the items presented, they were allowed to keep the money. Knutson noticed that another brain region, the insula, associated with such emotions as empathy, guilt, humiliation, and pride, lit up when subjects considered prices excessive. They would not make a purchase when their insulas were activated. On the other hand, when prices were deemed acceptable—especially when they were discounted during the experiment—the nucleus accumbens lit up like the Fourth of July, and those subjects consequently made their purchasing moves.[26] Once again, the argument for pure rationality in all economic decision making presents itself as an illusion. Yes, we are capable of making rational economic decisions, but we don't always do so.

The point is that we tend to be suckers for bargains, or what we perceive to be bargains. If and when we are confronted with a bargain, it's hard for us not to bite. My wife and I were in a chain specialty store recently, picking up some soft drinks and wine. After having secured the bottles and making our way toward the cashier, we happened to see a set of tables and chairs on clearance—marked 50 percent off. Since our son, at that moment, was getting ready to go back to college and was in need of two kitchen chairs (but not a table), we checked the chairs out. They neither matched his table nor were sturdily built, and when we had entered the store neither of us had said anything about looking for chairs (even though we had purchased chairs at this particular store before). Those considerations, however, were temporarily trumped by one thing: an unbeatable price. And if we didn't make our move soon, someone else would snatch up the great deal instead of us! At least that's what my nucleus accumbens was telling me. I was ready to make the purchase. My wife's insula must have been activated, however. She wasn't as impressed with the "bargain" as I was. We walked out of the store without the chairs; I later thanked her for her good sense. The chairs were dogs, but temporarily made to look good to me because of perceived ascendant value by a discounted price.

In his book *The High Price of Materialism*, psychologist Tim Kasser makes the bold claim that we live today with a worldview that says that the worth and success of persons are not ascertained by their apparent wisdom, kindness, or community contributions but by their possessions and material achievements. The stock price of this worldview rides high even in the face of mounting evidence that reaches the following conclusion: obtaining more money and material goods is not making people happier or more psychologically healthy. Kasser goes farther with his critique on materialistic society by saying that people with "strong materialistic values" are more closely associated with unhappiness than are those who are not imbued with materialistic values.[27]

The work of thinkers like Carl Rogers, Abraham Maslow, and Erich Fromm gives Kasser a framework to critique materialistic society. These three psychologists acknowledged that there is a baseline of material needs to be met for humans. When that pursuit crosses over or melds into pursuing materialism for its own sake, it then detracts from human well-being and happiness.[28] Does money buy happiness? Does accumulating possessions beyond a certain baseline make one feel better? If a little bit more is better, what would it be like to have an excess amount?

Kasser says that "the more materialistic values are at the center of our lives, the more our quality of life is diminished." According to Kasser, in 1984 and 1985 the first data emerged demonstrating a negative relationship between well-being and materialism. Business researcher Russell Belk published papers showing that unhappiness and dissatisfaction are linked to possessiveness, nongenerosity, and envy, traits related to a materialistic outlook. Subsequent studies have shown correlations linking materialistic values with depression and social anxiety. In the post–World War II era, materialist production won the day. There are enough material resources to feed, clothe, shelter, and educate the whole human family—with aplenty leftover. Yet, intriguingly, the world seems to be increasingly defined by two groups: *haves* living in relative luxury and excess, who strive to accumulate more and more, and *have-nots*, who struggle in poverty and deprivation. Concerning material needs, we all require enough to get by, but the continual striving for "just a little bit more" and much more—beyond a level that reasonably sustains our living—has not proven to make our lives happier or more satisfactory. According to Kasser, an overemphasis on materialistic values leads to a de-emphasis on satisfying other needs that are nonmaterial in nature, like self-esteem, connectedness, and authenticity.[29]

Kasser proposes that people who highly emphasize materialistic values are driven by unmet needs for security and safety. All humans require material resources and comforts to feel secure and safe. Our ancestors wanted to have a store of food they could rely upon for the lean times that inevitably came; we want to have money in the bank for emergencies and challenges that come our way. These are natural coping strategies. When children grow up in situations where family environments do a poor job of satisfying needs for security—food on the table, roof over the head, protection from instability—they have a propensity to become adults who adopt a value system that relies upon wealth and possessions.[30] This is especially true in our age when adopting such a value system is a realistic option.

Rockefeller obviously fits this description as his bigamous father was both absent and unreliable. Carnegie also fits the description; his father was one of many displaced (by machine) hand-loom weavers in Scotland, precipitating the family's immigration to the United States. Others that I have mentioned in this work, like Ivan Boesky, Ken Lay, and Alan Greenspan, also fit the description.[31] Having a personal history that gives incentive to hard work and earning money is not an indictment; using Kasser's explanation gives a more nuanced understanding of why the pursuit of "just a little bit more" is not the cure-all consumerist society generally treats it as. It can injure the common good, while not fulfilling its proposed intention.

A $750,000 mansion and $80,000 Lexus are not necessary for survival. Pursuing and attaining such items is typically seen, by those with materialistic values, as a grand achievement. Others, not so imbued with materialistic values, might see material pursuits and attainments as a symptom of an underlying insecurity and as a coping strategy for satisfying additional needs. This would help explain why numerous studies in recent years do not show any significant increase in life satisfaction for people as they attain greater personal incomes, beyond what is necessary for moderate survival.[32] Again, with our propensity to compare our own economic situation with those wealthier than us (and rarely with those poorer), we establish a new marker for comparison, like adding a story to a building that has no ceiling.

This Revolution Is Televised

During the late 1980s my wife and I lived in Chiclayo, Perú, the country's fourth largest city. I worked in a church setting as an intern pastor in a poorer, smaller town just outside Chiclayo, where the main employer was a local sugarcane cooperative. In this small town, San Antonio de Pomalca, house walls were constructed of mud bricks and roofed with heavy cane plants. Located on the northernmost strip of the Peruvian coastal Sechura Desert (one the most arid in the world), the area rarely saw rain. The sugarcane grew heartily in the Southern Hemisphere sun, thanks to ample irrigation. Though the people of San Antonio were poor, their town was established and supplied with electricity and water wells (but not with indoor plumbing). There were people living in other areas of Perú who were much poorer. *Pueblos jóvenes* ("young towns") is the optimistic name given to Peruvian shantytowns; many are located on the outer margins of the capital, Lima. The moniker fits well; these towns typically start as invasions of uninhabited or unwanted lands. Living in an unincorporated community, the residents begin the long struggle for formal recognition, legal incorporation, electricity, running water, and other services. One day while traveling south of Lima on the Pan American highway with a colleague, we ascended a slope that gave us an expansive view of a *pueblo joven* of Lima. This one was fairly established; it was supplied with electricity. My colleague called attention to the plethora of television antennas that protruded from the many flat tin roofs of the pueblo's dwellings. His statement about the vista has stuck with me through the years: "For better or for worse, television shows people what they don't have."

For rich and poor and those somewhere in between, television reinforces a materialistic value system. Studies show that individuals with materialistic value systems in Australia, Denmark, Finland, Hong Kong, India, and the United States watch significant—some might say excessive—amounts of television. The television shows not only depict people of mostly upper and upper-middle classes, but the advertisements supporting the shows also typically exhibit levels of wealth above societal norms. To quote Kasser: "People with a strong materialistic orientation were likely to watch a lot of television, compare themselves unfavorably with people they saw on television, be dissatisfied with their standard of living, and have low life satisfaction." In the study of materialism, Kasser defines discrepancies as the gulf between what one perceives his life or standard of living to be and that which he desires it to be. "Materialistic people overidealize wealth and possessions and therefore experience discrepancies that cause them to feel dissatisfied and to want further materialistic means of feeling good about themselves. But satisfactions from this compensation only temporarily improve their sense of worth, and soon they return to another cycle of dissatisfaction."[33]

A generation ago Neil Postman wrote *Amusing Ourselves to Death*, a critique of television and advertising that still speaks authoritatively today. Postman says during the Gilded Age advertising started to use *image* more than informational content. He says that in the 1890s advertisers first began to use slogans to pedal clients' products. Advertising's only mode of transmission at this early juncture was printed media—newspapers and magazines. However, printed word gave way to image as illustrations and photographs came to dominate in Gilded Age–era advertisements. Shortly thereafter, radio and television came to the fore—the shift from word-centered culture to image-centered culture would soon be completed.[34] This shift helped create and fortify a full-blown materialistic and consumerist society.

According to Postman, the next consequential step for our image-centered society to take was toward becoming an entertainment-based society. Yes, a picture is worth a thousand words, but an emphasis on images (film and television being thousands of pictures strung together) can suppress the content of ideas. Not so sure? Pay attention, if you are able, to political advertisements during an election season. The sacrifice of ideas and their content to mostly negative images and imaging in thirty seconds is what we have today for political campaigning. Postman says that the Abraham Lincoln and Stephen Douglas debates lasted up to seven hours. The pendulum has now swung absolutely to the opposite side. It is the nature of television—in this day and age of entertainment—to suppress complex ideas as it accommodates the requirements of visuality.[35] Television has shortened our attention span; what you see is what you get, and it usually doesn't go too deep. Politics is entertainment, sports are entertainment, food is entertainment, news is entertainment, and buying and selling is entertainment—and it's all televised.

Television celebrates affluence and, according to Postman, "television is our culture's principal mode of knowing about itself." We know this: television reveals *even to us* what we don't have and what we just might need. Former news anchor Robert MacNeil's quote "Television is the *soma* of Aldous Huxley's *Brave New World*" is still apropos a generation later, as Postman's end product of entertainment now shares the stage with consumerism. Complex issues have been replaced by superficial images; this revolution is not only televised, it's completely for sale.[36]

Since the early 1950s, when television sets en masse invaded American living rooms, television and advertising have been tightly linked. By 1953 two-thirds of American households had television sets, and by the mid-1960s, 94 percent of American homes had at least one. The "selling machine in every living room" was on an average of five hours a day in the 1950s (by the 2000s the average was close to nine hours a day). By the end of the 1950s, television advertising made up more than half of revenues at the big advertising firms; it's always been debatable whether advertising served entertainment or vice versa.[37]

In 1949 John Cameron Swayze hosted NBC's first news show, the fifteen minute *Camel News Caravan*. The tobacco company's sponsorship was visibly and vocally ("America's most popular cigarette") part and parcel of the production, with cigarettes, cigarette packages, ashtrays, and Camel logos prominent. Swayze was even encouraged to light up—as, of course, were viewers—during the broadcast.[38] Huntley, Brinkley, Cronkite—television news hit its high-water mark in 1969, the year Neil Armstrong and Buzz Aldrin walked on the moon. Fifty percent of American households tuned in to at least one of the three major network newscasts. That rate has been in decline ever since. Expanded programming and more channels, the advent of cable providers, satellite providers, and alternative media outlets have all contributed to the slide. But news programs have always been among the cheapest programming to produce. And even though their audiences are shrinking and aging (today's average viewer age is sixty), they do have money to spend.[39] Cue the pharmaceutical commercials: go and see your doctor, and tell her what the TV told you she needs to prescribe for you.

In 2010 Fox News amassed a net profit of $700 million, an impressive sum (mostly from cable company fees) based upon an average viewership for its nightly programs of only about two million. (Fox News has a whole bundle of shows shown throughout the day.) In comparison, the three network news divisions, with more than twenty million viewers between them, didn't make as much combined. Fox News has not always been as profitable as it is today, so it cannot be accused of profiteering solely on its right-leaning bias, because that slant has been a constant through times of both thin and thick profits. It can be accused, however, of helping dumb down (Fox News isn't the only culprit) the national conversation on just about everything it covers, from politics to economics to education. The traditional notion that Americans can share a common set of facts and ideas and then participate in civil debate is an anachronism to the Fox News mindset that lionizes the idea that the only legitimate dialogue today is the polarized variety, void of honest debate, often full of contempt.[40]

Infotainer comedians Jon Stewart and Stephen Colbert, each with a show on Comedy Central, have viewership numbers similar to Fox News. Decidedly left leaning, these shows use news bits to serve their higher purpose of comedy. In that they troll for laughs, the polarization accusation doesn't cut as deep. Satire is a subtle form of dialogue and less contemptible; it's smarter than plain old reactionary babble.

Good Ol' Polarization

Hype and reaction, however, sell. In the winner-take-all, egalitarian-forlorn society that has been dominant since the 1980s, reactionary polarization is much more accepted than it previously was. Remember the good old days when political opponents considered themselves adversaries and not mortal enemies? Republican President Ronald Reagan and Democratic Speaker of the House Tip O'Neill come to mind: they agreed that before 6:00 p.m. it was all politics—but after the designated hour they were cordial. Reagan and O'Neill shared meals together, including a seventieth birthday party for the speaker hosted by the president at the White House. The two Irish Americans told jokes, ate, and drank together.[41] Republican Speaker of the House John Boehner and Democratic President Barack Obama played golf together on June 11, 2011. It was a cordial game between two political opponents; they teamed up, beating Vice President Joe Biden and Republican Ohio governor John Kasich in the match. A few months later Hank Williams Jr. was a guest on the Fox News morning program *Fox and Friends*. He likened Obama and Boehner playing golf together to Hitler and Israeli Prime Minister Benjamin Netanyahu teeing it up together. The show's three cohosts were visibly uncomfortable with Williams's comments linking Obama to Hitler. A few days later Disney-ESPN-ABC dropped Williams's song that had been used as the opener for ABC's *Monday Night Football*.[42] It's good to know that polarization isn't accepted—at least when advertising or sponsorship money is up for grabs.

Moderation is a concept, like egalitarianism, that seems to have become decidedly passé. In the political sphere, moderates of either major party are becoming scarce in the nation's capital. Richard Mourdock, Indiana's former state treasurer and 2012 Republican nominee for US senator, is a tea party favorite who defeated long-time incumbent Richard Lugar in the Republican primary election. Lugar, having served since 1976, is well recognized as a moderate. Mourdock, no moderate, continued to leverage his extremist views after the primary victory: "I have the mindset that says bipartisanship ought to consist of Democrats coming to the Republican point of view."[43] Mourdock lost the race for US senator to Democrat Joe Donnelly, his extremist views ultimately dooming his candidacy.

Thomas Mann and Norman Ornstein have written seven books together in the past twenty years. Mann is associated with the Brookings Institute and Ornstein with the American Enterprise Institute. Both DC think tanks can be described as centrist, with Brookings leaning a bit to the left and American Enterprise a bit to the right. Both institutions have been around for decades. Mann and Ornstein's latest book dealing with Washington and the current political atmosphere, *It's Even Worse Than It Looks*, gives good historical perspective of lawmaker bipartisan cooperation. According to the coauthors, political polarization is currently at an all-time high (going back to Reconstruction). The World War II and New Deal years showed the least amount of polarization, with the Gilded Age era having shown the previous high for polarization. "Partisan polarization is undeniably the central and most problematic feature of contemporary American politics. Political parties today are more internally unified and ideologically distinctive than they have been in over a century."[44] The percentage of moderate senators and representatives continues to plummet—good riddance, Senator Lugar—as ideology takes precedence over pragmatism.

In 2011 Congress achieved a new high and low: its highest disapproval rating (82 percent) and its lowest approval rating (9 percent) in polling history. Mann and Ornstein trace the seeds of this current discontent to Newt Gingrich. When Gingrich entered the House of Representatives in 1978, representing the state of Georgia, the Democrats had held the House for twenty-four years. They would hold it sixteen more, until 1994, when the Republicans swept into majority power. Gingrich became the new Speaker of the House. *Time* named him Man of the Year in 1995. His strategy wasn't entirely new, but it was effective: destroy the institution in order to save it—throw the majority bums out. His method was to unite minority Republicans (prior to 1995) in refusal to cooperate with Democrats and to publicly label the majority as the party benefiting from entrenched corruption. Gingrich favored confrontations with political opponents; namely, Democratic Speakers O'Neill and Jim Wright, and felt that TV news coverage of the confrontations gave his minority party an advantage. Term limits and smaller government were a part of the 1994 Republican Contract with America, championed by Gingrich and fellow Republicans. Mann and Ornstein credit Gingrich with the following approach still used today: the minority party stymies and damages a president of the opposing party to its utmost. The new norm, post-Gingrich, is for colleagues of opposing parties to see each other as mortal enemies.[45] The Democrats, of course, adopted the same strategy, bringing about, in part, Gingrich's demise as speaker in 1998. As I've said before—it takes two to tango. Although Gingrich's fingerprints are all over the ideological gridlock we have today in Washington, both major parties have contributed mightily to its sustenance. And we wonder what is more important to certain politicians: party fealty or the communal good? The latter will always be invoked—achieved on paper, of course, by each of the partisan's specific methods—but the acute levels of polarization say otherwise. Today party loyalty and its accompanying winner-take-all philosophy are thoroughly excessive, and the common good suffers under their proliferation.

Excess Winners (and Losers)

As we saw before, Andrew Carnegie did have a concept of the common good and advocated it. (He also did a number of things, as previously mentioned, that worked against it.) He kept a maximum multiple factor of twenty between regular worker wages and his own; he campaigned against leaving the major portion of an earned fortune to the next generation of family members; he designated significant portions of his fortune to charity and philanthropic endeavors. Carnegie somehow knew that the new realities of excess—brought on by his and Rockefeller's (and others') endeavors—needed to be reined in. The world had not seen the incredible inequalities that the Gilded Age brought forth; Carnegie and some of his peers responded by redistributing their vast incomes on their own terms.

That was a hundred years ago, at the beginning of the long era of excess. In certain ways, it could be a thousand years ago. Many of today's CEOs—in the short era of excess since the late 1970s—have been neither as imaginative in their philanthropy nor as conscientious in their legacy. According to US tax return data, the richest of Americans (the top 0.1 percent) mostly consist of CEOs and financial professionals. Among the group is a spattering of professional athletes and team owners, high-end lawyers and doctors, real estate moguls, and megaranchers. These Americans, as a group, are significantly richer compared to their fellow citizens than they were a generation ago. Without question, the rich have gotten richer; they have a significantly less progressive tax code at the very top of the scale to thank for their increases. It's not that they've necessarily worked harder or better; it's simply that they pay less in taxes than had been the case before. Beginning in the late 1970s, the steeply progressive tax code, predominant after the post–World War II era, was slashed at the very top. This has continued for decades and currently remains the case.[46]

In 1980 executive pay started to go through the roof. In 1965, echoing Carnegie's maxim, the average CEO of a large US corporation made about twenty-four times the wage of a typical employee in that same company. By 2007, the factor was approaching three hundred times greater. In that same year, just before the housing bubble–inspired economic turmoil, CEOs in the largest 350 publically traded companies averaged more than $12 million in salaries—and that didn't include bonuses.[47] CEO bonuses *alone* were on average sixty-two times the wage of typical employees. Instead of paying out these bonuses, the companies could have hired dozens of additional employees, internally reinvested the proceeds, or distributed them philanthropically.[48]

American CEOs are paid considerably more—twice on average—than CEOs in other rich nations.[49] *Of course*, they are worth it. Remember when Home Depot actually lived up to founder Arthur Blank's proviso of keeping alive the values that were important to him, such as customer service?[50] In the early days, before Blank retired in 2000, I remember a Home Depot store I frequented in Houston that had great customer service.* The store seemed a veritable hangout for handyman types, who were dressed in the orange employee apron with a tape measure in the front pocket at the ready. Friendly, knowledgeable advice was quite common; I was confident that I could get any question I had answered and get what I needed for the project I was tackling. But then things started to change at Home Depot after the turn of the century: simply put, customer service disappeared. It became harder and harder to find a free employee to ask a question. I remember checking out at a Home Depot a few years ago and being asked the ubiquitous "Did you find everything you needed?" question by the cashier. I hadn't, but I wasn't about to blame her. It wasn't her fault that Home Depot slashed employee rolls greatly

---

* Home Depot has administered a stiff dose of efficiency to small, local hardware stores just like Walmart has done to surrounding local stores. I also frequented a local hardware store when we lived in Houston; one of my congregants worked there and his advice was just as good if not better than the folks at Home Depot. Like a lot of smaller hardware stores, they didn't sell lumber, putting them at significant disadvantage to Home Depot which stocks lumber by the truckloads.

so that stock prices could be maintained and executives could be paid more and more.[51]

Bob Nardelli, who took over for Blank in 2000 and de-emphasized that old-fashioned customer service, reaped a $210 million severance package when he was canned in 2007.[52] (That we have come to this—nine figure *severance* packages—is an indictment of the age in and of itself.) How many low paid part-timers (a Nardelli emphasis) could that severance package have hired instead? At ten dollars per hour for thirty hours a week, that would work out to about five extra employees (including additional payroll taxes and other expenses) at all of Home Depot's two-thousand-plus stores. I suspect a vote of store managers would choose the five extra employees over Nardelli's severance package. Or maybe they'd be happy simply to take two or three of the old-time workers Nardelli let go—just a hunch—who were really good with advice and customer service.

Angelo Mozilo, the former CEO and cofounder of Countrywide Financial, is roundly blamed as one of the main culprits in the 2007–08 economic crash brought on by the subprime loan mess in the housing market. Mozilo and his partner, David Loeb, started their mortgage brokering firm in the late 1960s. In those days, thrifts—savings and loans associations, credit unions—wrote the majority of mortgages. Mozilo busted his backside to drum up business for his firm, limited at that time mostly to low risk Federal Housing Administration (FHA) or Veterans Affairs (VA) loans. Good fortune came in 1968; Congress approved the Federal National Mortgage Association to buy a wider range of mortgages, not just those guaranteed by the FHA or the VA. Fannie Mae—the Federal National Mortgage Association (FNMA)—established in 1938 as a part of New Deal legislation, served (and still does) as a secondary market, buying mortgages from lenders and essentially re-freeing capital for further loans, home purchases, and other endeavors. As Fannie Mae was privatized in 1968, mortgages were pooled, pieced, and sold to institutional investors, with the interest payments on those loans passing through to the investors—the beginnings of securitization.

Freddie Mac, the Federal Home Loan Mortgage Corporation (FHLMC), came to be in 1970; its mission was to supplement Fannie's. Mozilo and others working like him had a green light. They could now resell a greater range of mortgages to Fannie and Freddie, refuel, and restart the cycle. Business was good—and at this point mostly legitimate—for Countrywide, and the thrifts crisis of the 1980s made it even better. Rising interest rates and losses hampered the thrifts; Mozilo not only sold mortgages brokered by his own employees but also signed up independent brokers to work for him (a number who had worked for the thrifts) *who were paid a commission only if they sold a mortgage.* His partner,

Loeb, was unfavorable toward working with independents because regulations were weak, and the only guard against them working unscrupulously was a well-functioning moral compass. Loeb acquiesced, however; Mozilo trudged forward and Countrywide would soon become a Wall Street darling.[53]

As the 1990s gave way to the 2000s, Mozilo got in deeper with what were called subprime loans. Adjustable rate mortgage loans (ARMs), Alt-A loans (where borrowers weren't required to disclose income information), jumbo loans (over $400,000), and other nonconforming loans brought Countrywide more and more originations—and easy profits. Whereas previously Countrywide wrote a large majority of conforming loans, after 2005 the majority of loans that Mozilo's company wrote were nonconformers. An especially egregious example of a nonconforming loan was the pay-option adjustable rate mortgage. The loan was sold with an extremely low teaser rate (sometimes 1 percent); after two years the rate rose according to a formula linked to market interest rates. Mortgage holders had the option of continuing to pay the low rate, but in doing so, their unpaid interest was added to the principal of the loan—negative amortization. By the fifth year of the loan, it was transformed into a conventional loan—usually by that time with brutal rates and payments, the principal larger than when the loan originated. California attorney general Jerry Brown sued Mozilo in 2008 for deceptive advertising, accusing Countrywide of writing risky loans with the sole purpose of profiteering, because they would immediately attempt to sell these loans on the secondary market. Not only that, but Mozilo also paid his employees and brokers higher commissions when they sold these loans. A settlement ($8.7 billion) eventually was reached with Brown and other attorneys general, after Bank of America had purchased Mozilo's floundering company. Valued at some $25 billion in its heyday, Mozilo's company was purchased for only $4 billion.[54]

My wife and I had a Countrywide loan on our home for ten years. We moved to Austin in the late 1990s, closed on our home with a smaller mortgage company that, within months, sold our mortgage to Countrywide. We were treated well by Countrywide; we eventually refinanced our loan with them to a seven-year/thirty-year ARM. We were committed to getting out of that loan—either by refinancing again or by selling—before the initial seven years had passed. We refinanced in 2004, the height of Countrywide's power and glory. Just four years later as news of Countrywide's turmoil became public, we were looking to get out of that ARM loan. Our first option was to stay with Countrywide; we thought it was simplest and, as I said, we had been treated well by those we worked with at the company. It didn't turn out to be a viable option; obviously, something had changed at the company. As we tried to negotiate—trying to use some leverage as reliable customers who hadn't missed a payment in ten years—we only met up with inflexibility. We eventually refinanced with our local credit union. At the time, I had trouble trying to figure out why Countrywide didn't want to keep good customers. Now I know: pedestrian monthly interest payments weren't enough. Mr. Mozilo didn't want a little bit more—by that time he needed much more. But it just wasn't there as the housing market spiraled downward.

In October 2010 Mozilo settled federal charges against him personally that he misled investigators about Countrywide's shoddy loan portfolio. He paid a fine of $22.5 million along with forfeiting $45 million of ill-gotten gains. At that point, his was the largest penalty ever levied by the Securities and Exchange Commission against a senior level executive of a public company. Mozilo did get something for giving up some of his Countrywide cash—he didn't have to admit to any wrongdoing.[55]

Nardelli, a poster boy for astonishingly overpaid executives, left his Home Depot and Chrysler (2007–2009) CEO posts, in part, over the prospect of decreased pay and benefit packages. It was deemed better for him to leave Chrysler and for Chrysler to declare bankruptcy than to take federal bailout money that would have capped its executive pay.[56] Mozilo, whose wrongdoing was substantial, didn't hurt himself by giving discounted sweetheart loans to people in high places: including Chris Dodd, the former US senator (Democrat) from Connecticut and powerful former chair of the Senate Banking Committee, and the two former heads of Fannie Mae, Jim Johnson and Franklin Raines.[57] It's so good to know that Angelo took care of his friends—and bought a little Washington influence along the way.

As CEOs, Nardelli and Mozilo are stunted in many ways compared to the former CEO and founder of Microsoft. Bill Gates, born in Seattle, is the modern-day Rockefeller: ruthless in business, rich beyond compare, and one of the greatest philanthropists the world has known. Like Rockefeller's Standard Oil, his company also has been accused of monopolizing practices. Both Rockefeller and Gates, their genius and drive indisputable, exhibited business acumen that bested the competition again and again. The comparisons are striking; Rockefeller excelled at buying or squeezing out smaller competitors while Gates excelled at bringing smaller players along for the ride (with the gargantuan Microsoft), only to dispose of them once their particular code was incorporated into existing Microsoft codes and then tweaked (or outright purchased). Enough of a change in a computer code—too bad Gates couldn't have advised George Harrison when the Chiffons weren't so fine with "My Sweet Lord"—and infringement was a nonissue, especially with Microsoft lawyers so suitably financed. And as Rockefeller wasn't a participant in the beginnings of oil refining, neither was

Gates the progenitor of the operating systems (generically referred to as OS or DOS) that serve as the backbone of small computer software systems. Gates has the computer giant IBM to thank for a lot of the success that came his way. IBM, working together with Gates and Microsoft in the early 1980s on its new product—the personal computer—was still focused primarily on business computing, which it saw as its main livelihood. Deciding that personal computers were lightweight, IBM let Gates and Microsoft cofounder Paul Allen keep the rights to MS-DOS, the operating system on IBM's new PC, the 5150. A decade later, as personal computer sales exceeded all expectations, IBM and Microsoft split ways. Microsoft's Windows 3.0 would eclipse IBM's OS/2; and because of Gate's business model of incorporating and conquering,* Microsoft became one of the world's most valuable companies and Gates the world's richest person. Gates, a whiz at writing computer code, didn't write MS-DOS; he bought its progenitor version from Tim Paterson, a computer genius himself, who borrowed heavily from another precursor version written by another Seattle computer whiz, Gary Kildall.[58] Gates is brilliant, but he's not as self-made as is typically assumed.

Gates's father, William Gates Sr., a retired lawyer, is not someone who is taken in by the fiction of the self-made man. In the spirit of egalitarianism, he has been a tireless spokesperson for progressive taxation of the rich, those who have the incomparable *ability to pay*. In 2001, following George W. Bush's inauguration, tax reform was given high priority by the new administration. The estate tax, or "death tax," was one of their reduction targets; in the post–World War II era its highest rate was consistently held at 77 percent. During the Reagan years it was reduced to 55 percent, and the Bush administration desired to reduce it further, if not to fully repeal it. In the spring of 2001, Gates Sr., with an opinion piece in the *Washington Post*, became a vocal opponent of tax reductions for the rich; two years later he also coauthored the book *Wealth and Our Commonwealth: Why America Should Tax Accumulated Fortunes*. Gates argues that the estate tax helped America maintain the egalitarian spirit that differentiated its founding from aristocratic Europe. During the height of the Gilded Age, eighteen states of the Union adopted inheritance taxes—Andrew Carnegie (not surprisingly) was one of many wealthy supporters of the new laws. Estate taxes, according to Gates, serve "as a practical, democratic restraint on massive concentrated wealth and power." Repeal of the estate tax "would widen the growing gap in economic and political influence between the wealthy and the rest of America."[59] As of this writing in 2013, the United States yet employs a tax on the right to transfer property at death.

---

* Author Harold Evans says, "Hundreds of small innovative companies have died in Microsoft's bear hug." Harold Evans, *They Made America: From the Steam Engine to the Search Engine,* Little Brown (2004), 418. Rockefeller and Sam Walton would be proud.

Gates Jr. has become the most generous philanthropist in the history of the world—Rockefeller and Carnegie would be impressed. Gates and investment magnate Warren Buffet joined forces to create The Giving Pledge: "an effort to invite the wealthiest individuals and families in America to commit to giving the majority of their wealth to philanthropy." As of 2013, more than 110 individuals or families have joined the pledge to give at least 50 percent of their fortunes away. Others making the pledge include Sandy and Joan Weill, David Rockefeller, and Michael and Lori Milken. No member of the Walton family has yet to sign on.[60]

Bill Gates's place as the richest man in the world has been taken over in the last few years by Mexican phone mogul Carlos Slim Helu. Slim purchased the state-owned telephone company Telmex in 1990 and has consolidated his customer base in the country ever since. He owns 70 percent of the Mexican wireless market today. Mexico's economic inequalities stretch deep and wide; an Organization for the Economic Cooperation and Development (OECD) report accuses the Mexican telephone industry, monopolized by Slim, of overcharging its customers in the multiple billions of dollars. The majority of Mexicans use pre-paid phone plans sold by Slim's company. As with Rockefeller's accomplishments with a basic product like kerosene, pay-as-you-go phone plans making Slim the richest man in the world is hard to comprehend. But monopolistic market dominance can do that for you. Slim, on record saying that job creation fights poverty better than charity, has been skeptical of Buffett's and Gates's philanthropic endeavors. As of 2010 Slim has started to show some philanthropic interest, but his giving is relatively paltry compared to heavyweights like Gates and Buffet (pledging to eventually give away, respectively, 95 and 99 percent of their fortunes) and amateur compared to trendsetters Rockefeller and Carnegie.[61]

Let's All Make Lots of $$$

The plane neared its destination; we looked out the window with excitement. Halfway expecting to see tumbleweeds and brown stretches of barren land, we saw green terrain and trees—lots of trees. My wife and I, both from the Land of Lincoln, were flying to Houston for my first interview at a church; it was 1990 and neither of us had been to Texas before. We were pleasantly surprised by what we saw out the plane window. The particular Texas stereotype that we brought with us, constructed of sagebrush and desert, was crushed by reality. Houston was lush and—as we would find out later—got its fair share of rain. Over the plane's intercom, the friendly Continental Airlines flight attendant, complete with Texas twang, informed us of the local time and temperature. What we heard next, however, from our hospitable hostess shockingly showed us that not all our Texas stereotypes would be poleaxed: "Y'all have fun in Houston and hope y'all make *lots of money!*" My wife and I looked at each other with mouths agape, our faces betraying abject disbelief over what we had just heard. Did she really just say that? Our Upper-Midwest sensibilities took a direct hit; we wondered, what awaited us in this land of big profits and tall talk?

Truth be told, that jarring introduction to Texas more than twenty years ago didn't scare us away. We love it in Texas—and for many reasons: the people, the mix of cultures and traditions, the food, the opportunities. Texas is unique historically; a big part of that history is commercial boldness. When we came to Houston in the early 1990s, low crude oil prices had made parts of the city go bust. Earlier, when the rest of the country suffered economically because of the Middle East oil embargo, Houston boomed. High oil prices were and are good for Houston; the romance of the energy business is reflected in its sprawling urban geography and lack of zoning laws. Houston, in the words of Enron chroniclers Bethany McLean and Peter Elkind, was "wide open to opportunity and worshipful of money." Houston hasn't changed. In 2011 *Forbes* named Houston the fastest growing millionaire city in America. The reason? It's still oil and gas.[62]

It was most appropriate that Halliburton moved its headquarters to Houston (from Dallas) in the early 2000s. Halliburton and its previous subsidiary, Kellogg, Brown, and Root (KBR), made a mint off government contracts during the 1990s. What it made from those contracts in the 2000s made the previous decade's earnings seem piddling in comparison. Before becoming vice president, Dick Cheney led Halliburton from 1995 to 2000. Before leading Halliburton, Cheney had a twenty-five-year career in the nation's capital, representing Wyoming in the House of Representatives and serving by appointment in the Ford and (first) Bush administrations. Cheney's DC contacts were considerable. During Cheney's tenure at Halliburton, the company won $2.3 billion in US military contracts. This doubled the amount won by Halliburton in the five years previous to Cheney's appointment. When Cheney returned to Washington as vice president, the Halliburton take on government contracts—many of them "no bid"— thoroughly outpaced any previous totals. In the new century, the US Department of Defense began to carry out war differently than before. With the Cold War over in the 1990s, the US military budget shrinking and military personnel numbers decreasing through that decade, and new conflicts in Iraq and Afghanistan, *outsourcing* became the solution for an overextended military under the Bush-Cheney administration. During the Iraq war, the ratio of military personnel to contract employees—Halliburton being a major supplier—was nearly one to one.[63]

War carried out differently means that stationed troops don't have to tend to the basics of making camp anymore: cooking and cleaning. Food, water, and much more, are shipped in and distributed by an array of workers—some foreign (Fiji, Philippines, Egypt, Sri Lanka) and paid cheaply—contracted by companies like Halliburton. An all-volunteer army, not the conscripted ones from previous eras, needs additional incentives to stay the course. This is the rationale behind the change, and the necessary adaptation to having a smaller military force (especially when overstretched, as was the case under Bush-Cheney). And the incentives are impressive: PXs (Post Exchanges) stocked with CDs, DVDs, TVs, bicycles, microwaves, steak, lobster, and Xbox consoles; and the presence of American fast-food outposts (Burger King, Pizza Hut, Subway, Cinnabon) and Internet cafes. The PX that was your grandfather's morale booster post–World War II, with a bag of peanuts and pack of cigarettes in Europe, is now a mini-Walmart and a mall food court transported to Mesopotamia. Yes, indeed, war is carried out differently than it used to be: the *consumerist-materialist* religion is not left behind in America but transported to the battlefield. The Army and Air Force Exchange Service (AAFES) provides the goodies, a well-meaning (and appreciated) service that can also cross the line into *too much*. A civilian worker (an American citizen who worked in Iraq for KBR) I interviewed told me of TVs and other electronic equipment casually tossed in the garbage—by both military personnel and privately hired workers—when transfer orders came their way. In February 2010 General Stanley McChrystal, commander of United States and NATO forces in Afghanistan, ordered a number of AAFES installments closed in Afghanistan. Burger King, Orange Julius, Pizza Hut, the Oakley Stores, and Military Car Sales all had to close up shop. Apparently, materialism and consumerism were hindering the combat mission. A McChrystal aide commented, "This is a war zone—not an amusement park."[64]

KBR, in Iraq and Afghanistan, ran a kingdom that was a microcosm of the globalized economy. People doing the same type of jobs and work but paid very differently, depending from whence they came. Lowest on the scale were locals, who were paid in cash (US); foreign workers were next up the line; contracted American civilians were paid best, making double and triple what enlisted military personnel were paid. The localized war-zone market supported this stratified wage scale. Local Afghanis and Iraqis were happy for any work in their war-torn homelands; they ran the risk, however, of disapproval (including death) from fellow citizens who opposed the American occupation. Asians and other foreigners were making more than they could have at home—yet with *promised* pay and *actual* pay, many experienced the predictable bait and switch tactic. American civilians wouldn't have been lured to work for KBR in a war zone unless they were paid more than they could have made at home—typical yearly pay was $80,000–$100,000.* KBR and Halliburton, however, made out best: awarded at least $19.3 billion in contracts for the war effort.[65]

After a decorated military career, Major General Smedley Butler of the US Marine Corps wrote a scathing pamphlet entitled *War Is a Racket*. He had a long military career, including service during World War I, retiring from the Marines in 1931. Of the many profiteering millionaires made during the war, he asked:

> How many of these war millionaires shouldered a rifle? How many of them dug a trench? How many of them knew what it meant to go hungry in a rat-infested dugout? How many of them spent sleepless, frightened nights, ducking shells and shrapnel and machine gun bullets? How many of them parried a bayonet thrust of an enemy? How many of them were wounded or killed in battle?[66]

So many things change, yet so much stays the same. The new face of war, due to a civilian support staff, frees up soldiers for duty, mission, and service. Halliburton through its subsidiary KBR, with the help of former CEO Dick Cheney, was best positioned to profit from that new face—and profit they did. David Lesar, who succeeded Cheney as Halliburton CEO, was a CPA who worked for Arthur Andersen—see if this sounds familiar—on the Halliburton account. According to investigative reporter Peter Elkind, Enron wasn't the only company that hired friendly Andersen auditors and consultants. Halliburton came calling for Lesar in 1993—fortunately for the CEO-to-be—before Andersen went down with Enron. During the Iraq war, accusations of waste, graft, inefficiency, and excessive profits—war profiteering—led Halliburton to eventually spin off KBR. From the 2003 invasion of Iraq to the spin-off of KBR in 2007, Lesar averaged some $20 million a year in total compensation as Halliburton CEO. His personal company stock holdings in 2005 were valued at more than $125 million. Halliburton is principally an oil and gas company, but during the Iraq war a lot of company revenue came courtesy of US taxpayers.[67]

The Military-Industrial-Counterterrorism Complex

On January 17, 1961, President Dwight Eisenhower—a five star general in the US Army who served as supreme commander of Allied Forces in Europe during

---

* This practice, in turn, drove up reenlistment bonus pay for military personnel. Stiglitz & Bilmes, 12.

World War II—gave his farewell speech after eight years in the White House. The Cold War dominated his remarks, which focused on war, peace, and freedom. He alluded to Hebrew scripture when he stated that previous to the Cold War, American manufacturers of "plowshares" could make, when necessary, "swords as well." After World War II and because of the Cold War, Eisenhower explained that "we have been compelled to create a permanent armaments industry of vast proportions." This was the irony of the Cold War: in order to maintain peace and freedom, the United States had to build up a large military establishment whose own burgeoning existence threatened to become a garrison of influence beyond its original intention and scope—threatening the very freedom it was called into being to protect. Eisenhower then uttered the words that would be the most remembered from his address: "In the councils of government, we must guard against the acquisition of unwarranted influence, whether sought or unsought, by the military-industrial complex."[68] Were he to utter such an exhortation today, the beloved Ike would be branded an unpatriotic, antibusiness heretic. What would Ike say if he knew that today's US military budget is almost equal to the amount spent on military defense by *all the other nations of the world combined*?[69]

The US Air Force is the largest and, arguably, the most technologically advanced air force in the world. Russia's air force is the second largest, but has been in decline for decades. China's air force is the third largest and growing. After these largest three, the air forces of the other countries in the world are significantly smaller. Yet another air force is just as strong as either Russia's or China's, but not many know about it. The air force of the US Navy, with more than 3,700 aircraft, easily rivals that of Russia or China.[70] When *one* country has the *two* largest air forces in the world, three things can be said: first, that's a strong military; second, that's a lot of budget expended; and third, there's ample opportunity for inefficiency and waste.

In the post-9/11 atmosphere of fear, politicians are loathe to debate, much less comment upon, the incredible inefficiencies and waste that inflict our military branches. The majority of military leaders and troops are not culpable; they serve in a system where competition for appropriations, budget allotments, new equipment, and power is on overdrive. According to historian James Carroll (whose father was an Air Force general), it's been like this since World War II, when militarism expanded in the United States. "Rivalry is built into the military ethos . . . It was inevitable that the service branches would fall to squabbling over dominance." The US Navy was established in the early days of the republic; it has traditionally seen itself as the ultimate guardian of American security, first as coastal defense, and second as the mobile projection of American power across the oceans. When the US Air Force was established as freestanding in 1947, naval hegemony was challenged, especially as the USAF was appointed custodian of the new atomic bomb. The air force could fly to world outposts considerably faster than the navy could sail—and, again, the air force had the bomb. Army and navy rivalry was long standing. The air force breaking free from the army (during World War II the air force was part of the army, the Army Air Corps) made for a triangular relationship rife with envy, tensions, and turf guarding.[71]

Carroll explains how the Pentagon was invested with so much money, power, and cultural energy that it—as feared by Eisenhower—began to take on a life of its own; namely, the *enterprise* of national security. "Tensions among the power centers in the Pentagon, particularly those of the inter-service rivalries, generated a force field of expansion that no one foresaw and no one controlled. Every American military entity organized itself against two enemies: the Communist monolith and every other American military entity." According to Carroll, interservice rivalry is the engine that for more than sixty years has driven Pentagon budget requests.[72] More than two decades ago, Yale historian Paul Kennedy argued forcefully that hegemonic powers in the modern era—Spain, Holland, France, Russia, Britain—have had an unfortunate common trait: excessive military spending that eventually became overly burdensome upon their economies, leading to their downfall.[73] The Soviet Union's downfall, happening after the publication of Kennedy's *The Rise and Fall of Great Powers*, fit the description adeptly. Only time will tell if America's so-called exceptionalism will save it from similar fate.

In the post-9/11 world, counterterrorism follows the same path, taking excess to new levels. In their book *Top Secret America*, investigative journalist Dana Priest and *Washington Post* columnist William Arkin claim that the US intelligence system has grown so vast that nobody knows how many people it employs, how much taxpayer money (some of it wasteful) supports it, and how much of its work is duplicated. Nine-eleven created a perpetual fear that exerts its influence on American society. Priest and Arkin assert that "a culture of fear has created a culture of spending to control it." Fighting terrorism is a necessary and important cause; there's no question, however, that it has been a lucrative pursuit for federal and state agencies and a mechanism by which a plethora of new agencies— public and private—have been created and funded.[74]

Priest and Arkin cite numerous examples. When the Office of the Director of National Intelligence (DNI) opened in the spring of 2005, it had eleven employees, gathering in the New Executive Office Building located one block from the White House. Three years later, the DNI was permanently housed in its new digs, a 500,000-square-foot superstructure in well-to-do McLean, Virginia. Between the DNI and the adjacent National Counterterrorism Center, some 1,700 federal employees and 1,200 private contractors do their work. The two organizations share a police force, canine unit, and a jumbo-size parking lot that would make Sam Walton proud. This is just one example where *more* is often seen as the best solution. Priest and Arkin's count as of 2010: 1,074 federal government organizations and nearly 2,000 private companies working in the fields of counterterrorism, homeland security, and intelligence—spread among 17,000 US locations. Two hundred sixty-three of these organizations were newly formed after 9/11; the biggest growth, however, has come in agencies and corporations—already in existence—that have grown exponentially in the post-9/11 aura of fear. The Pentagon's Defense Intelligence Agency had 7,500 employees in 2002—eight years later, it had 16,500. General Dynamics, the high-tech defense contractor located in Fairfax County (Virginia), more than doubled its employee ranks in the first decade of the new century and tripled its revenues. The company expanded considerably with the acquisition of numerous and smaller defense-related companies—no doubt made feasible by its reliance on a hefty portion of the governmental counterterrorism pie. Priest and Arkin continually ask the following pragmatic question of the enormous counterterrorism industry: who can possibly keep track of all the material and information that is being produced?[75]

In 1986 the Goldwater-Nichols Act (Department of Defense Reorganization) was passed by wide margins in both chambers of the US Congress, its purpose to streamline the military chain of command and to fix the problems of interservice rivalry and duplication of duties. For forty years, interservice rivalry was reflected at the highest level in the Joint Chiefs of Staff (made up by the leaders of the army, air force, navy, and marines), the representative leaders, political equals on the committee, advocating their own branches more often than not. Goldwater-Nichols, signed into law by President Reagan, made the role of chairman of the Joint Chiefs supreme—as the principal military adviser to the president. The failures of the Vietnam War and the problematic 1983 invasion of Grenada fueled momentum for the change;* Goldwater-Nichols forced the military branches to work together more effectively and efficiently. Though the military's internal rivalries are still strong (the bidding for new equipment during the Iraq war by the navy and the air force, while the army was favored and fortified proves the point), Goldwater-Nichols has modified some of the entrenched parochial culture.[76]

---

* According to Priest and Arkin (98), the majority of military brass opposed Goldwater-Nichols. It's no small irony that Goldwater-Nichols was signed into law during an era of military-industrial excess.

The intelligence community, post-9/11, is in need of its own version of Goldwater-Nichols. While the nation debates the size of government—the Republican Party being most vocal about the need to shrink government—the federal payouts to agencies doing intelligence work, public and private, swells. This has been the case under both the Bush and the Obama administrations. Six out of the ten wealthiest and best-educated counties in the United States are found in the suburban area surrounding Washington, DC. Government agencies and private companies doing intelligence work employ, as we've seen, thousands. For the five years immediately following 9/11, defense and intelligence spending soared by more than 50 percent; many Pentagon employees left public service for more lucrative private employment in the same fields they had previously worked—still paid, essentially, by the American taxpayer. In 2008 a wide-ranging expense report on the network of intelligence agencies was prepared for Defense Secretary William Gates. It determined that while contractors made up 29 percent of the workforce, it garnered the equivalent of 49 percent of its compensation budgets.[77]

Pharmaceuticals Gone Commercial

The counterterrorism industry hasn't squeezed out all other players from DC, however. The pharmaceutical industry, one of the biggest spenders among lobbyists in the capital, has a presence and effect like no other industry. The United States is the only developed country in the world that does not regulate prescription drug prices; the United States and New Zealand are the only two countries that allow drug makers to advertise directly to consumers. The pharmaceutical industry is notoriously enamored with profits; its legions of lobbyists far outnumber the legislators who receive their attentions. Americans spend more money on medications than the people of any other nation, and 65 percent of all Americans—including an increasing number of children (and pets)—take prescription medicines. No other country comes even close to this rate.[78]

In 1925 George Merck became president of the pharmaceutical company his father had led for close to three decades. In those days "pill companies" were not held in high regard; medical doctors placed little trust in the industry as a whole and scientists chose not to risk their reputations by working for the industry. Merck was instrumental in helping change that reality; he hired scientists and promised them the freedom to disclose their findings at professional meetings with colleagues and in scientific publications. Pharmaceutical giants-to-be Squibb and Lily followed Merck's lead. These were important days for the industry and its nascent modernization. At this time, there was no regulating body to protect the public from industry incompetency or bottled chemical speculations.* After a deadly elixir produced by a Tennessee drug maker in 1937 killed children who had taken it for nothing more than a sore throat, FDR signed into law the Food, Drug, and Cosmetic Act, empowering the Food and Drug Administration (FDA) to require companies to test for safety before selling medicines. It then became standard procedure that pharmaceutical labs were manned exclusively by trained scientists—more than 58,000 worked in the field during the 1940s, up from only a few thousand in the 1920s.[79]

Penicillin had been discovered in the late 1920s, but its mass production had not been achieved even as the United States became involved in World War II. The government attempted to involve the pharmaceutical companies in mass production of penicillin—for the troops. From our vantage point today, it's surprising that none of the pharmaceutical companies were interested; the time and money investment was prohibitive. George Merck, after repeated entreaties from the government, eventually changed his mind and persuaded three other pharmaceuticals to join Merck & Company in the effort to mass produce penicillin. Thanks to their successful efforts, penicillin supplies were sufficient to cover all the wounded troops on D-day. In those days, profits and the idea that medicine is for the people were kept in balance. It wasn't a perfect balance, but it was at least an active balance. Those egalitarian days sometimes saw doctors and scientists serve the common good by giving patents for life-saving medicines to public trusts. Those days are long over; today's pharmaceutical industry overwhelmingly and consistently chooses profits over people.[80] Medicines help people heal, cope, and thrive; many are grateful to the pharmaceutical industry for what it does for society. Yet, the pharmaceutical industry is no different than so many other industries that, beginning in earnest in the late 1970s and early '80s, have taken the spirit of "just a little bit more" to excessive measures.

Americans spend upward of $300 billion on medications per year—almost $1,000 for every man, woman, and child in the country.[81] How did we get to such a place? In earlier days Americans could get medications from their local pharmacist. The 1951 Durham-Humphrey Amendment changed that, modifying the 1938 Food, Drug, and Cosmetic Act by assigning medications to two categories—prescription and over the counter. The miracle that was penicillin gave pharmaceuticals a boost beyond imagination. At that time, amputation was a

---

* The predecessor body of the FDA was established in 1906 but had no practical jurisdiction over pharmaceuticals.

common option for stubborn infections. Penicillin transformed the understanding and reality of infection: no longer was an infection feared as we might fear cancer today. Penicillin raised the bar for the pharmaceutical industry; it was expected that novel medications could perform similar miracles, and eventually pharmaceutical marketing strategies fully encouraged this new faith.[82]

The immediate post–World War II era was the golden age for pharmaceutical progress. Cortisone had been identified and reproduced, penicillin's discovery was followed by other antibiotics; polio and tuberculosis were significantly ameliorated, and advances were made against childhood leukemia. Soon enough, however, the rate of significant discoveries slacked off. At this time marketing and promotion came to the fore in the pharmaceutical industry. Competition within the industry amped up as well—"me-too" drugs, where companies copied competitors' products, became commonplace. Like Bill Gates would later do with computer code, a slight tweak in the makeup of a particular drug allowed for a newly copyrighted one. Tennessee Senator Estes Kefauver held hearings on the pharmaceutical industry in 1959, the hearings proving true what was generally suspected: the industry was addicted to profits. The hearings revealed that the Upjohn Company was spending close to 30 percent of its budget on promotion and only 9 percent on research. Upjohn wasn't alone in emphasizing marketing over research. For more than fifty years, this has been standard industry practice. In the late 1990s the number of pharmaceutical marketing personnel almost doubled that of research and development; this trend continues unabated.[83]

Melody Petersen, an investigative journalist and author of the book *Our Daily Meds*, casts ample doubt upon pharmaceutical executives' oft-repeated claim that they need to charge high prices for their products (while they lobby Congress for copyright extensions on particular drugs) in order to cover costs for research and development on newly discovered drugs. The pharmaceutical industry plays the same game of beefing up the stock price for investors on Wall Street—courting, in the process, the usual suspects of beguilement, deception, and hype—and routinely hires medical doctors and university professors to help pitch their products, often not disclosing these for-pay relationships.[84]

In 1996 marketing and promotion ticked up for the industry as the FDA allowed medications to be advertised on television. Print advertising had been used by the industry for decades; television, however, was the promised land for marketers and executives. Claritin was the first mass-marketed medication. Its producer, Schering-Plough, spent $136 million on Claritin ads in 1998, the most ever spent to advertise a drug. Sales consequently skyrocketed. That same year saw another drug introduced, however, that eventually made Claritin's sales meager in comparison. It was also heavily advertised by its maker, Pfizer. Early ads, later banned, featured two little, red devilish horns coming forth from the user's head upon taking Pfizer's new wonder drug Viagra. "Lifestyle drugs" treating the problems and irritations of aging have become a major focus for the industry in recent decades.[85]

One task of pharmaceutical marketers—in concert with paid physicians—is to name new disorders (overactive bladder, social anxiety disorder) or rename old ones with the purpose of creating demand for their cures. In the case of male impotence, there are many potential causes, but declining heart function is the clear-cut leading culprit. Current Viagra ads (and those of "me too" competitors Cialis and Levitra) feature active forty- and fifty-something males who are generally fit and healthy looking. None are overweight or fit the typical profile for someone afflicted with heart disease. Erectile dysfunction (an industry-produced name) is made to seem as if it's a normal occurrence for the American male once he crests forty-five or so.[86] Normal, yes, if he has diabetes, high blood pressure, high cholesterol, depression, a spinal cord injury, or *heart disease*. The Viagra website—smoking can be a cause of impotence as well—is more forthcoming than its TV ads.[87]

The pharmaceutical industry for decades has had substantially higher average profit rates (up to three times greater) compared to other Fortune 500 industries, helping accelerate the spiraling costs of health care in the United States. It has corrupted its relationship with physicians and the medical industry with commercially sponsored research. More often than not, "expert" medical reviews are written by doctors (or company ghostwriters) who have direct financial ties to the companies whose drugs are being reviewed, a clear conflict of interest. And the industry has a despicable record of overpromoting drugs that either do not do what they are advertised to do or, worse, inflict damage or death upon their subjects—men, women, and children. The notorious "science" supporting hormone replacement therapy (HRT) for women dealing with the changes brought on by menopause was called by a research physician nothing more than "a house of cards." The treatment itself increased the risks of heart disease, stroke, and cancer in women. Twenty million American women were subjected to HRT in the last quarter of the twentieth century. Vioxx, Bextra, Baycol, Propulsid, Paxil—treating arthritis, high cholesterol, and anxiety—are some of the other medications that have been blamed in severe patient illness and death.[88] Promotion and profits go together—at great cost to the people who suffer and even die in the process.

Health Care—Not Getting What We Pay For

Health care spending and costs in the United States are the highest in the world by any measurable standard: gross expenditure, expenditure per person, and percentage of GDP. In 2011 total spending in the United States was $2.7 trillion, an average of $8,680 per person, 17.9 percent of GDP. As with its significant military spending, the United States claims between 40 and 50 percent of the world's total expenditure on health care, outspending the majority of other OECD countries per capita by two and three times. The GDP percentage of health care spending in the United States has doubled since 1980; the other OECD countries have not experienced such a surge in spending as percentage of GDP: France comes closest to the United States at just under 12 percent, while Japan spends the least at just over 8 percent. *Of course: the United States spends the most because it has the best health care system in the world.* Unfortunately, by many measurable data, that is not the case. For starters, both Japanese and French citizens have a higher life expectancy than Americans. The same can be said for Canadians, Italians, Spaniards, Greeks, and others, and their per capita spending on health care is significantly less than the US level.[89]

The United States is the only industrialized nation to not provide universal coverage to its citizens, lending a sense of incomparability with the other OECD nations. America's health care reality is more akin to underdeveloped nations: first-rate health care for the well-to-do (arguably, the best in the world), and for others, stratified levels of care generally related to job status and income. A variant of the "work to eat" credo, one of every six Americans are not insured at all. Yet, almost half of these uninsured Americans are working Americans.[90] Consequently, in this arena the credo is not persuasive. Rising health-care costs increasingly make it difficult for employers (the traditional source for health coverage) to offer the benefit. As corporate revenues have been siphoned upward to management and ownership, less revenue is available to allocate toward the rising cost of health care benefits. America's workers, at an increasing rate, are not insured by their employers. From a high-water mark in the early 1980s of nearly 75 percent, the percentage of those with employer-based health coverage has fallen under 50 percent (based on 2011 figures).[91]

The Commonwealth Fund is a nonprofit research organization that was started in 1918 by Anna Harkness, the widow of a Standard Oil director, Stephen Harkness. Mrs. Harkness was the first American woman to establish a public foundation. The mission of the foundation from its early years has been to "promote a high-performing health care system that achieves better access, improved quality, and greater efficiency, particularly for society's most vulnerable, including low-income people, the uninsured, minority Americans, young children and elderly adults." The Commonwealth Fund advocates greater efficiencies in the overall health care system. Financial journalist Maggie Mahar agrees, calling the US health system "extravagantly inefficient." Neither one is knocking American doctors and nurses, whose skills and dedication are not in question; health care in the United States costs more because we pay more for the same services (compared to other OECD countries), pay higher administrative costs, duplicate medical tests, and have a propensity to perform more complex and specialized procedures. In addition, medical bills are a leading cause of personal bankruptcy in the United States (along with credit card debt), with many of those bankrupted having had medical insurance, albeit inadequate coverage.[92]

The American population is aging and in need of more care, contributing to the rise in health care costs. Also contributing, some argue, is the ever-present threat of malpractice litigation, forcing doctors to pay exorbitantly for malpractice insurance and carry out "defensive medicine"—ordering multiple tests to rule out potential causes of illness. Yes, these have their contributing effects, but they are tempered by the facts that most of the other OECD countries also have aging populations and that as an overall percentage of health care spending, malpractice awards in the United States are in line with those of Canada, the United Kingdom, and Australia. The principal reason costs in the United States have risen exponentially in the last thirty-five years, according to Mahar, is the power shift in the health care system from physicians to corporations. Many of today's decisions about health dollar allocations are marketing decisions: drug makers, device makers, and insurers decide what gets done based partially or wholly on the profit motive.[93] Typically, we expect the market to help make the system more efficient; this hasn't happened. And the marketization of the health care system isn't making us any healthier either.

Egalitarian societies, where income and wealth are distributed more equably, are healthier societies. Highly economically stratified societies—the United States sharing the same level of socioeconomic disparities with countries such as Cameroon, Jamaica, and Mozambique—are associated with lower life expectancy, higher rates of infant mortality, and greater occurrence of depression. The Commonwealth Fund ranks the United States last in a select group of industrialized nations in five areas of comparative health care: quality, efficiency, access to care, equity, and the opportunity to live a long, healthy life.[94] Being last while spending the most—that's enough to make some of us sick.

Keeping Up with Barbie

The pharmaceutical industry isn't the only lobbying group to invent terminology for conditions in need of cures. The plastic surgery–cosmetic industry coined *micromastia*: the disease of having small breasts. Houston is where the first breast implant surgery occurred, and Houston currently remains the boob job capital of America. Houston's celebrated Medical Center, a conglomeration of hospitals, schools, and health-related practices in the central-south part of the city, hosted the first breast augmentation surgery in 1962. Dow Corning made the first breast "prosthetics"—silicone bags filled with silicone gel—and Thomas Cronin and Frank Gerow, plastic surgeons, pioneered the surgery. For women who needed breast reconstruction—due to mastectomies, accidents, or deformities—Cronin and Gerow's innovation was a marked improvement over what had previously been available (mostly injections). The line between want and need quickly vanished, however, as breast augmentation became mostly an elective surgery for enhanced patient quality of life. By 1985 one hundred thousand women were going under the knife each year; by 1992, two million women in the United States had implants, propping up a $450 million industry. Today it is the most popular plastic surgery procedure, with three hundred thousand women subjected to the knife every year.[95]

The entertainment and porn industry quickly caught on to the financial benefits of the procedure. Rick's Cabaret, a strip club franchise founded in 1983 in Houston, has an interesting history. For a time Rick's supplied more models to *Playboy* than any other strip club, became at one point American Express's largest charge customer, and helped make strip clubs legitimate commercially by being the first to be publicly traded. After a relentless climb, the company's stock price topped out at $28.24 at the end of 2007. It has since sagged to under $10 per share; it's no surprise that its stock price mirrors the rise and fall of other companies that rode the inequality wave of the early 2000s until it could no longer be sustained. The top-heavy models who worked Rick's stages and tables knew tip size corresponded with tit size.[96]

While Houston led the way with implants, Las Vegas continued with the easier and cheaper option of silicone injections (some of it industrial grade), even though silicone had been regulated as a drug by the FDA since 1965. As of 1975, more than twelve thousand women had received injections into their breasts in the casino capital, thanks to a robust underground network. Death, infection, gangrene, necrosis, and amputation were some of the undesirable results. It wasn't long, however, before trouble with the first generation of implants started to emerge; FDA regulation of implants commenced in the late 1970s. Eventually,

Dow Corning was sued ad nauseam for defective and ruptured implants; the company declared bankruptcy in 1995. Business history repeated itself once again: one group (manufacturers and doctors) profiting with an unproven product off another group—both groups, perhaps, having equally mixed motives. Plastic surgeons continue to treat micromastia—creating Barbie doll-like measurements for some women who, in their own minds, just don't measure up.[97]

Journalist Florence Williams, in her 2012 book *Breasts*, aptly describes a new reality, born two generations ago in Houston:

> Thanks to the alliance of two kinds of silica-based technologies— breasts and computer chips—most young people learn about bodies and sex from the Internet; they have seen many more factory-made breasts than real ones . . . Big, fake breasts have so thoroughly saturated mainstream entertainment and media that they've created a new standard by which boys judge girls and girls judge themselves.[98]

Athletic Excess

Lance Armstrong used to be a national celebrity; he was a hero in Austin, where he resides, for having survived cancer and winning seven Tour de France titles. Yellow Livestrong bracelets supporting the Lance Armstrong Foundation's fight against cancer were proudly displayed by the young and older all over Austin. Armstrong was beloved for his spirit of survival as much as his unparalleled invincibility on his bicycle. When he gave up his fight against the US Anti-Doping Agency (USADA) in 2012 (consequently losing his Tour de France titles), most Austinites were not only shocked but also outraged at the USADA. But when he eventually admitted to cheating in 2013, some of that outrage was deflected back his own way. Liar, cheater, and bully were the new epithets hurled in his direction.

Another Austinite, John Hoberman, is a historian who teaches at the University of Texas. In 2005 his book *Testosterone Dreams* was published to scant notice. An excellent book, it ambitiously covers athletic performance and related topics such as health and aging, including male menopause, or (thanks to pharmaceutical marketers) Low T. Testosterone, produced synthetically as an anabolic steroid in 1935, was initially touted as a cure for homosexuals and revitalization for old men. Hoberman reveals that professional cycling, a sport that has been dirty (beginning with amphetamine use) since its inception at the turn of the twentieth century, has enjoyed medically supervised doping of cyclists since the 1950s. Because the '50s was the golden era of pharmaceuticals, there was at that time no moralistic attitude that opposed a *professional* athlete, working with his doctor, benefiting from the new scientific enhancement of drugs. On the other hand, amateur athletes were expected to be clean and clear of the use of drugs as a performance enhancement. Money made a difference—it was generally accepted that professional athletes, earning a living with their physiques, needed the extra boost. The ignorance of steroids' side effects also made a difference. The first known professional cyclist to die related to doping was Knud Jensen of Denmark in the 1960 Olympic Games in Rome.[99]

The World Anti-Doping Agency and the related USADA didn't come into being until 2000. The grand irony is that for more than sixty years the societies of the developed nations—especially the United States—have increasingly relied on pharmaceutical science for healing and enhancements. Hoberman states that there is a "growing acceptance of pharmacological solutions for an expanding catalogue of human problems." This reliance and acceptance goes hand in glove with American society's obsession with performance. College students take Ritalin to help their concentration for studying and exams. Police officers are known to take steroids to meet the physical demands of police work, ultimately serving public safety. USAF pilots took the amphetamine Dexedrine to boost performance when flying missions during the Gulf War. The steroid era in Major League Baseball (further detailed below), which saw record numbers of home runs hit by beefed up players, brought the game back to life for many fans who had previously lost interest in America's pastime.[100]

Armstrong confessed to interviewer Oprah Winfrey that the culture of professional cycling is as Hoberman and others have documented: the use of performance-enhancing drugs is commonplace. Most likely all were cheating, and if so, the Tour's playing field in some sense was leveled. The sport has been compromised for decades; besides crossing the finish line first, the other main factor affecting cycling results is who actually gets caught doping.[101] Steroid-masking agents are as much a part of the doping regimen as are the drug enhancements. Armstrong's confession perfectly illustrates the credo of "just a little bit more" taken too far: "When I was diagnosed (with cancer) I would do anything to survive. I took that attitude—win at all costs—to cycling . . . My ruthless desire to win at all costs served me well on the bike but the level it went to, for whatever the reason, is a flaw."[102] Good and evil *yetzer*: The same drive that helped him overcome cancer led him to become an intimidating and vengeful bully who considered only his own reputation as he repeatedly crossed lines—ruining others' reputations and livelihoods—in the attempt to keep his own name clean.

Starting in August 1994, Major League Baseball (MLB) suffered through a bitter strike that lasted into 1995. For the first time in ninety years the World Series wasn't played as MLB became the first major sport to lose an entire postseason due to a labor dispute. Outraged fans stayed away from ballparks and attendance plummeted 20 percent the following season. The national pastime was indelibly tarnished. The game (and its beloved statistical records) that had not changed much in one hundred years—enhancing baseball's continuity and likability for generations of fans—was now infected with greedy owners and selfish players that simply weren't able to share an enormous revenue pie (close to $2 billion). As the NBA (Michael Jordan era) and the NFL (the Dallas Cowboys—America's Team—won three Super Bowls in four years) became ascendant, MLB needed something to retain its former glory. The well-chronicled steroid era saved the day. That players used performance-enhancing drugs was an open secret; home run records that had stood for decades were pulverized by muscle-men Barry Bonds, Mark McGwire, and Sammy Sosa.[103] It's not ironic whatsoever that the steroid era, starting in the 1990s, coincided with the short era of American excess. More home runs, more tickets sold, more profits, more excess.

The National Football League (NFL) now provides America with its most popular sport. There are no outcries about doping in the NFL, although the use of steroids has been ongoing since the 1960s. Steroid use was made illegal in the NFL in the late 1980s when the league began its testing policy. But the profuse popularity of the sport works against it ever coming completely clean. As long as the rewards—emotional and financial—are as elevated as they are, cheating will be just another part of the game. And that's true for any game, including the biggest game of them all—the one played on Wall Street. Hoberman summarizes, "In short, systematic doping must be understood as resulting from a social system and its values."[104] One hundred years ago Rockefeller not only gave permission to but also sanctified the philosophy of winner-take-all; it's been a dominant social value in the United States since the late 1970s.

Today's pay breakdowns among players in professional sports reflect the pay inequalities that exist in society. This is a recent development, reflecting some of the same pay inequalities that have emerged for CEOs and Wall Street executives in the last thirty years. Professional teams consist of those who have skills that are highly coveted and rightly rewarded more so than others on the same team—we see this same principle at work in general society. A state governor needs to be compensated better than a janitor working in the state capitol; LeBron James is compensated better than teammate Mario Chalmers. Professional sports free agency (instituted in the four major professional sports leagues in North America from the mid-1970s to the mid-1990s) has accomplished two things: made the best players extremely rich and exacerbated the pay difference between those exceptional players and their teammates. The National Hockey League (NHL), the NBA, and the NFL all operate with overall team salary restrictions—a salary cap. MLB doesn't have a salary cap, but has a required "luxury tax," which is levied upon teams with payrolls that surpass a specified amount. Any luxury tax collected by the league is redistributed to competing teams not surpassing the set taxed amount.

Amar'e Stoudemire and Carmelo Anthony are two of the top players in the NBA. Both play on the New York Knicks. For the 2012–13 season, both stood to make $20 million, comfortably putting them in the top ten of league salaries. The NBA salary cap for the season was set at $58 million (the NBA employs a "soft" cap, allowing teams to go over the cap amount, but requiring them to pay a luxury tax above $70 million). Two players on the Knicks were consequently taking close to two-thirds of the team's allotment toward the cap. This is a common practice on many teams, with the top players garnering the majority percentage of team pay. (In 2012 Kobe Bryant was the highest paid player in the league at more than $27 million.) The Knicks, however, aren't that good of a team. They qualified for the playoffs in both the 2011–12 and the 2012–13 seasons, losing ten of their seventeen playoff games. They lost their 2012 playoff series against the eventual league champion Miami Heat. The Heat's best player, LeBron James, was paid less money than Stoudemire and Anthony for the season. While the two star players for the Knicks have maximized their pay potential, the team won't get that much better. These two players have taken up sizable salary cap space, leaving little leeway to sign other good players. LeBron James, on the other hand, could have made as much or more than either Stoudemire or Anthony—he chose, however, to be paid less for the opportunity to be on a better team.* He didn't maximize his pay potential, and his team won two championships.[105] One could argue that James (and his team) has won it all due to his refusal to take as much as possible—Rockefeller's permission be damned.

James's abnegation of the biggest bucks possible, however, doesn't help a family of modest means come to the arena and watch a live game. In 2012 the average ticket price for an NBA game was close to $50, with the New York Knicks of Stoudemire and Anthony leading the way at $117. The Miami Heat of LeBron James averaged $67. NBA salaries and sports' salaries across the board have escalated incredibly in the last thirty years, blowing away the inflation rate.[106]

---

* A couple of qualifier statements are needed. At the time he signed his contract with the Knicks, Stoudemire was a top player. His gimpy knees have since mitigated his superiority. James, with a contract that pays him less, makes considerably more money in endorsements than do Anthony and Stoudemire combined.

If our hearts are found where we place our treasure, we look no farther than our TVs to find both. Movies still help tell our cultural story; televised sports, with their incredible popularity consequently enabling players, coaches, and owners to "earn" vastly exaggerated sums, reveal that we supremely value entertainment and performance, no matter the cost. Many can't afford to go to the game in person, but viewers are the meat and bones of television contracts that have contributed to escalating revenues and salaries. America is a performance-oriented society; that reality helps explain why we countenance Alex Rodriguez (another steroid user) of the New York Yankees being paid $30 million a year for hitting and catching a ball and Wall Street executives making just as much for doing what they do.

The Ultimate Game

What is it that they do on Wall Street? Professional athletes provide entertainment at an extremely high level; their physical feats—artificially enhanced or not—are truly impressive. Their art is not as sublime as that of accomplished painters, musicians, or playwrights. Athletic feats, individually and collectively on team sports, however, contribute a sense of cohesion for fans and represented cities (and nations), uplift economies, and encourage youth to develop their own sense of artistry via athletic endeavor. On the other hand, Wall Street types make money. Their work employs co-workers at the firm or bank; and, some argue, the wealth "created" is then available for loans and societal development. Commentators and former Wall Street employees, however, question that social good is produced at all on the Street. It increasingly is compared to Monte Carlo and Las Vegas—a place to gamble with money simply to make more money. Social purpose is an afterthought at best. Making money on Wall Street has become the ultimate game in a society that expects to be the best—at sports, in military might, and at money making.

In their book *Drilling Down*, anthropologist Joseph Tainter and engineer Tad Patzek explain the concept of the energy-complexity spiral. Sure, American ingenuity and hard work helped create the American way of life, but according to Tainter and Patzek, considerably more crucial to the development and maintenance of American society has been the *availability of inexpensive, high quality energy*. Coal powered the nineteenth century, with oil and gas predominant in the twentieth century (with coal still providing significant power for electricity). A gallon of gasoline, for example, has the energy equivalent of four hundred person hours of work. After having lived in Perú for two years, I realized the biggest difference between my lifestyles in North and South America was that I was able to get so many more tasks done on a daily basis in the United States. The same person—all other things being equal—has a different level of productivity based upon societal context. Cars, roads, buildings, sewer pipes, and bridges require ingenuity and *energy*—the cheaper and more available the better—for their production and maintenance. The discovery of petroleum in the United States, its subsequent development into multiple products, and its availability—thank you, Mr. Rockefeller—helped give America its exceptional momentum. It has also contributed to American society's unprecedented complexity.[107] Energy and complexity proceed together in Tainter and Patzek's spiral as society attempts to solve the myriad problems it confronts.

Remember when your car (no remembering necessary if you drive an older model) had a crank handle for the window? Operating it could sometimes be a hassle, especially when your hands were already occupied or when the handle mechanism became slow and stubborn or simply broke. It didn't work that well if you had a bum shoulder or arm, either. Automatic windows, now standard on all new cars, help solve the problems associated with crank window handles. Automatic windows are great—except when they break and cost six hundred dollars or more to fix. Complexity: I used to crank the window up or down, expending energy, whereas now a small machine, using energy, does the work for me. The same can be said, of course, for the evolution of automatic transmissions, power steering, and brakes. Less work for the driver and more work done by mechanisms. This exchange has happened continuously in countless areas of our lives. The house painting that my graduate school buddies and I did decades back was often aided by the knowledgeable guy at the paint store who by eye and hand could match the color from an old paint can lid or siding sample: *experience and feel*. Nowadays, when you go to the big box home improvement store hoping to match a color to an item previously painted, the *computerized* mixing machine, equipped with a camera, takes a picture of your paint-stained lid or siding sample and does the rest. The computerized mixing machine does a good job; it requires, however, significant financial commitment, steady maintenance, and plenty of electricity. The paint store guy simply needed a proper "Good morning" and a cup of coffee in order to do a good job. Energy and complexity spiral together upward, and to maintain modernity (better and advanced solutions) we need to find more energy to sustain the momentum. Complexity will continue to increase—cheap energy allows for it.[108]

EROEI is the acronym for *energy returned on energy invested*. In the 1940s, the EROEI for American oil production was 100 to 1—it has declined today to 15 to 1. Think of the incredible amount of planning, work, hardware, computer software, expertise, and *energy* necessary to extract oil from reserves below the waters of the Gulf of Mexico or the North Sea. (The Gulf was the site of initial offshore oil drilling, starting in the 1940s.) Tainter and Patzek report that to power a complex modern society a net energy ratio of at least 5 to 1 is needed. The politically charged Canadian tar sands, scheduled to be piped down to the Texas coast for production and refining, have an EROEI as low as 3 to 2.* In the business of worldwide petroleum extraction, most of the low-hanging fruit has already been picked. Tainter and Patzek are among numerous observers who conclude that *peak oil*—the point of declining worldwide oil production—was reached in 2005. Today's innovation in the petroleum industry comes with much harder work and at exponentially greater expense (the doomed Deepwater Horizon cost $1 billion to construct) than it did decades ago.** Generally speaking, many other industries are experiencing a similar slowdown in productivity of innovation. The energy-complexity spiral again helps explain: there just might be economic limits to innovation. The number of new patents worldwide steadily declined through the twentieth century; the peak of US innovation (percentage of patents per population) has also been in steady decline since reaching its apogee in 1915. Patent teams (recognized authors) and scientific research teams (published papers) continue to increase in size—more work input, fewer results output—another demonstration of a slowdown in the productivity of innovation.[109]

What's all this got to do with Wall Street? The same principle applies. Wall Street (the same can be said of the pharmaceutical industry) has had to work harder and harder to come up with innovative ways to *create* wealth. More than thirty years ago, staid actor John Houseman (he was superb in many roles; Dobbs in *My Bodyguard,* alongside Ruth Gordon, is a little-known treat) told us, in advertisement, that the Wall Street investment firm Smith Barney made money the old-fashioned way: they *earned* it—with research and smart investment strategy. Those days, if they did in fact exist, are long gone. *Derivatives*, a general term to describe a wide range of financial products, are often purposely so complicated that neither brokers nor regulators—much less investors—understand completely how they work. Derivatives are financial instruments related to, or derived from, other securities. *Complex derivatives* can sometimes include options to buy or sell certain stocks or bonds at future dates; the packaging of derivatives involves combining potential values from different underlying securities and calculating their supposed worth by means of elaborate mathematics that can approach the level of computer code. Mortgage-backed securities, anyone? The development of increasingly complicated investment products follows the principle of the energy-complexity spiral, and many of these dense products carry significant risk

---

* EROEI for solar energy and wind energy are 13 to 2 and 20 to 1, respectively. Tainter & Patzek, 203.
** Hydraulic fracturing, "fracking," will be discussed in chapter 8.

for the investor. Combined with selling and processing fees, Wall Street isn't so much creating new wealth with its complex derivatives but confiscating existing wealth. Economic writer Yves Smith states:

> Big financial firms recognized that product complexity was their best friend, offering all sorts of hidden traps and snares by which they could take more money from unwitting clients. Big financial firms became increasingly inclined to prey on their customers and, ultimately, the societies in which they lived.[110]

Traditional research (the kind John Houseman talked about) is becoming anachronistic on Wall Street—more than half of stock trading today is done automatically by computers with other computers (flash trading), using algorithms, based solely on information extracted on price patterns and trades.[111] The new research is purely motivated by profit—no other considerations need apply.

Phil Gramm's political campaigns, like those of many politicians from both sides of the aisle, were buttressed with contributions from Wall Street firms. Perhaps the big checks from supporters helped him feel the holiness of Wall Street; however, others who have worked in Wall Street firms tell of a markedly different spirit on the Street. Old school misogyny, dog-eat-dog competitiveness, greed, and the primacy of profits over people are the descriptions given by those who have actually worked in the financial firms. Nomi Prins, Frank Partnoy, Nassim Nicholas Taleb, and Michael Lewis have written extensively and convincingly about their not-so-holy Wall Street experiences. They describe similarly the self-serving money culture that existed in the 1980s and the 1990s on Wall Street, and still exists today.

Steven Weinberg won the 1979 Nobel Prize in Physics for his work on the unified theory of weak and electromagnetic interactions. He teaches at the University of Texas at Austin where he is the director of the Theory Research Group. In a 2011 interview published in the *Austin American-Statesman*, he was asked about the tendency of physics students to migrate to the financial industry in order to use their brains and mathematical genius on Wall Street.

> My experience is that the students who really are so good that they can feel they are going to be part of the effort of discovering the fundamental principles of nature or answering deep questions about cosmology, those students stay in the field. It's the students who are not so sure of that who migrate into Wall Street. I don't know of any cases where a student was

doing really first-rate work who then moved into Wall Street. I mean, *all they can offer is money.* [112] (Italics mine.)

Wall Street has been the destination for America's top university students for the past two decades. In the 1990s those with MBA degrees started to get some competition. Students of finance, math, engineering, computer science, and physics—with either undergrad or graduate degrees—began to arrive, and they had the ability to formulate the complex financial products that became the exclusive tag of Wall Street. Harvard, Yale, and Princeton grads are aggressively recruited by the banks and firms of Wall Street; in today's weak job market a promised position is a good option for those grads who have loans to repay (the soaring rate of college tuition is yet another example of the culture of excess). But there has been recent pushback: students and alums at these aforementioned schools, as well as Stanford, have led protests critical of Wall Street firms' access to top students. The protesting students are learning—and telling school administrators and professors—that the modus operandi of Wall Street is antithetical to the civic mission the schools purport to lift up. Princeton's motto "In the nation's service and in service to all nations" takes a bit of a beating when Wall Street comes with its recruiting pitch. Anyone interested in public service? Teaching? Nursing or medical research? How quaint. When Wall Street *offers the money*, the game is simultaneously on and over. [113]

Not only upper echelon students receive recruitment attention from Wall Street's best firms; expert *poker players* are also getting good looks. A Wall Street insider described what a good trader and a good poker player have in common: "a penchant for risk-taking and a dispassionate regard for large sums of money." [114]

Before his conviction of insider trading in 2011, Raj Rajaratnum, the former manager of the Galleon Group hedge fund, was lionized as one of Wall Street's savviest investors. Rajaratnum, a native of Sri Lanka, earned his MBA at the prestigious Wharton School of the University of Pennsylvania. A court of law, however, revealed that a lot of his investment "research" was insider-trading knowledge. Along with Rajaratnum, twenty-five additional individuals from various Wall Street firms were indicted. Most of them cooperated with prosecutors and pled guilty. One of Rajaratnum's former employees testified against him, claiming that the firm did its homework—meaning research—but it also "cheated on the test." Galleon at one point boasted $7 billion worth of assets, with Rajaratnum reputed to have had a net worth of more than $1 billion. Like many professional athletes, Rajaratnum is said to be "very competitive." As we've seen, as long as the rewards are great, cheating will be a part of the game.

Regulations, like referees in athletics, help combat the natural propensity toward cheating.[115]

Frank Partnoy did his Wall Street time at First Boston and Morgan Stanley. Partnoy liked to gamble; he fine-tuned his card-counting strategy—useful at the blackjack tables of Vegas and Atlantic City—through discussions with co-workers on the Street. Casinos consider card-counting cheating. If a blackjack player is suspected of card counting, muscular casino employees escort the player to the door and tell him not to come back. Partnoy and his buddies weren't the only Wall Street types who liked to gamble—gambling has been a mainstay activity of traders for generations. Michael Lewis, in the aptly titled account of his Wall Street days *Liar's Poker*, likens the casino floor to the trading floor, with one exception: the equivalent of some of the bets wagered on the trading floor of Wall Street firms—complex derivative options and futures with heavy leverage—wouldn't be allowed in Vegas, because the bettor couldn't back them up.[116]

Greg Smith worked for Goldman Sachs for twelve years. He resigned from the firm in March 2012 with a showy *New York Times* op-ed piece. Smith, a Goldman executive director, criticized the all-encompassing pursuit of profit entrenched in the firm: clients being persuaded to invest in products that weren't very profitable, including derivatives that were opaque and hard to fathom. Many in the financial community were critical of Smith's indictment of Goldman: did Smith expect Goldman to behave like a nonprofit? All the same, Goldman clients being swindled to the point of having their "eyeballs ripped out" (trader talk for making a profit from a sale to a client) says plenty about the culture that exists.* Goldman is no nonprofit enterprise and only hints at pursuing something akin to a common societal good. In 2010 Goldman started an ad campaign that featured its support—by raising capital—of socially beneficial projects, such as wind farms. But like a disgraced politician attempting to reshape public perception, creating a new reality for a Wall Street firm is oftentimes an uphill battle. Smith's disclosure—along with the eye-rolling of insiders—only adds to the impression that Wall Street is out of touch, insular, and thoroughly invested in serving its own interests first.[117]

Wall Street offers the ultimate game, where competition is fierce for society's ultimate reward: money. It's similar to why people go to Vegas. But Wall Street sticks to its main business without any wiggle room—make money or get out—while Vegas offers many other attractions besides gambling. Though *Fortune* magazine makes fun of someone like Greg Smith, he speaks a truth that few are willing to articulate: private interest and social purpose must be balanced.[118]

---

* Partnoy similarly refers to traders profiting off clients as "ripping their faces off." F.I.A.S.C.O., 61.

They Saw It Coming

In his 1776 book *The Wealth of Nations,* Adam Smith, the Scottish social philosopher, famously wrote of the market's "invisible hand." Individuals, acting out of self-interest, would produce beneficial results for general society. An invisible hand would work better than a manipulating hand. Smith was able to see the future because of an adverse condition: mercantilism—government control of foreign trade—still dominated commerce. By today's standards, mercantilism was a manipulating hand. Smith's ideas—new and innovative—were crucial to the development of the market system, which came to the fore in the nineteenth century and caused the pendulum to swing back in the other direction, away from mercantilism. Now that market ideas and practices have flourished successfully for more than two hundred years, the resultant globalized market can be said to inhabit the other end of the pendulum's arc. Context is still important, however. The conviction that self-interest will *always and forever* lead to the best communal outcomes—an idea that borders on religious-type belief—is an abuse of Smith's original concepts. Balance is the key: private returns (for individuals) were subdued in a mercantilist system; *social returns can be subdued in the modern market system.* To seek a relative balance between private and social returns is hard but necessary work. Market systems are not entirely or automatically efficient—something that Smith himself recognized.[119]

Markets obey the laws of desire; when markets become detached from the communities they serve, they do not work in the way Adam Smith envisioned they would. Community—including social mores, neighborliness, and cooperation—is the lynchpin of Smith's economic philosophy; without these positive communal characteristics, the twin engines of self-interest and desire join as if one runaway train. In this day of excess, commercial successes have the ability to erode the communities that have traditionally maintained civil society. Professor and Smith scholar Jack Weinstein concurs: "Adam Smith's philosophy bears little resemblance to the libertarian caricature put forth by proponents of laissez faire markets who describe humans solely as homo economicus. For Smith, the market is a mechanism of morality and social support."[120]

In the aftermath of the financial crisis of 2007–08, only a free market ideologue or a Wall Street lobbyist would suffer the shame (the latter for a price) of proclaiming faith in the idea that collective self-interest always produces the best common good. Avaricious Wall Street types, criminals robbing houses in your neighborhood, and terrorists serve a self-interest that doesn't benefit the common good. Laws serve to protect life and property—regulations serve to keep a check on unenlightened self-interest.[121]

In 2001 Charles Lindblom foresaw the results that excess profiteering and greed in the market would bring. "In our time the greatest threat of worldwide disorganization of the market system may lie in reckless banking and incompetent governmental regulation of financial markets."[122] He was right.

Partnoy, in 2003, also foresaw what was coming:

> Today, the risk of system-wide collapse is greater than ever before. Although a handful of regulators and Wall Street managers have known about some of the systemic problems, individual investors have been largely oblivious to the fact that they have dodged, not a bullet, but a nuclear meltdown. The truth is that the markets have been, and are, spinning out of control.[123]

He was also right. Both Lindblom and Partnoy were right because they've seen this before; Alan Greenspan and others were convinced that we had entered an era of "new economy." They were wrong; this time is not any different than previous eras—the Gilded Age or the 1920s—when rampant inequalities led to economic disasters.

JP Morgan Chase, the biggest bank on Wall Street, admitted to a loss in its derivatives trading department of more than $5.8 billion in May 2012. See if any of this makes sense: a London-based Chase employee in their Chief Investment Office (CIO), working with complex derivatives valued at $100 billion, with the purpose of protecting the company in the event of an economic downturn, instead caused the company's "value at risk" measure (how much the bank stood to lose on a given day) to increase dramatically, due to "changes in the synthetic portfolio held by the CIO."[124] Complexity in the service of pure profit turned out to be a loser.*   The question to consider is the following: When this bank loses $5.8 billion, how does that affect the common good? Or, to what extent is the common good inhibited in a society where companies can haphazardly gamble away a sum greater than five thousand eight hundred million dollars? [125]

---

* The writers of endnoted article—Fitzpatrick et al.—admit that they themselves and other analysts have difficulty understanding the CIO group and its workings. The confusion, at least, makes sense to me.

CHAPTER 7

INEQUALITY IS REGRESSION

In June 1906, John D. Rockefeller and his wife, Cettie, traveled to France to visit their daughter and son-in-law. Bessie and Charles Strong had lived in Cannes for two years. Bessie suffered ill health; Mom and Dad Rockefeller hoped their visit would lift her spirits. The Rockefellers planned to sail incognito from New York aboard the *Deutschland*, their names discreetly deleted from the passenger list. A reporter for the *New York American*, William Hoster, ascertained Rockefeller's travel intentions and purchased a ticket for the crossing. Despite never having met the world's richest man, Hoster had written a number of articles about the great oil baron. Hoster had a particular hunch about Rockefeller that he shared with his inquisitive readers: Rockefeller was traveling to France to visit a specialist to treat his ruined stomach.

To Hoster's surprise, the Rockefeller he observed and met on the *Deutschland* was far removed from the stereotyped demon he had created in his written conjectures. His stomach was obviously fine—Hoster witnessed the titan robustly consuming three meals each day. He also saw Rockefeller make merry with children, play shuffleboard, and entertain fellow passengers at the captain's dinner. Rockefeller was no isolated grouch, untouchable or unapproachable. He was human—regular and vigorous, with clear eyes that betrayed no sense of guilt or remorse for the great riches that set him apart.

Hoster, however, wasn't the only one to experience the deflation of a speculated stereotype during the trip's fortnight. Two years removed from Ida Tarbell's scathing judgments, Rockefeller gave no quarter to reporters. When he initially encountered Hoster, Rockefeller played his usual hand, acting as if he never read his critics. The circumstances of being dislodged from his normal environment perhaps led him to lay his cards down for Hoster to see; Rockefeller knew who he was and had read his stabs in the dark. Rockefeller confronted his intruder and expressed his agitation about the fabrications Hoster wrote about Rockefeller's health and other aspects of his life and business. To Rockefeller's great surprise, he learned that Hoster was sincere and—perhaps remembering his own early working days of urgency and ambition—understood that Hoster and other writers sometimes had no choice but to invent stories, because they lacked accurate information about and access to their subjects.

Exhibiting the panache that helped make him the world's foremost businessman, Rockefeller did an about-face. He invited Hoster to accompany his party inland to France. Rockefeller converted Hoster into his traveling companion for a season. They dined and golfed together; Rockefeller even taught Hoster how to ride a bicycle. Hoster was impressed with the strong sense of populism he spied in Rockefeller; his interactions with common folks were animated and natural.

Hoster—ever the reporter—did ask Rockefeller if a certain rumor was true: Was he worth a billion dollars? Rockefeller responded hastily: "Nothing like it—not by one-third of that amount! I want to make clear to you the injury that is done to me by these persistent stories that I am worth a billion dollars. *They provoke in the minds of thousands thoughts which lead to great unhappiness*" (italics mine). Rockefeller's confession: he was quite aware, even in those nascent days of hyperdisparity, that inequalities of income and wealth were unhealthy for American society.[1]

The Original 1 Percenters

The protest movement named Occupy Wall Street (OWS) began on September 17, 2011, in Zuccotti Park in Lower Manhattan of New York City. OWS chose to base its protest there because of the park's proximity to Wall Street. The movement galvanized the phrase *the 99 percent versus the 1 percent*, which calls attention to the increasing gains that the superwealthy, the 1 percent, have been making in the short era of excess over and against the rest of the population, the 99 percent.

Here's an idea: the Greek gods were the original 1 percenters. Powerful, influential, and resourceful, they emerged from wars and intrigue to reside on Mount Olympus, from whence they ruled and enjoyed their leisure. They had staffs and servants who tended to them. Their whims from on high determined how life was carried out on the lower plain, where mortals resided. The exploits of the Greek gods were, for the most part, highly dysfunctional; promiscuity, manipulation, deceit, and betrayal filled their days. They did some good things— Athena gave the olive tree, Dionysus gave the knowledge of wine making— that hinted at their superhuman status. Through and through, however, these Olympians were also thoroughly human, exhibiting the full measure of tarnished glory that has defined humans from the earliest days.

Eric Mazur, cited previously, observed that gods were society's first celebrities; their fame was derived from stories told of their deeds. Supermarket tabloids—if they had existed in ancient Greece—would have sold well, covering the philandering ways of Zeus or the doomed courtship of Orion and Artemis. The maximized fame and notoriety of the divines allowed them to do things mere mortals were not able to do.[2] The Romans, succeeding the Greeks and borrowing heavily from their mythology, took that fame and notoriety and incarnated it into their political rulers. Caesar Augustus was proclaimed divine and his deeds of power were bullishly related to the conquests of his army. The emperor and Rome were synonymous with victory—anyone who dared to protest or resist would be punished. Although not an Olympian goddess, Victoria (borrowed from the Greek goddess Nike) was the celebrated and visible goddess of military victory. Her likeness graced statues, coins, and flags; Roman senators, upon entering court, burned incense for her. Ruling Romans not only celebrated victory, they also worshiped victory.[3] The scenes and plots of two films depicting the brutality of life and death in the Roman Empire, *Spartacus* and *Gladiator*, were not fabricated from thin air. Rome dictated terms and Rome was accustomed to dominating and winning—no other way about it.

Roman senators were among the wealthiest 1.5 percent of the empire. Senators were required to be worth at least one million sesterces (a common brass coin); many senators were much wealthier than this basic requirement. Control and influence, prestige and honor—even as the emperor consolidated his own power—defined life for Rome's elites.[4]

Modern democracy put into practice an idea that had been around since the time that hunter-gatherers enjoyed their leisure and, perhaps, honed the skills of reverse dominance hierarchy: humans, in essence, are equal. This idea—or ideal—stimulated the initial blossoming of political democracy among the same ancient Greeks who lifted their eyes to Mount Olympus. As Niebuhr said, the ongoing march of civilization includes better *and* worse. Whereas the few elites—humans or gods—aim to project their voices over and beyond all others, the democratic ideal gives voice to all. The right to vote is one of the crucial characteristics of democracy; modern democracy has slowly yet steadily relinquished links between voting rights and certain requirements: property ownership, race, gender. (Slavery, of course, was completely antithetical to the democratic ideal.) The challenges to democracy, however, continue in our day as racism, prejudice, and sexism have not been purged completely from democratic societies.* Beyond these impediments, the greatest challenge to democracy is the increasing concentration of power and wealth in the hands of the few. As it was for the ancient gods, power and wealth give elites the ability to do more than mere mortals, or citizens. Democracy, the governing of the people by the people, is one

---

* The current voter ID law movement has obvious parallels to Jim Crow–era disfranchisement of minority voters.

of humanity's greatest social achievements. It is a precious achievement precisely because it works to keep in check the natural human tendency—recalling Bell's "thin coat of civilization"—of wealth, power, and fame to dominate. As Supreme Court Justice Louis Brandeis said in the early twentieth century, "We may have democracy or we may have wealth concentrated in the hands of the few, but we can't have both."[5]

The US Senate traditionally has been the gathering hall of the wealthiest Americans. The median net worth of US senators in 2012 was better than $900,000; this figure is skewed lower because it does not include a primary living residence. Close to sixty congressional leaders are worth more than $10 million. Median net worth among US citizens, including all real estate assets, as of 2009 was $96,000. In terms of wealth status, the majority of citizens are dwarfed by national senators. The threshold of belonging to the wealthiest 1 percent is reached at the income level of $350,000, easily qualifying most members of the Capitol's north wing.[6] That the senators have been "successful" perhaps explains why they were elected to leadership in the first place. Yet, economic (or inheritance) successes don't obscure the reality that wealth has the ability to contort and bias one's outlook and perspective.

Mitt Romney, the 2012 Republican presidential nominee, never has served as a US senator; he fits the mold, however, and attempted to join the club, but ran unsuccessfully against Ted Kennedy in 1994. He did serve as governor of Massachusetts from 2003 to 2007. *Forbes* estimates his net worth at $230 million.[7] During the presidential campaign, Romney, with two telling statements, exhibited the shortsighted bias that wealth can impart. The first statement was his admission that his "wife drives a couple of Cadillacs." He made the statement during a campaign stop at the Detroit Economic Club; the remark was not in his prepared notes. He made the comment to endear himself to Detroit car manufacturers, but its lasting effect was to reinforce a common critique of the former governor: that he's out of touch with average Americans—those not part of the two Cadillacs crowd—because of his wealth. Detroit, the home of General Motors' Cadillac, has the highest poverty rate of America's biggest cities.

Romney's second comment was delivered to a group of college students in Ohio. He encouraged them toward entrepreneurial enterprise: "Take a risk. Get the education. Borrow money, if you have to, from your parents. Start a business." Romney illustrated his exhortation with the story of Jimmy John Liautaud (founder of Jimmy John's Sandwiches) whose father loaned him $20,000. The number of parents who have $20,000 to loan their children is not what Romney might think it is. In 2010 school loan debt totals in the US surpassed credit card and car loan debt, approaching an aggregate of $1 trillion.[8]

How is it that wealth skews or distorts one's point of view? In the last thirty years Americans have been steadily sorting themselves into more homogeneous communities, neighborhoods, and social groups. Bill Bishop's insightful book *The Big Sort* makes this claim with supporting data and subsequent interpretation. As an example, in 1976 less than 25 percent of Americans lived in counties where the presidential voting results could be categorized as landslide (the winner taking 60 percent or more of the vote)—in 2004 nearly 50 percent lived in landslide counties.[9] Increasingly, upper-middle and upper class Americans clustered together in homogeneous neighborhoods *don't know anyone who is poor*. Their living is secluded; being rich can be limiting in a way that hinders and constricts—like going through life with blinders on. This certainly applies to some US senators, solidly ensconced in the wealthiest 1 percent. When you don't know anyone in a particular socioeconomic group, it's much easier to make judgments or create stereotypes about the members of that group. This argument goes in both directions—rich to poor and poor to rich. Yet US senators, collectively charged with the responsibility of leadership for all Americans, have to work extra hard to *not* make decisions that serve only their interests, the interests of their fellow wealthy, and that of lobbying interests. Economist Joseph Stiglitz calls the Washington, DC, lobbying system "corruption American-style": legions of lobbyists and loose campaign contributions, a system financed and supported by the rich much more so than by the poor, decide matters on Capitol Hill and in American courtrooms.[10] Princeton philosophy professor Jeffrey Stout says that "power minus accountability leads to domination."[11] Politicians in Washington are much less accountable to voters than they are to moneyed interests. The Greek gods lived and breathed as Stout describes; democracy has the grand challenge of keeping the powerful accountable—for the common good. Inequality, its upper hand on power and privilege, is a decidedly regressive counteraction to political egalitarianism (democracy), which is decidedly progressive and modern.

Child Poverty, Et cetera

Austin, Texas, rightfully has a reputation for being a spirited city. Music, food, outdoor activities, sporting events, high tech, and eclectic folks are just a few of the things that make Austin attractive. Here's a secret about Austin that no one wants you to know: the city has a child poverty rate (29 percent) higher than the state of Texas (27 percent) and higher than the national average (23 percent).[12] In fairness to Austin, its ranking is about average for larger US cities. Yet Austin, which doesn't suffer from job losses as places like Cleveland and Baltimore do, should be doing better. Why are almost one-third of children in a progressive city like Austin living in poverty? The answer: social inequality. The rich have gotten richer while the poorest continue to make no headway.

Social inequality describes why the United States—arguably the wealthiest country in the history of the world—has such an abysmal child poverty rate. According to a 2012 UNICEF report on child poverty, among thirty-five of the world's richest nations the United States ranks an atrocious next to worst with a 23.1 percent child poverty rate. Romania, with its rate of 25.5 percent, spares America the shame of having the highest rate of child poverty.[13] Some observers—from their perches far removed from poor neighborhoods—make the argument that America's child poverty rate is so high because of poor parental choices, laziness, or indifference. These reasons explain some causes of child poverty, but the argument is flawed, saturated with ethnocentrism. Child poverty rates in the United States have increased significantly since the mid-1970s; the increase can also be attributed in part to growth in Latino population (currently 35 percent of US Latino children live in poverty) and in general immigrant populations. Yet, these reasons alone don't account for the stark reality that almost one in four American children lives in poverty.[14] Social inequality caused by immense disparities of wealth—a category in which the United States ranks extremely high—explains the elevated child poverty rate and other characteristics of social failure.[15]

Evidence is coming to light that shows a high correlation between escalations in social problems and elevated income inequality in societies. It's been known for some years that violence and poor health are more prevalent in economically unequal societies. But other social problems can be added to the list: mental illness, teenage pregnancy, obesity, high imprisonment rates, anxiety, increased use of illegal drugs, and low economic mobility. The widening gulf between rich and poor in the United States explains why the wealthiest nation in the world also has (per capita) more mental illness, more obesity, more prison inmates, and shorter life spans than other developed nations.[16] (Among developed nations, only Singapore's income gap between the richest 20 percent and the poorest 20 percent is larger than that of the United States.) In their book *Drilling Down*, Joseph Tainter and Tad Patzek speak of "topping out," meaning the crest of peak oil has most likely passed, less energy is returned on initial energy invested, rates of key innovations are diminishing. Topping out gives a reality check to the ideology of unlimitedness. British researchers Richard Wilkinson and Kate Pickett, in their influential 2009 publication *The Spirit Level*, make a similar argument: "Further economic growth in the developed world no longer improves health, happiness or measures of well-being." For affluent societies, further gains in income and wealth don't give citizens the improvements once seen in the societies' earlier and less affluent days. For example, Cuba and the United States are equal in life expectancy rates. In other words, regarding social well-being, we've gotten close to the end of what economic growth can do for us.[17]

Comments like these from two British epidemiologists are fighting words for American devotees of the commerce, materialist, consumerist creed. This critique of the dominant American way of life—unlimited growth benefiting all—is rarely given serious attention. Popular movies, television, advertising, politicians wanting to be reelected, and most newspaper editorial pieces operate in a zone where the cult of unlimited growth is unassailable—only a heretic (or "socialist" or "Marxist") would utter apostasies to the contrary. But the critique is valid. The majority populations in affluent countries take for granted basic necessities like clean water, full stomachs, and functional shelter. This is a good thing—and evidence of the great power of economic growth in its early and middle stages for the developed nations of the world. But where are we to go from here? Blenders with even more buttons? Phones that do the laundry? Cars that can be switched to autopilot so that drivers can fall asleep at the wheel while cruising the interstate? Wilkinson and Pickett do not relent: "Economic growth, for so long the great engine of progress, has, in the rich countries, largely finished its work. Not only have measures of wellbeing and happiness ceased to rise with economic growth but, as affluent societies have grown richer, there have been long-term rises in rates of anxiety, depression and numerous other social problems. The populations of rich countries have got to the end of a long historical journey."[18]

The Fueling of Inequality

President Jimmy Carter's infamous "malaise" speech of July 1979 called Americans to self-discipline, sacrifice, and conservation. OPEC was driving up the price of oil, the Iranian Revolution was cresting, Russia would soon invade Afghanistan, and American confidence was waning. Carter never used the word *malaise* in the speech, but the description stuck, and critics claimed that Democratic defeatism was televised, watched by more than one hundred million Americans. This was a watershed moment for American politics of the last four decades. Ronald Reagan—treating conservation and material sacrifice like the plague—defeated Carter handily in the following year's election. Since that time, Reagan's summons has obliterated Carter's: not one leading national politician has been brave enough (or foolish enough, politically) to question the ongoing sustainability of our lifestyle and to ask for limits on consumption.[19]

After more than thirty years of growing social and economic inequality, Carter's speech, revisited, reveals certain insights more apropos of a social critic or philosopher than a president.* "Too many of us now tend to worship self-indulgence and consumption. Human identity is no longer defined by what one does, but by what one owns. But we've discovered that owning things and consuming things does not satisfy our longing for meaning. We've learned that piling up material goods cannot fill the emptiness of lives which have no confidence or purpose."[20] *Meaning*, Carter intimated, isn't sold at the mall.

Carter's speech was initially well received; Americans flooded the White House with approving phone calls and letters.[21] But the tide turned quickly, and the newly elected Reagan contrasted his bold optimism with the supposed somber pessimism of his predecessor. Carter, however, was not announcing or advocating American demise. The speech has turned out to be a prophetic decree of daring that called the nation to self-examination. Its message harkened to the egalitarian spirit that helped forge American society. But the proclamation has been widely ignored. More than thirty years of unexamined commitment to unlimitedness, as if it's the only way forward, begs critique. Wilkinson and Pickett call for America and other wealthy nations to move away from the idea "in which people regard maximizing personal gains as a laudable aim in life."[22]

America is not *done*; hard-won innovations, discoveries, and efficiencies will undoubtedly tell part of the societal narrative for the remainder of the twenty-first century. The other part of the narrative, crucially, will be determined by the struggle between private and social returns. The struggle will intensify, because, economically speaking, the sky is not the limit. That the United States is on a path different from the one taken by previous fallen world powers—those that didn't avoid the excesses of financial market bubbles, outsized military spending, and massive debts—is a delusional faith beholden to the idea that "this time is different."[23] The two most recent economic upswings turned out to be bubbles (1990s' tech, 2000s' housing), yet the expectation is for that type of unhealthy growth to be the norm. For the last thirty years, Alexander Hamilton's credo—great reward for great risk—has been besting Jefferson's—prosperity as the reward for hard work and thrift—to the detriment of the common good. If American society is to remain ascendant in the twenty-first century, Jefferson's credo must attain a

---

* Why do Lincoln, Teddy Roosevelt, and FDR have significantly more profound quotes as compared to the most recent crop of commanders-in-chief? Neil Postman blamed the culture of entertainment, consisting of TV sound bites, among other things, that by definition lack profundity.

measure of balance with Hamilton's.* The next generation of Americans is not hopeful about their economic future: the wealth gap between older and younger Americans is the widest on record, and mounting public debt—resulting in higher taxes, weaker and decaying infrastructure, and further slowed economic growth— paints a bleak picture for the future.[24] The days of excess are not sustainable.

Slightly more than one hundred years have passed since sales of gasoline became dominant among crude oil's many derivatives. Gasoline, along with diesel and jet fuels, make up more than 75 percent of the typical refinery yield for a barrel of oil in today's world.[25] A by-product of twenty million years of marine biomass chemical transformation caused by underground heat and pressure, petroleum is a flammable substance that is essentially converted solar energy. All fossil fuels are stored solar energy. Plants use sunlight to grow and thrive, animals eat plants, and their fortuitous decay brought about the coal, natural gas, and petroleum that have fueled our modern industrial life for two hundred years. It won't last forever. Tainter and Patzek say we're living off "the geological equivalent of an endowment from a long-dead ancestor . . . a subsidy that allows us to support levels of complexity that otherwise we could not afford." In a sense, the way we live now (the wealthiest 20 percent of the world's population consumes the majority of the world's energy) is a heightened aberration of history, a radical departure from what has been the norm for nearly all of human history. We can't and won't go back to what used to be, but we can teach our children a truth that is widely overlooked in our modern world: high-gain energy (relatively easily attained and highly productive) is *precious and rare*, and it behooves our respect and right use for the common good.[26] It is highly unlikely that this aberration will be ongoing. Just like a lucky run at the poker table, all good things do come to an end.

The first chapter of this book covered Rockefeller's permission, which allowed for disparities of wealth previously unknown in the history of the world. We can now say that these disparities were made possible *because of oil and other fossil fuels*—their discovery and commercialization. The potential energy formed over millions of years in and by the earth has been unleashed over the past two centuries: it fueled the first and second industrial eras, forged the advances of Darby, supplied Edison and Ford with the power to innovate, made Carnegie the king of steel, produced Rockefeller's titanic wealth, and provided the foundation for the incredible advances of the middle and latter parts of the twentieth century.

---

* Actually, a bastardized, excess version of Hamilton's credo has been dominant since the late 1970s. Case in point: excess pay for CEOs. When business is good, performance bonuses are proffered over and beyond regular pay. When business is bad, the bonus still comes and is described by the modifier *retention*.

On the other side of the ledger, however, the energy unleashed has also fueled economic inequality, which has increased significantly in the last one hundred years, bringing along its accompanying social ills. Niebuhr said it so well: progress in better and in worse.

Violent Inequality

"Despite the modern impression of the permanence and universality of inequality, in the time-scale of human history and prehistory, it is the current highly unequal societies which are exceptional. For over 90 percent of our existence as human beings we lived, almost exclusively, in highly egalitarian societies." Wilkinson and Pickett go on to say, as we've seen before, that hunters and gatherers lived in relative egalitarianism and that modern inequality began with the development of agriculture.[27] We saw previously that the ancient Jews equated unmitigated personal riches with violence perpetrated upon the poor. Inequality—which began millennia ago with the beginnings of civilization—has in the last two hundred years hit three high points: the Gilded Age, the 1920s, and the past thirty years. These eras of escalated inequality have been accompanied by their fair share of social violence. The Gilded Age saw violent unrest between laborers and owners— Carnegie's Homestead tragedy in 1892 and Rockefeller's Ludlow Massacre in 1914 stand out—and plenty of worker injury and death due to dangerous working conditions.[28] The 1920s saw the virulent restart of the Ku Klux Klan, with its venomous violence toward blacks, Catholics, and Jews.* The last twenty years, on the other hand, have seen decreases in violent crime and homicide rates in the United States. Are economic inequality and violence coincidental partners? Studies show that increased inequality raises the stakes for status competition, which is a main component of violent offenses, especially those perpetrated by young males.[29]

James Gilligan is the preeminent American psychiatrist working in the area of violence studies. He currently lectures at New York University and for thirty years directed Harvard Medical School's Center for the Study of Violence. After

---

* The Klan held a march and rally in Washington, DC, in August 1925, with thirty thousand participants. The weather was warm, humid, and foreboding. Eventually, close to one hundred Klansmen and women were overcome by the heat and ended up in area hospitals. As the columns of marchers gathered for scheduled speeches near the Washington Monument, thunderclouds rolled overhead. The host speaker intoned, "It will not rain. We shall pray. Never yet has God poured rain on a Klan assembly." The supposed streak came to an abrupt end in minutes—the deluge steady and the Klan speakers drowned out. Wyn Craig Wade, *The Fiery Cross: The Ku Klux Klan in America*, Simon & Schuster (1987), pp. 249–50.

decades of work and research, he explains that violent acts are "attempts to ward off or eliminate the feeling of shame or humiliation—a feeling that is painful, and can even be intolerable and overwhelming—and replace it with its opposite, the feeling of pride."[30] Perceived threats to pride—acts that instigate feelings of shame and humiliation—serve as triggers to violent acts. Violent acts are attempts to undo the loss of face suffered by perpetrators. Daniel Bell, a generation previous, called crime, because of its disproportionate concentration in the lower classes, "a form of unorganized class struggle."[31]

Both wealthy and poor people commit violent acts. When shame and humiliation confront people of middle- or upper-income status, their status markers are not depleted, and they have greater potential for maintaining a sense of status. Also, they might have more to lose by committing a violent act. Young men at the bottom socioeconomic levels in society, on the other hand, possessing fewer status markers, have a greater tendency to react explosively and violently when threatened, shamed, or humiliated. For them, there tends to be less to lose and more to gain by committing a violent act. The competition for status demands a response to incidents (real or supposed) of disrespect or humiliation. The ratio between rates of imprisonment for African Americans and whites in the United States is 6 to 1, meaning the risk of imprisonment for blacks is six times higher than it is for whites. The poverty rate among African Americans is 27 percent compared to 10 percent for whites.[32] Wilkinson and Pickett call inequality a type of "structural violence"; societies that are more egalitarian economically have built in buffers and protections—humiliations suffered are not always triggers or excuses for violence.[33]

A correlation does exist between economic inequality and violence. What about the drop in overall crime and homicide rates in the United States over the last twenty years? James Alan Fox,* a criminologist at Northeastern University, offers four reasons for the drop: increased incarceration, improved law enforcement strategies, the wane of the crack cocaine epidemic (1984–1990), and the aging of America's large baby boomer population.[34] The United States has the highest rate of incarceration of developed countries at 576 people per 100,000. Studies do show a direct correlation between economic inequality and incarceration. Certainly, numerous criminals are behind bars, and the median age

---

* In the bestseller *Freakonomics*, authors Steven Levitt and Stephen Dubner ridicule Fox for wrongly forecasting an increase in the US crime rate in 1995. Levitt and Dubner make the case that the legalization of abortion in 1973 is the greatest factor for the drop in crime rate. This hypothesis, however, has been subsequently questioned for flawed calculations. "Oops-onomics," December 1, 2005, *The Economist* website, http://www.economist.com/node/5246700, retrieved November 12, 2013.

of the country's citizens continues to increase, from 32.9 years in 1990 to 35.3 in 2000 to 37.2 in 2010.[35] We're getting older, slower, and thankfully, less violent—but economic inequalities and many of their other consequences haven't gone away.

All Things Being Relative . . .

When my brother and I were kids, our mom (perhaps as did yours) encouraged us to clean our plates at dinnertime by invoking the numerous starving hordes in China—or was it in Africa? Either way, the argument's effectiveness was marginal at best. I had not visited either place as a kid, and there was no steadfast image in my mind's eye of a comparison between my blessed lot and the unfortunate lot of other children, unknown and elsewhere, starving. I am, however, a card-carrying member of the clean plate club. This categorization is informal—my parents, having grown up in immediate post–World War II America when food was scarcer, do remember President Truman's rallying call to waste no food in order to help feed a recovering Europe. My parents, therefore, were official members of the club. Their influence on my brother (also a plate cleaner) and me most likely came from our observing their behavior, which reinforced what my mom had to say to us concerning table habits. We assimilated this part of our parents' table habits because it made sense in our own immediate environment.*

Wilkinson and Pickett make a similar point about the relative nature of poverty and inequality within a given society: income differences *within* wealthy countries matter more than differences between countries. Socioeconomic differences within the United States matter more than differences between, for example, the United States and China or the United States and Africa. If my mom had used the example of hungry kids in the city of Chicago—we lived in the suburbs—perhaps I then would have eaten my cooked asparagus quicker. Would you rather live less well-off in a richer society or well-off in a poorer society? Most choose the latter—even when the latter income is less than the former, all other considerations being equal. Prominent economic deprivation in relation to the rest of society—especially when the society in question is a wealthy one—is what subverts the common good. Social comparisons have an important effect upon the

---

* We didn't adopt all of our parents' habits or preferences. To Jean Piaget's theory of assimilation I'll propose a companion phenomenon, which I'll call "dissimilation"—the adoption of a habit, in the development of self-identity, precisely because it is different than what was modeled. I purposely didn't drink coffee as a young adult—a decision cast in childhood—because I didn't want to be like my parents, whom I accused of being coffee addicts! I've since changed my convictions as I've aged and come to understand the benefits of caffeine, along with the sublime smell and taste of the roasted bean.

self-worth of individuals in communities, which, in turn, have repercussions for issues such as public health, levels of violence, community trust, and incarceration rates in the greater society.[36]

The argument that poor people in the United States are better off in comparison with poor people elsewhere, in places like Belarus or Zimbabwe, is nuanced. Every situation has its own context; people living on the streets, regardless of the country, don't have it easy. Generally speaking, poor people in the America can count on a larger safety net than poor people in less developed nations. That is undoubtedly advantageous. Social comparisons, made not with unknown individuals in Belarus or Zimbabwe but with fellow citizens speaking a common language and sharing similar cultural understandings, are what ultimately determine ideas of fairness and acceptable (relative) living standards within a given society.

Inequality increases status competition within a society, making less well-off people struggle to keep up and helping well-off people distinguish themselves. Inequality fuels consumption; the rich and poor and those in the middle are vulnerable to purchasing goods primarily for their social value more than for their pragmatic usefulness. Economists call this the Veblen effect. British economist Richard Layard claims that the wealthy's consumption reduces the sense of satisfaction among other members of society. "Keeping up with the Joneses" stokes consumption, which, it can be argued, is good for business. It also, however, can produce long-term declines in savings and crippling increases in debt. This has been the case in both the United States and Britain, which are two of the most economically unequal countries on the face of the earth. Layard proposes that a dissatisfaction cost, like Major League Baseball's luxury tax, be imposed on the consuming rich for their part in spurring status competition through consumption. Bankruptcy claims have spiraled upward dramatically in the United States in the last thirty years, and there is a direct correlation between the rise in bankruptcies and inequality where economic disparities are most prominent.[37]

Outside upper-level CEOs, top athletes, financial industry leaders, and other 1 percenters, wages have been essentially flat for the majority of Americans during the last thirty-five years. The "politically engineered inequality"—marginal tax rates slashed from 70 to 28 percent and the capital gains rate cut from 35 to 20 percent—that began in the early 1980s primed the pump for the escalation of social status competition by making the wealthy wealthier. Excess, as we saw, defines the eras that became increasingly more unequal. Average Americans tried to keep up; going into debt was the most common way to pull it off. Advertising cooperated; it's not surprising that greater advertising expenditures also correlate with a country's higher rates of inequality.[38] Rising consumption pressure, part and parcel of the national commitment to materialism and excess, has not produced greater health and happiness. This holds true not only for the middle class but for many in the upper class as well. A 2011 Boston College study, funded in part by the Gates Foundation, concluded that many of the superwealthy (those having assets greater than $25 million) interviewed for the study don't consider themselves financially secure.[39] In 1987 Bono and U2 sang, "I still haven't found what I'm looking for." After more than thirty years in the short era of excess, neither have we.

All We Are Saying Is Give Egalitarianism a Chance

When I was in seminary, a report emerged from one of the dormitories about a late night game of Monopoly. Two African students, being taught the intricacies of the great American board game, decided quite spontaneously to join forces midgame as their individual prospects to win the competition dwindled. At first their American mentors tried to tell them that joining together was against the rules and not permitted. The Africans stood their new ground, infusing some religious teaching and some of their own culture into the rules: the good of the community—the two students together—was to be exalted over individual gain. Their fellow students saw the light, and the novices ended up winning the first game of Monopoly they ever played. They also exposed some cultural biases about competition and challenged the notion that rules are somehow unbiased. More often than not, those who determine the rules leave their distinctive fingerprints and biases all over them. That doesn't mean that the rules are necessarily bad or overly partial; but it reminds us that they are constructed from a given point of view, for better and for worse.

Envision a world that operates by different economic rules or standards than what we have now. The suggestion to imagine something new doesn't mean that what we have now is bad or evil. What we have now is good for millions of the world's inhabitants. But what we have now is not good for other millions of inhabitants—and we are capable of doing significantly better. The idea that we can choose between only one of two extremes is erroneous and shortsighted. The supposed choice between a market economy and a centrally controlled economy is concocted. Centrally managed economies have proven themselves not as capable as open markets to create capital. But the idea that an open market society creates fantastically wealthy individuals like Rockefeller and Gates out of ontological necessity is one that carries an inherent bias. It's a biased idea that is not scientifically proven—economic theory has not and will not achieve scientific status anytime soon. The bias comes from those who especially benefit from the idea. Do not wealthy individuals and corporations past and present use their great stores of excess wealth to influence political decisions? (The Supreme Court's five-four decision in the 2010 *Citizens United v. Federal Election Commission* case is the latest show of support for the interests of the wealthy over other interests.) Take it from an outsider, albeit one who had his economic training in the United States but infused it with a different bias: that of the underprivileged. Muhammad Yunus, the Nobel Prize winner from Bangladesh, says, "The rule of 'strongest takes it all' must be replaced by a rule that ensures everybody a place and a piece of the action. 'Free trade' means freedom for the weakest."[40] Of course, many would scoff at Yunus's notion, invoking Adam Smith's invisible hand, proclaiming the mantra of individual gain—without any restrictions—as the best recipe for public gain. As previously discussed, such an interpretation of Smith has its own built-in bias. There are other interpretations of Smith.

Yunus represents an alternative reading of Smith: "The world has interpreted 'self-interest' as equal to profit maximization." It's as if human beings have but a singular overriding motive in the economic realm (and all realms, for that matter): personal gain. Undoubtedly a strong motivator, personal gain has rivals. Sometimes it is bested by compassion and empathy, and other times by generosity. The economic realm is multifaceted and is not governed solely by profit maximization. Soldiers enlist for military service—not all of them do so primarily out of financial motivation. Humans and their motivations are complex. When push comes to shove and the "thin coating of civilization" is breached, self-interest and survival can mesh into one. In such a time, motivations such as compassion and empathy become rare luxuries if not downright fantasies. But the world as we know it currently is (yet) civilized. Generosity and honor are not rare luxuries but common and present realities. In such a world, the unlimited quest for personal gain has to compete against mitigating circumstances. Justice, fairness, and the quest for the common good keep self-interested profit maximization in check. Egalitarianism is that strain of thought—preexistent to American democracy and part of its very founding—that bundles justice, fairness, and the pursuit of the common good. It simultaneously fights against interests that favor rich over poor and privileged over disadvantaged.[41]

Yunus claims that without regulation, the rich win out over the poor every time. This has been especially true in the last thirty-five years. Conventional wisdom posits that checks on self-interest are both harmful and unnecessary, and that middle and lower class citizens benefit best in a society where the upper class is unrestricted in its pursuit of wealth, capital, and profits. The gains of the wealthy are to cascade down upon the lesser classes. As the rich have gotten richer in the

United States in the short era of excess, the lesser classes have not made economic gains.[42] As previously discussed, wages have been stagnant for middle and lower class Americans during this time span, while the richest Americans have seen their takes of income and wealth swell considerably. The spirit of egalitarianism is not against profit; it is opposed to unfair advantages, those *without checks and balances*. By definition, democracy is not government as demanded by the highest bidder.

Swiss historian and economist Jean Charles Léonard de Sismondi, a contemporary of Adam Smith, warned that "Humanity should be on guard against . . . the error of identifying the public good with wealth, abstracted from the sufferings of the human beings who create it."[43] Sismondi proffered his conviction at the beginning of the industrial era. His point: those with wealth will tend to use it to their own advantage at the expense of those who helped create it, if societal common good is simply a laissez-faire by-product of maximum individual profit. The point still holds true. Labor laws, regulations, unions, and societal pressures have done their part for almost two hundred years to maintain a balance between owners and labor within the market system and to keep the voice of wealth in check.

The balance, however, between the self-interested concentration of wealth and purposeful societal common good has eroded in the short era of excess. The *Citizens United* case created the super PACs (political action committees) of the 2012 presidential election season. It allowed wealthy individuals (as well as corporations and unions) to contribute cash without limits, and the PACs were not required to disclose donor names. That the PACs are prohibited from coordinating with a particular candidate makes for a system thoroughly lacking accountability.[44] The checks and balances upon PACs are few, save the powerful voice of the public's vote. The Supreme Court decision hinged on the interpretation of the First Amendment's free speech clause: it's no small irony that the majority of ultrawealthy contributors conspire with PACs' desires to keep donor identities hidden. *Free* political speech is quite costly in today's United States, and again, a commitment to unlimitedness does damage to societal common good. An egalitarian law (as was the McCain-Feingold Act of 2002, which was defeated in *Citizens United*) would set limits on contributions. Slush funds for college athletic programs are rightly categorized as cheating—it's about time politics caught up. For the nation that once prided itself as the champion of democracy, legal political slush funds bankrolled by millionaires and billionaires do not represent a great advancement. It's tough to spread democracy—*people power*—when money does all the talking for only a miniscule minority of the people.

Egalitarianism Lives

Japan has one of the most egalitarian societies among the developed nations. Its people have the highest life expectancy rate of industrialized nations, the smallest gap between its richest and poorest, and a median net worth for individuals more than three times greater than the level for Americans ($141,410 and $38,786, respectively).[45] America's egalitarian strain officially began with the republic's founding in the late eighteenth century; its origins can be traced back to the Mayflower landing at Provincetown. Japan has been governed by monarchical and oligarchic rule for much of its history; post–World War II era democracy commenced in 1952 with the end of American occupation. Japan's egalitarianism, it can be argued, is an American import, a by-product of the promoted post–World War II ideal of American democracy. In Japan, American influence brought forth land reform, women's equality (including voting rights), education reform, union organization, and the breakup of prewar family trusts and their accompanying concentrations of economic power.[46] Demilitarization guaranteed that precious postwar public expenditures supported these transformations.

Japan, however, now sixty years into its modern democracy, has a number of problems. It has one of the higher suicide rates in the world—twice that of the United States, its ratio of government debt to GDP is the highest among industrial nations, and its social safety net for its aging population is in jeopardy because of Japan's near zero birthrate and its restrictive immigration policies (reducing the pool of workers supporting the social security system). Japan is the most ethnically homogeneous of the developed nations.[47] The 2011 Tohoku earthquake, a great tragedy on many levels, has further imperiled Japan's mounting debt. A nation that had a net energy import rate over 80 percent before the calamity, Japan currently has only a few of its fifty-four nuclear reactors online and functional. The multiple nuclear accidents caused by the tsunami and subsequent internal social pressure against the use of nuclear energy will drive both the energy import rate and energy prices higher.[48]

The Scandinavian countries of Sweden, Norway, Denmark, and Finland are also highly egalitarian in terms of income. Whereas Japan achieves it via relatively equal pretax market incomes, the Scandinavian countries are well-known for higher tax rates and redistributive measures. While Japan and the Scandinavian countries approach economic egalitarianism differently, the countries share multiple similar characteristics. Except for Finland, the other four nations have obesity rates at least two times lower than the United States; levels of social trust—the belief that most people can be trusted—are significantly higher in all five of the countries as compared to the United States; and social mobility rates (Japan excepted) are far greater than those in the United States. Life expectancy rates of the four Scandinavian countries exceed that of the United States, and imprisonment rates are lower for Scandinavians.[49]

The United States has significant differences—culturally, historically, and otherwise—with Japan and the Scandinavian countries. My point is not that the other countries are better than the United States. America has had an egalitarian tradition for much longer than these five countries; American egalitarianism's balancing strain—individual freedom in the pursuit of wealth—has trampled egalitarianism in the last three decades and the social markers tell a decided story. Some may counter this line of reasoning—as did Alexander Hamilton early on in the American narrative—by claiming that social inequality is simply the price paid for freedom championed, economically and otherwise. Even so, there is a greater price to pay for social inequality. A society free from great disparities in wealth among its citizens was a principal idea that helped form this country. America has a strong egalitarian tradition; it would be an unthinkable tragedy if it were quashed by its competing strain.

Idolatry of Ideology

Song poet Bruce Cockburn sings derisively of those who use democratic means as a cover to consolidate power and money. How are these consolidations different from those sought by many monarchs and all despots in days gone by? In the song "Call It Democracy," the phrase "idolatry of ideology" is Cockburn's description of societies and individuals who profit wherever and whenever possible—as if this is *freedom*—regardless of the consequences for those who suffer on the other side of the profit equation.[50]

Ideologists have always been with us—religious and political leaders, philosophers, militarists, scientists—for better and for worse. Ideology, generically understood as a system of ideas, has helped humans delve deep into physical mystery—the splitting of the atom. Yet ideology has also been behind some of humanity's worst atrocities—the Jewish holocaust. Ideology for humanity has been a boon and bane, both helpful and hurtful. Ideology is usually helpful in a specific and localized realm—such as nuclear physics—but potentially dangerous when aggrandized for societal consumption or control.

An ideological construct (whether imperialism, totalitarianism, or fundamentalism), in the words of Rabbi Jonathan Sacks, is "the attempt to impose a single truth on a plural world."[51] The diversity inherent to this world is what keeps it operational and vibrant; there are multiple ways to complete tasks or tackle problems. Modern democracy by definition welcomes diversity and abhors absolutism or a single, dominant ideology. The market system reigns supreme as the structure that best provides widest prosperity; market fundamentalism feigns to be the be-all, end-all explanation and solution of all things economic (and beyond). Unrestrained, free markets produce inequalities—during the Gilded Age, the 1920s, and the short era of excess beginning in the late 1970s—that devitalize societies and their communities within. Practically all political ideologies— including some manifestations of socialism and democracy—produce social inequalities. American democracy, with an infrastructure in part consisting of egalitarianism, was constituted to be different. Egalitarianism was, and is, the mitigating force that keeps inequalities from dominating.

The restless advance of the complementary emphases of consumerism-materialism and economic growth—globalization—is a mingled blessing. Goods are produced, workers and their families are provided for, societies advance, peaceful and pragmatic interchanges occur between nations, and capital is created. When these collaborative enterprises cross the line and become ideologies, however, they become a curse. Local autonomies and cultures are desecrated, workers are victimized, families suffer, social problems escalate, and capital is ultimately hoarded. People's lives, squeezed into the shrinking crevice between needs and wants, become casualties of the economic monolith.

The idolatry—excessive and blind adoration—of market fundamentalism threatens societal progress in the twenty-first century. True societal democracy— as diverse in ideas as it is in citizenry—still thrives, and it has implications not only for the political realm but for the economic realm as well.

CHAPTER 8

ECONOMIC DEMOCRACY

Economic democracy is a relatively new term.* It doesn't have a precise, single definition; its use and popularity have increased in the past few decades as the practice of corporate capitalism—economic and political decisions made by the powerful few—has become more entrenched. An understanding of corporate capitalism helps define what economic democracy is not. Economic democracy seeks a wider share of power and decision making through the balance of political equality, political liberty, and economic liberty.[1] This chapter highlights five characteristics of a capitalist economic system less governed by concentrated power and more so by shared power (the very definition of democracy).

Limits

The first characteristic of this shared-power economic system is limits. A good friend of mine had a habit that he eventually grew tired of—excessive drinking. He wasn't a drunk; he was a good family man working hard and steady, going to church regularly. He was fully functional in society and family life—but when he played golf or poker with his buddies, he had a tendency to drink beer after beer after beer. He wasn't able to stop after two or three—and he eventually grew tired of his inability to control his drinking. By January 1, 2012, he had had enough. He decided to quit drinking, but it wasn't a promise between himself and the man in the mirror. Acknowledging his weakness, he openly and honestly told others about his decision to change his ways. Aptly fitting the cliché, he has become a changed man. He no longer drinks, he started an exercise program (losing twenty-five pounds), and continues to tell others about the new freedom he found in self-limitation.

Most families deal with the burdens of dependency and addiction. Alcohol and drug abuse account for untold suffering, family and societal dysfunction, and death. Most estimates of American alcohol and drug abusers (age twelve and older) number around twenty million, slightly less than 10 percent of that specific population.[2] Although numerous treatments options exist for those desiring to become liberated from addiction, traditional 12-step programs have had the

---

* British author C. H. Douglas, an engineer, published a book in 1923 with the term as its title.

most success, benefiting millions in the United States (where the programs were developed) and around the world, crossing cultural boundaries with a common understanding that confronts the afflicted human condition: *there is freedom from addiction in accepting limitation.*

The first step (of twelve) is to admit that there is a problem—that one is powerless in the face of the addicting substance. Confessing weakness, individuals then join with others who confess to the same weakness. In traditional 12-step understanding, community is formed by those who share a similar and specific vulnerability. Ironically, as common weakness is acknowledged and explored, a shared group strength emerges. Acceptance of limitation is the key to freedom from chemical dependency. My good friend still plays golf and the occasional game of poker, but with a new understanding that his golfing and card-playing friends respect: no beer for the guy who decided to quit drinking.

Ernie Kurtz, the preeminent historian of the Alcoholics Anonymous movement, describes various segments of modern society as inherently addicted, replicating the behavior of the habitué: "The striving always harder for the ever more that always satisfies ever less." "Just a little bit more"—Rockefeller's legendary admonition—shows its dark side. Kurtz notes the overreliance on rationalization and intellectualization that leads to the denial of nonmaterialist perspectives; for example, the supposed supremacy of blood pressure medications—in all cases— over yoga (and changed diet) for a person suffering with high blood pressure. He also implicates the overpursuit of control, which leads to conflicts and problems from wars to rebellious behavior in teenagers. Kurtz claims that we moderns equate limited ability with inability. In our day, it's seemingly better to seek complex (and expensive) solutions rather than simple ones. When the insatiable desire for more inevitably meets limitations that do exist, the limiting barrier must somehow be made to succumb. An all-or-nothing mentality understands abeyance or compromise as defeat.[3] This thinking goes hand and glove with today's dominant materialist-consumerist religion, which eschews limitations. People enslaved to the winner-take-all attitude have great difficulty understanding the advantage of limitation: at certain times and in certain places *less is more.*

Social critic Richard Heinberg is one of many commentators questioning the reliance on (more and more) economic growth to solve all our problems. "Through the one-time-only process of extracting and burning hundreds of millions of years' worth of chemically stored sunlight, we built what appeared (for a brief, shining moment) to be a perpetual-growth machine. We learned to take what was in fact an extraordinary situation for granted. It became *normal.*" The underlying assumption in our society is a contradiction: unending growth in a finite world.[4]

Truth be told, economic growth has slowed since the 1980s. Certainly, China and India have experienced expansive growth, but overall, according to World Bank data, world economic growth since 1980 has averaged 1.4 percent per year. In the 1960s and '70s, it was double that rate, averaging more than 3 percent.[5] Proponents of economic growth counter that substitution (hydrogen power for oil, as an example), innovation, and efficiency will allow us to continue on the path of greater growth. But addicts are apt to do most anything to assure that ample supplies continue. Limits exist for some people, perhaps, but not for those who need more and more.

Financial advisor and writer Paul Kedrosky concurs: "I want to believe in innovation and its possibilities, but I am more thoroughly convinced of entropy."[6] Economic growth, from the Industrial Revolution until post–World War II in America, flourished in a perfect storm. European refugees left behind staid economic opportunity to embark on an adventure of new possibilities in America, replete with vast stretches of open land, prodigious forests, undisturbed animal and fish colonies, and virgin mineral deposits. Cheap labor—forced, coerced, and otherwise—helped fortify the economic gains. Many benefited and many became rich. Two world wars in Europe further helped shift riches and power toward America. But not all good things last forever. The long-term economic spurt principally fueled by Rockefeller's gooey black gold is slowing down.

Concerning oil and other precious resources, the low-hanging fruit is mostly gone—for the United States and the world. Oil production has been levelling off,* world grain production per capita peaked in 1984, water scarcity and stress are more prevalent than ever before, global marine seafood capture peaked in 1994, and most metal and mineral extraction hit their peaks long ago. Joseph Tainter and

---

* The recent boom of American oil and natural gas production notwithstanding—"fracking" is a complex, laborious, and resource-exhausting process that is hampered by low EROEI rates and rightfully critiqued for its unfavorable environmental impact. Whereas numerous proponents foresee a re-do of 1950's style American economic dominance because of rising energy production, sober commentators are calling the boom a temporary second wind that will not change the foundational reality that oil and gas are limited resources.

"The age of cheap oil is over," according to International Energy Agency chief economist Fatih Birol. While America's dependence on foreign oil will decrease, the incentive to conserve fossil fuels will continue to be precariously low. The boom delays significant action to combat human factors in climate change as economic growth will continue to trump all other considerations. The next generation will have to solve the problems associated with the burning of fossil fuels while suffering their potentially intensified consequences. See Mason Inman, "US Oil Fields Stage 'Great Revival,' But No Easing Gas Prices," February 10, 2012, *National Geographic* Daily News website, http://news.nationalgeographic.com/news/energy/2012/02/120210-us-oil-production-increasing/, retrieved December 12, 2013.

Tad Patzek are succinct: "In human societies, at least, high-gain phases do not last very long."[7]

The high-gain phase of the financial sector—*financialization*—started in earnest in 1980. It was reminiscent, of course, of what had happened in the 1920s. Economist Thomas Palley describes it in depth:

> Financialization is the process whereby financial markets, financial institutions, and financial elites gain greater influence over economic policy and economic outcomes . . . its principal impacts are to (1) elevate the significance of the financial sector relative to the real sector, (2) transfer income from the real sector to the financial sector, and (3) increase income inequality and contribute wage stagnation.[8]

The size of the US financial sector more than doubled (as measured by percent of GDP) from the mid-1970s to 2008, just before the sector's breakdown.[9] The United States and the United Kingdom led the way, from the early 1980s, with financial deregulation posited as the key of economic growth.[10] As discussed in chapter 5, the repeal of Glass-Steagall in 1999 was the coup de grace that helped bring about the worldwide financial meltdown in less than ten years.

The popular wood block game Jenga, created by British board-game designer Leslie Scott, provides an apt metaphor for the instability of the financial sector. The game consists of fifty-four wood blocks, stacked in layers of three, alternatively stacked crossways, to build a tower of eighteen stories. The purpose of game is to build the tower higher and higher by taking individual blocks from the lower stories and placing them on top. As one can surmise, the tower can be built only so high—limits—before it is no longer sustainable as a structure. Economist Ha-Joon Chang likens the growth of the financial sector in the past few decades to the final stages of a Jenga structure: "an increasingly tall structure of financial assets teetering on the same foundation of real assets."[11]

Limits are a natural part of life's order and the world we inhabit. To think that in the realm of economics limits somehow don't apply is reckless. Religious adherence to the ideology of growth, refusing to recognize that limits cannot be ignored, is misplaced faith. A commitment to economic democracy accepts the reality of limits, both physical and financial, as a positive constructor of the common good.

Balance

The second characteristic of a capitalist economic system governed by shared power is balance. Golf provides a useful analogy. The golf swing, when executed properly, is done so with exquisite balance. Like the pendulum and its two sectors of one arc, the golf swing consists of complementary sectors—left and right, back and forward, up and down—that must work together for the overall mission of the golf shot (distance and accuracy) to be achieved. Tiger Woods has spent a lot of time in the weight room sculpting his six-foot-one-inch, 185-pound frame; it's been time well spent. Woods has an impressive athletic body that can hit a golf ball farther and (usually) straighter than other professional golfers. Northern Irishman Rory McIlroy, who in 2012 emerged as Woods's main competitor for dominating golfdom, stands no taller than five feet nine and weighs 160 pounds. Unlike Tiger, Rory hasn't spent much time in the weight room, and it shows. McIlroy, however, can pound the golf ball just as far as Tiger can, and he hits it with just as much accuracy. Hitting the golf ball long and accurately does not depend on bulging muscles but upon timing, tempo, and balance. Big muscles are no guarantee either for coaxing six-foot putts to find the bottom of the cup.

Golf rewards limitations and punishes excesses. As with a ball of clay between the palms of your hands that you are trying to shape into a perfectly smooth, round ball, there must be cooperation and coordination between opposing strengths, a mutual limiting of powerful forces. Balanced control between the left hand and the right hand makes the golf ball travel straight. (If the right hand dominates, the ball generally goes left, whereas if the left hand dominates, the ball generally goes right.)* Not only that, hitting down on the ball makes it vault gloriously to the heavens, and a slow and easy tempo is finer than a fast and forceful one. Limitation is important—overswinging is overkill, defeating any fantasies of triumphant glory. Overcompensation, where a golfer hits it to the right because she didn't want to hit it left (avoiding a pond), is a manifestation of too much control. Sometimes you simply have to let go and trust, because overfocus on the *desired* results takes away from the process of producing *actual* results.

Balance and limitations might benefit one's golf game and one's eating habits, but those who support today's financial growth machine have no need of restrictions, because (they claim) the latter get in the way of the all-knowing invisible hand of the market. Since the late 1970s, Milton Friedman's mantra—limitations on self-interest are both unnecessary and harmful—has been echoed

---

* To speak with generalizations concerning golf ball flight is somewhat treacherous. As any golfer knows, for better or for worse, anything is possible as concerns ball flight.

over and again by US economists; it's the cornerstone of the national mythic religion. In 1934 T. S. Eliot, the great American-British poet, wrote a play called *The Rock*. Eliot was by that time a devotee of the Anglican Church. He described the religion of the church in contrast to the ways of the world. The church is tender where the world is hard, and hard where the world is soft, "men" are caught between: "they constantly try to escape from the darkness outside and within by dreaming of systems so perfect that no one will need to be good."[12] Eliot's characterization fits the convenient interpretation of Adam Smith, according to the materialist-consumerist religion, perfectly. This interpretation claims that self-interested, even greedy, economic actions inputted into the market system come out somehow and always benefiting the common good. Truth be told, Smith himself warned that unenlightened self-interest can lead to injustice and societal ruin.[13]

Chrematistics, like plutocracy, is a word that has ancient Greek origins. Aristotle contrasted *oikonomia,* which is management of the household so as to increase value for the long run, with *chrematistics,* which is manipulation of property and wealth for the purpose of short-term gain. Like the word *plutocracy* and its derivatives, chrematistics needs to be reintroduced to today's dictionaries. According to Aristotle, the practice of chrematistics was perverted, unnatural, and detrimental to the common good. Adam Smith advocated oikonomia— economics—and its longer vision much more than he did the short-term gains of chrematistics. Much of the activity in today's financial markets is better described as chrematistic, profiteering and maximizing for short-term gain, than it is economic, focusing on long-term benefit for the common good. According to its original meaning and context, true economy is *balanced* and seeks to benefit the common good; chrematistics, on the other hand, is unbalanced, unlimited, and mostly interested in enriching some at the expense of others. Oikonomia knows when enough is enough—chrematistics only knows that more, however attained, is better.[14]

"America's inequality is the result of market distortions, with incentives directed not at creating new wealth but at taking it from others." Economist Joseph Stiglitz made this claim in 2012, judging the current period as the era of wealth transfer. "The rich are getting richer, the richest of the rich are getting still richer, the poor are becoming poorer and more numerous, and the middle class is being hollowed out."[15] Despite its foundational egalitarianism, contemporary American society increasingly makes class warfare a present reality. Social mobility, as previously discussed, has become a lost American virtue. Even Warren Buffett, who is part of the very richest of the rich, agrees: "There's been class warfare going on for the last twenty years and my class has won."[16]

Nobel laureate Muhammad Yunus sees the lack of balance and the embrace of unlimitedness in today's global economy as the main contributors to the poverty that still exists for too many of the world's inhabitants.

> The thought that always energizes me is that poverty is not created by poor people. Poverty is an artificial imposition on the people. Poor people are endowed with the same unlimited potential for creativity and energy of any human being in any station of life, anywhere in the world. It is a question of removing the barriers faced by poor people to unleash their creativity to solve their problems.[17]

Of the seven billion people that inhabit the earth, how many live in poverty? Most who are living in the developed world don't know, and frankly, many don't care. Our national religion, guided by self-interest, dictates the terms: we take care of our own issues; and poverty—by an invisible hand?—will go away, or better, isn't our worry. The World Bank estimates that by 2015, 1 billion people will be living in *extreme poverty*, surviving on $1.25 or less a day. While the number of people living in extreme poverty has decreased since 1981, the number of people living in poverty—on $2.00 or less a day—has remained steady at roughly 2.5 billion people. Many of these, of course, are children.[18] We want to believe that, as we are told by Friedman and his disciples, the system we live in is perfect enough to convert our self-interest (for ourselves) and our disinterest (for the poor) into something good. Borrowing from musician Lou Reed, it takes a "busload of faith" to believe the Friedman ideology in today's world; the ideology is not scientific but a contextualized assessment, applicable in certain situations, yet not applicable in all situations.

Scottish writer James Buchan argues that economic theories tend to confirm or deny the privileges or fantasies of the social classes.[19] Adam Smith, a Scot who lived more than two hundred years ago, is interpreted differently by different economists. Muhammad Yunus, from Bangladesh, a developing country, sees the world differently than did Milton Friedman, who grew up the son of hardworking immigrants in early twentieth century Brooklyn, when social mobility (both directions) in America was still dynamic. Friedman's free market ideology—which assumes lively social mobility—uses an uncomplicated, straightforward interpretation of Smith. This interpretation worked for post–World War II America because an essential ingredient that Smith advocated was present: a restraining, positive moral force of shared community values. The pendulum had swung away from the avaricious values of the 1920s that brought about the Great Depression; abject greed was taking a brief holiday. Friedman's interpretation had some validity for his time and place. But then as another era of greed emerged in the late 1970s,* and social mobility waned; Friedman's approach became problematic. Friedman understood government intervention in the market as undesirable—but his ideology had no guard against the market's potential to deplete moral capital. Yunus's voice (and many others) has been corrective: policy making—a leading function of government—can be an extension of societal values. For Yunus, the market needs checks and balances beyond supply, demand, and price determination. Returning to our metaphor of the highway, globalization makes for a multilane superhighway. Friedman would say that the fastest and biggest transporters rule—those smaller and slower transporters need to watch out lest they get squashed. Yunus, on the other hand, would say "Not so fast. Let's make the highway work for all who have an interest. Fast lanes and slower lanes can coexist; let's see how we can make it happen."[20]

Can Friedman's and Yunus's ideas work together? Or are they necessarily and diametrically opposed? The image of the pendulum is once again helpful. Within the arc there is ample room for both dynamic forces. As a matter of fact, both sides need each other. Together they seek balance; when one side dominates, there is imbalance. To construct our metaphorical superhighway and to make it work will require ingenuity, commitment, resolve, conviction, and smart regulations. Trains, trucks, cars, motorcycles, bicyclists, pedestrians, and even the rickshaws of Bangladesh all can be accommodated. Both Friedman and Yunus can make claims to truth, but neither of them has all of it. The trouble with ideology is that the ideologue cuts himself off from other possibilities and, in the process, has to force contexts—which tend to be complex and ever changing—to fit his description of reality. Balance is sacrificed for a forced orthodoxy.

Accommodation for all—in the spirit of egalitarianism—is a great challenge in our day. Our economic system, generically referred to as capitalism, is more specifically referred to as corporate capitalism by those in this short era of excess who have a watchful eye and mind. Political scientist Robert Dahl, in his book *A Preface to Economic Democracy*, speaks of the two competing—or balancing—strains (covered throughout this book) going back to Thomas Jefferson and Alexander Hamilton that define American democracy and economy. Dahl's description enlarges our definitions: the well-ordered democratic society (Jefferson) seeks to balance political and economic liberties with political equality, understanding the right to self-government as primary; the society of unrestricted liberty (Hamilton) seeks to encourage the most prosperous society possible, understanding the right to property as primary. Dahl's description of

---

* Some argue the new era of greed emerged precisely because of Friedman's ideology and its influence.

the Hamiltonian strain fits what is dominant today: corporate capitalism, with corporations taking the role originally intended for individuals. It was in the Gilded Age of Rockefeller, Carnegie, and Ford that corporations became the largest employers in US society; it's a reality that has continued to our current day.[21]

Dahl explains that Alexis de Tocqueville, in his great admiration of early American society, held onto one main concern: that the pursuit of equality would crush liberty. Until the turn of the twentieth century, the majority of Americans were employed in agriculture. In that era of precorporation dominance (outside the South, with its numerous large plantations worked by slaves), most farms were small and family owned. Equality (for white males, at least) and liberty were new societal rights. There was one major impediment to equality and liberty: concentrated power. Monarchy and aristocracy had already been rejected; those particular ways of old Europe would be given no quarter in the new republic. The only other foreseeable manifestation of concentrated power was the "tyranny of the masses."[22] To the point, the writers of the US Constitution created the Electoral College to guard against such tyranny and the masses' possible preference for president. The framers feared that the combination of a candidate's power of manipulation and the ignorance of the citizenry could bring about undesired results.* The relatively wide distribution of previously guarded commodities—equality and liberty—was a new experiment. Lurking on the edges in those early days was legitimate fear of what the new found freedom might produce; the maintenance of equality and liberty required a delicate balance. A give and take between the two would be required. The biggest battle, however, would still be waged against concentrated power. However, none of the framers or their observers foresaw another manifestation of concentrated power that could threaten the new experiment: the colossal corporation.

Corporations have been around for a long time. The pilgrims' arrival in America was supported by corporate activity, much of the world exploration by Spanish, Dutch, and British adventurers was of corporate endeavor, and a number of the initial expeditions into the North American continent also were corporate ventures. The crown (Spain) and fledging governments (America) were not able to sponsor it all. *Corp* means "body"; people joined together in purpose can do more than separate individuals. Shared mission, shared risks, and shared (it is hoped) profits. But profit seeking then wasn't the be-all, end-all that it has become in our day. Nations—like eighteenth century Britain—granted legal protections to corporations because of an understanding that the common good would be

---

* The parallel to today's manifestation of concentrated power, the super PAC, is telling.

served as a result of the corporation conducting its business. Even in the extreme example of slaving, economic gains generated through the loathsome practice were understood to benefit general society. (William Wilberforce and other abolitionists eventually swayed public opinion to the understanding that British societal common good included even slaves and their freedom.) Whether an early corporation from three hundred years ago or today, corporations carry out their best purpose when profit and intentional public service are in balance.[23]

Adam Smith, the reputed father of modern economics, was first and foremost a moral philosopher. His work *The Theory of Moral Sentiments*, published in 1759, preceded his more famous work, *An Inquiry into the Nature and Causes of the Wealth of Nations*, by seventeen years. The two works are not contradictory; the best interpretation of the latter necessarily includes understanding the former. Smith, like his fellow students at the University of Glasgow and Oxford, was trained in history, politics, and morality (philosophy). In *The Theory of Moral Sentiments*, he argued that conscience is learned and adopted from social relationships.[24] Modern-day, unbalanced interpretations of Smith cherry-picked the notion that rational people maximize personal gains—doggedly pursuing wealth first and foremost. Smith realized that an actor in the market might try to maximize leisure or social station or moral standing rather than profit. Participation in the market wasn't only and always about maximizing financial assets or income. There were (and are) social relationships to be maintained and nurtured. In Smith's world, the system of the invisible hand wasn't yet perfect enough to turn greed into good.[25]

Taking advantage of others for gain—on a personal or corporate level— happens when the power relationship is unbalanced: neighborhood bully versus ninety-eight-pound weakling; white slavers versus black subjects; colossal corporations versus societies around the world. Since the creation of wealth is held to be the highest good in the national creed, corporations that make money are ipso facto serving the common good.[26] But if Smith were around today, he would say that enriching the common good involves more than simply creating wealth. Smith would have rejected outright the notion that wealth creation divorced from social responsibility benefits the common good. Angelo Mozilo and Countrywide's independent mortgage agents signing clients to nonconforming loans (wealth transfers to Mozilo and his agents, and creation of crippling debt for clients) in order to receive higher commissions, for example, would have alarmed Smith just as they alarm us. For Smith, a capitalist was assumed to be a national subject whose identity was defined by the social relationships within his community and country of birth. Self-interested economic actions were carried out—most always—in one's own community, smaller or larger. For Smith, private interest and communal interest were intimately linked. The invisible hand worked within a web of societies, communities, and individuals that had overarching mutual interests.[27] Today's aura of corporate capitalism allows for companies to understand their own corporate community as primary, divorced from the surrounding communal web—despite the occasional advertising campaign to the contrary. It's survival of the fittest—competing companies and even nations be damned.

Corporations—the power of people working together—have the potential to do great good, directly and indirectly. Many have throughout the last three hundred years. However, colossal corporations unencumbered by outside checks and balances can operate within the self-imposed parameters of their own universes. In 1911 the US Supreme Court busted up the Standard Oil trust into thirty-four independent subsidiaries, including Standard Oil of New Jersey and Standard Oil of New York. The former would become Exxon, the latter Mobil. Eighty-eight years later, in 1999, the two companies were rejoined. ExxonMobil is one of the world's most tenacious, forceful, and powerful corporations. (ExxonMobil and Walmart typically alternate at the top spot as the world's biggest revenue-producing corporation.) Author Steve Coll claims that ExxonMobil still owns the reputation for ruthlessness and self-interest that its progenitor company had forged during the Gilded Age. In addition, the CEO at the time of the merger, Lee Raymond (who retired in 2005), was expert at exhibiting hyperpartisan boosterism for the company. He discarded global warming as a hoax, let governments—including the United States—know that doing anything to curtail economic growth was an abomination, and proclaimed often that the common good was subservient to the greater goal of profits above all other things. "I'm not a U.S. company and I don't make decisions based upon what's good for the U.S." Raymond's faith in economic growth is understandable—oil is the lifeblood that runs through the veins of America's mythic religion. But once again, how much is enough? His level of compensation was and is inseparable from his advocacy. Raymond's retirement package crested $400 million with the inclusion of an open-ended $1 million-a-year consultancy.[28]

According to Coll, numbers tell the story that corporate power is as dominant now as ever. "Corporate profits in 2011 made up a larger share of American national income, when compared to workers' wages and small business income, than at any time since 1929."[29] Activist shareholder and corporate governance expert Robert Monks also fears the swelling corporate hegemony:

> Maximizing wealth has shed its obligations to the general good.
> Almost everyone now understands wealth a worthy explanation
> of a corporation's objectives and goals even if that means

quashing other concerns about corporate citizenship such as pollution, deceptive accounting, or tax evasion. Good deeds are for Eagle Scouts. Big Business's goodness is measured in profit and loss.[30]

Add in the US Supreme Court *Citizens United v. Federal Election Commission* decision in 2010, allowing corporations to spend without limits to influence elections, and corporate hegemony is approaching another zenith of influence and control.

Monsanto calls itself a "sustainable agriculture company." This description signifies a recent transformation. From its founding in 1901, Monsanto has been a leading chemical company worldwide, having manufactured a wide array of products, some beneficial, others harmful. The short list includes saccharin, caffeine, PCBs, DDT, Agent Orange, aspartame, bovine growth hormone, and the herbicide glyphosate (Roundup). In the 1980s Monsanto enlarged its undertakings to include genetic modification of seeds and plants. Monsanto has become the world's largest seed company; when selling its patented soybean seed laced with genetic immunity to glyphosate, it requires farmers to sign an agreement stating they will not save the harvest's seed for replanting. Monsanto aggressively pursues any offending farmers—*its own customers.* It won a unanimous Supreme Court decision in support of its patent rights in May 2013. In 1980 a previous composition of the high court ruled five to four that genetically modified organisms can be patented. Monsanto has led the way ever since, with hundreds of biotechnology patents. Is it right for corporations to hold exclusive patents on living organisms *for profit?** Indian environmental activist Vandana Shiva calls the patenting of living things an extension of the imperial and colonial eras. She explains that European sovereigns granted "letters patent"—a seal-bearing official document—granting adventurers the right to conquer foreign lands and peoples in the sovereign's name. Shiva asserts that the territorial conquests from centuries past and the biological conquests of today, by new "sovereigns" like Monsanto and other private-sector corporations, share the same primary goal of economic dominance (control of the food supply is both economic and political power). The other well-meaning goals of genetic engineering—feeding the world and using less water and energy to do so—are necessarily subordinate to the

---

* The Green Revolution (roughly 1945–1975) was produced by a public-private partnership helping feed many millions, with important initial funding coming from the Rockefeller Foundation. The Gene Revolution—mostly a private venture—has similar potential to nourish millions, but the inherent conflict between private profit and social returns obstructs its success. Farmers in poorer countries (especially African)—hindered by exorbitant pricing by for-profit seed companies—are essentially excluded. See Felicia Wu and William P. Butz, "What the 'Gene Revolution' Can Learn from the Green Revolution," *Rand Review*, Fall 2004, vol. 28, no.3.

profit motive in Monsanto's neocolonial world. The jury is still out concerning genetically modified organisms. Does food produced from GMOs increase allergic reactions and contribute to increasing antibiotic ineffectiveness? What will be the consequences from uncontrolled gene transfers escaping into the wild? Yet, this for-profit company—with numerous employees going back and forth through the revolving door of federal government and Monsanto leadership—has no balancing or competing power. How long until Monsanto applies for the patent to own nature?[31]

Corpocracy exists when corporations have too much economic and political power. Corporations as wealth producers have been an unparalleled success in the history of the world. Yet blessing and curse are often two sides of the same coin. Pollution and resource depletion are two common excesses of the activity of corporations; the curses they bring to society have long been accepted as the necessary tradeoff for job creation. But have we created a great wealth machine that will eventually destroy us?[32] "Moderation in all things" is an old concept; its wisdom, however, is not yet depleted. Checks and balances—as we see them operate in the American political structure—have historically operated in the economic realm to the benefit of societal common good. In the latter part of the nineteenth century the voices of John Dewey and Oliver Wendell Holmes Sr. decried the growing concentrations of wealth; private capital was a dynamic benefit to society, but its excesses (resulting in abusive labor practices and unjust social conditions) mitigated a portion of the gains.[33] Balance—curbing harmful excesses—is a constant charge and challenge of an economic democracy. A century after Dewey and Holmes, Supreme Court Justice Byron White, in dissent, wrote eloquently in *First National Bank v. Bellotti* (1978) of the need for balance in the economic realm, "preventing institutions which have been permitted to amass wealth as a result of special advantages extended by the State for certain economic purposes from using that wealth to acquire an unfair advantage in the political process . . . *The State need not permit its own creation to consume it.*"[34]

Development

Development is a third characteristic of a shared-power economic system. Development and growth are not one and the same. A child grows, and does so for fifteen to twenty years until physical maturity is attained. Physical maturity is typically reached before emotional and psychological maturity. Physical growth comes first, and then it slows to a stop. Biologically and physiologically, the cessation of growth allows other aspects in and of the person to develop and prevail. Physical growth is limited; development of one's character, spirit, psyche—the whole person—is potentially a lifelong process. Growth deals with quantity, development with quality. The earth, for example, had its period of formation and growth some four billion years ago; the earth's development is a current and ongoing project carried out jointly by nature and humanity. The same can be said of economies.[35]

Commitment to unlimited growth is part of America's national mythic religion. George Gilder, rightly categorized as a high priest of the Hamiltonian strain, opined without restraint in his 1981 bestseller *Wealth and Poverty* on the ideology of unlimitedness. "The United States must overcome the materialistic fallacy: the illusion that resources and capital are essentially things, which can run out, rather than products of human will and imagination, which in freedom are inexhaustible."[36] Gilder's sense of stretching the boundaries—for positive gain—is admirable; behind the dissuasion, however, is a grand leap of faith that grants "human will and imagination" limitless possibilities. Robert Burton, a neurologist, contends to the contrary: "Any concept of free will assumes that we possess a portion of mind that can rise above the biological processes that generated it." Freedom, as concerns the human mind, is partial illusion. Far from being limitless or having the ability to produce inexhaustible possibilities, the human mind is bound by physical parameters and is notoriously capable of self-deception and self-delusion. Burton refers to the *myth of the autonomous rational mind* as the belief "that we can step back from our thoughts in order to judge them." Burton assures us that we are not robotic; our minds are a complex and curious mix of free thoughts, biases, and unconscious determinations flowing from the hardware—genes, neurons, synapses—with which each one of us has been endowed.[37] Also, personal and societal experiences considerably influence our thoughts. There is some freedom of thought, but it's not unlimited; the freedom we experience occurs within the parameters of physical limitation.

Unlimitedness, inherently synced with growth, doesn't have the patience for development. We live in an exponential growth society—thanks to relatively cheap and abundant energy—that depends heavily upon the continuance of further exponential growth for sustainability. Unfortunately, this type of growth is simply not supportable ad infinitum. To say so, of course, is to contradict the national mythic religion.[38] To reiterate: energy ultimately comes from the sun; the discovery and use of fossil fuels unleashed stores of compressed energy, and we've been rapidly depleting them ever since. To act as if fossil fuel reserves are somehow inexhaustible or that we'll come up with some other energy source *so that we can continue on the same consumption trajectory we've been on* *for the last two hundred years* is narcissistic and irresponsible.* Others will come after us; their common good is a part of our own and the greater common good.

The age of exponential growth is over. China and India, yes, are experiencing the tail end of it, but collectively we are on the backside of the growth wave. The new wave we are riding, unfortunately, is the dark wave of debt. Herman Daly and John Cobb contend that "the growth of wealth is physically limited while the growth of debt is not."[39]

I was born in 1961; my formative years and my family's socioeconomic status (white middle class) gave me the understanding—unexamined though it was—of economic growth as completely normal, expected, and necessary. My adult working years, with wages relatively flat for the vast majority of working Americans, have slowly led to an examination of my ingrained assumptions. We would like unlimited growth to be the norm so that life can continue as we've known it—for ourselves and our children and grandchildren. We assume that things are always supposed to improve. That can still be the case, but it's time for us to adjust our assumptions and mindset: sustained development, not continued striving for unlimited growth, is our future's solution.[40]

The expectations we've had (individually, collectively as society, and as expounded by government leadership) for continued growth have resulted in enormous amounts of consumer and governmental debt.[41] Nations that have had financial difficulties and austerity measures imposed in the last thirty years—Greece, Argentina, Ivory Coast, Malaysia are but a few—were not able to service their debt. The United States, undeniably, is following in their path. But we Americans, often forgetful of our own history, would never consider our own nation as having to take on *austerity measures*: that is what other "lesser" nations have to do. And besides, we'll just grow our way out of it.

To spur growth, some politicians (and economists) talk about cutting taxes. It's what Ronald Reagan did and George W. Bush did. As we've seen, the United States has experienced some economic growth since 1980, but it hasn't been as robust as it was during the post–World War II era (when income taxes were considerably higher). Starting with the Reagan tax cuts in 1981, the share of income Americans have paid in overall tax has fallen. In fact, Americans (2010 figures) are taxed less than citizens of nearly every other developed nation.[42] The

* Methane hydrate is the latest natural resource touted as the next great energy source. Following George Gilder's ideological cue, proponents speak glowingly of a seemingly infinite supply of energy, while pooh-poohing externalities such as pollution and increases in greenhouse gases. Charles Mann, "What If We Never Run Out of Oil?", April 24, 2013, *The Atlantic* website, http://www.theatlantic.com/magazine/archive/2013/05/what-if-we-never-run-out-of-oil/309294/, retrieved December 16, 2013.

argument that Americans are taxed too much, thereby stifling economic growth, is not accurate as far as the last sixty years are concerned. David Wessel, Pulitzer Prize–winning journalist and economics editor at the *Wall Street Journal*, says that America's current love affair with growth as panacea for all things economically askew, started in earnest with Reagan's supply-side theory. While taxes were cut, governmental spending was not. Reagan left office leaving federal spending, adjusted for inflation, 20 percent higher than when he took office. The 1980s, under Reagan, broke a pattern in which the federal government ran large deficits only during wartime.[43]

George W. Bush's tax cuts combined with two wars—again, counting on unlimited growth to make up the difference—was disastrous, creating more suffocating debt. There was economic growth, but it turned out to be the sham growth of the housing bubble, which in turn brought about bailouts and buyouts, creating even more debt. Under Barack Obama, federal government debt has ballooned, almost doubling during his first term in office, from $6.3 trillion to $10.6 trillion. That works out to a debt of $90,000 per American household, or nearly 70 percent of GDP, the highest it has been in the last sixty years.[44]

While most politicians support tax cuts, only a few talk of cutting benefits or modifying the qualifications for social programs such as Medicare, Social Security, and other social programs. Not too many political consultants champion to their bosses the idea of cutting benefits—that would make for a tough election season. The tea party movement, with a number of elected representatives in Congress who adhere to the movement's platform, advocates cuts in spending and social programs. It's a bold stance; limits on spending, as we've seen, are not the American way. But the tea party movement is just as zealous about cutting taxes as it is about cutting social program spending—all the while trusting that tax cuts will spur economic growth.

The tax cuts of the last thirty years have accomplished two things: first, they have made the rich richer, creating greater income and wealth inequality; and second, they have further burdened our children and grandchildren to live under the crushing debt that continues to increase, soon, exponentially. Peter Peterson served in the Nixon administration (secretary of commerce) and has had CEO stints at Bell and Howell and Lehman Brothers. He cofounded an extremely profitable private equity firm in 1985; he was one of the wealthiest Americans before joining the Gates and Buffett Giving Pledge, and supported (with $1 billion) his own foundation that works to confront what Peterson considers to be the nation's greatest challenge: unsustainable long-term national debt.[45]

Peterson combines the fiscal responsibility exhibited by the tea party movement—social programs must be cut—with sober acceptance that tax revenues must be increased, especially on those who have the ability to pay: the rich. Peterson is adamant: "On our current course, we are headed toward an unthinkable situation in which the federal government spends more than four times as much on interest than it spends on education, research and development, and infrastructure, combined. This effectively would mean *spending much more on our past than on our future,"* (italics mine). Unlike many of the wealthiest Americans, Peterson advocates higher taxes on the rich. "I prefer to think of [tax cuts] as a tax increase on my own kids and grandkids. And I find that a fundamentally unacceptable immoral position."[46] Peterson, for one, is not waiting on the input of aggregate self-interest into the market system—the alchemy that turns vices into virtues—to save the day.

Peterson advocates cutting spending *and* raising revenues (through increased income tax rates), the two things most people do for their private household economies when things get tough. Why should it be any different for our nation? "There is no solution to this problem that does not require shared sacrifice in terms of reductions of benefits and revenue increases."[47] His concept of the common good does include those who will be coming after us; making future generations pay for our inability to live with limits and balance—as we stagger under the incantations of "more unlimited growth"—is simply unjust and abhorrent.

It's time to accept the reality that economic growth solves some problems, but creates other ones. Growth has done much good in the last two hundred years of industrial and economic advance, but more problems are being created today as resource peaks are crested and economic progress is expected to keep up with if not surpass previous levels of growth. Booms that have been, in part, shams—the dot-coms, housing, financial—lead to genuine busts that enrich precious few and burden the rest of us with cratering debt. Our obsession with unlimited growth is described by Australian author and economist Clive Hamilton as a fetish: "an inanimate object worshipped for its magical powers." Growth is the alleged solution to poverty, unemployment, social funding deficits, ecological reform, and income inequality. But reliance on unlimited growth to solve all our problems is ultimately a false hope; the unexamined pursuit of growth in a finite world only makes our problems worse and hinders us from seeking and implementing actual solutions.[48]

I'm not a doomsday theorist. I'm one who is hopeful for the future as I consider the past and the present. Our human will and imagination, when used to pursue sustainable development rather than unlimited growth, can bring us to a place of greater common good.

Sustainability

A fourth characteristic of economic democracy is sustainability. When I was in junior high school, I played football in a community league in the suburban Chicago city of Mount Prospect. Midget Football (the name has since been revised) was the real deal—tackle football. Our head coach would gather the team, look off into the distance while rubbing his chin, assume the role of philosopher, and tell us over and again: "Boys, a tie is like kissing your sister." At age thirteen, I had a vague sense of what he was getting at. He wanted us to play to win our games; there was a lot more to football and life than putting in work and coming to a draw. Our record that year in spite of the sage musings from our coach: one win, five losses, and four ties. Yes, we had four ties! I suppose that's why we heard the analogy over and again. The year was 1975; ties were still an accepted (albeit undesired) result in team and individual amateur athletic endeavor. That was the time, however—as the short era of excess commenced—when ties became an unaccepted outcome in the professional team sports of football and hockey. Baseball (extra innings) and basketball (overtime) have always determined winners of individual games, but professional football in 1974 and professional hockey in 1983 instituted (for regular season games) extra periods of tie-breaking play, with elaborate rules to further determine a winner (hockey) if the stalemate continued beyond the initial extra periods. College and high school football later followed suit with their own complex versions of overtime play to determine a victor. Ties, once part of athletic competition and its teaching milieu, were disappearing. American society and culture were changing.*

We live today in a culture that places incredible value on the outcome and difference between winners and losers. Since the late-1970s, we have been living in an age not only of *more* but also of hypercompetition. It's not all bad—but it's not all good either. We are told that the free market produces winners and losers. What we see on the athletic courts and fields—that ties are not allowed—reflects what happens on Wall Street, with its fixation on gain at all costs, and

---

* Professional soccer, the world's most popular team sport, yet subordinate in the United States to baseball, basketball, and football, is still fairly accepting of ties in regular season games. Also, Japanese professional baseball allows for ties at the end of twelve innings.

in Washington, DC, where hyperpartisan thinking and bickering dominate.* Moderation and compromise don't sell or pull in any viewers. Neil Postman was right; competition, entertainment, and communication have merged, and content has been diluted to a simple outcome we can all understand: who won and who lost. Whether a presidential debate, a new law passed by Congress, a Walmart opening on what used to be farmland, a winter storm barreling down from the north, or the late game on the West Coast, turn on the TV and find out who the winners and the losers are. CNN, NBC, Fox News, the Weather Channel, and ESPN will break it down and keep it simple—wins, losses, and not too many ties.

We're no longer *a society that has a market economy* as one of its important contributing components; we have morphed into a *market society*, where market values have become national values and market considerations consistently trump others ones. Are young students having trouble learning how to read in school? Let's pay them to succeed. Is there a shortage of donated blood? Let's commercialize it and pay people to donate. The cost-benefit analysis is rightly applied to many societal situations and dilemmas, but it isn't appropriate for all situations. The commodification of certain things—reading, writing, and blood donation—degrades their inherent value.[49] Not all things can be bought and sold.

Heinberg is one of a growing number of economists and commentators who are critical of gross domestic product being the unequivocal measure of economic well-being. "Calculating a nation's overall health according to its GDP makes about as much sense as evaluating the quality of a piece of music solely by counting the number of notes it contains." Chang also chastises the unchecked regard for GDP with a musical analogy: "If a string quartet trots through a twenty-seven minute piece in nine minutes, would you say that its productivity has trebled?" [50] GDP is useful, but it's solely a measure of quantity, not quality.

Erich Fromm, the German psychologist, was critical of economic growth as a primary societal value:

> The development of this economic system was no longer determined by the question: What is good for Man? But by the question: What is good for the growth of the system?   . . . We must put an end to the present situation where a healthy economy is possible only at the price of unhealthy human beings.

---

* Today's youngest athletic competitors are all awarded trophies, whether finishing in first or last place. Many complain about this change of the last few decades, but perhaps something tells us that our overemphasis on winning and losing is toxic.

Fromm asserts that language usage has changed in the postindustrial era: more nouns and fewer verbs used, meaning more emphasis on having and possessing, and less emphasis on being and doing. The answer to the ontological question "Who am I?" is a combination of what one possesses and consumes. Fromm then asks the critical question: if disaster strikes and all is lost, "Who then am I?"[51]

"The belief that more money makes us happier has all the characteristics of an addiction, one on which the survival of consumer capitalism depends." Clive Hamilton, who refers to those living in materially abundant societies as "prisoners of plenty," bemoans the reality that so many don't know how to live with abundance. Hamilton calls this the "tragedy of consumer capitalism."[52] What John Stuart Mill called the "cultivation of the art of living" is not necessarily enhanced by mechanical inventions, be it the sewing machine of his day or the automatic windows of this day.

Sustainability is not a new concept; Mill wrote of it in 1848 as the industrial era was reshaping Britain. The "steady state" economy—of stable size after initial economic growth and in line with ecological limits—was also envisioned by John Maynard Keynes, Nicholas Georgescu-Roegen, and E. F. Schumacher in the twentieth century. Herman Daly continues to advocate it in the current day.[53] Sustainable development balances present needs with the needs of those who will be coming after us. Sustainable development advocates ecological, biological, and cultural diversity, recognizing that diversity is the key to the survivability of all life forms. Hamilton points out a great incongruity of the present era, with its fervent adoration of the ideology of economic growth: "One of the ironies of the modern world is that choice has been elevated to supreme status precisely at a time of social and cultural homogenization across the globe."[54] With Walmart in 27 countries, Burger King in 73, and McDonald's in 119, the homogenization of choice is yet another expression of neocolonialism.[55] True choice would entertain the possibility that economic growth is not the unquestioned cure-all it is assumed to be.

The economic pie is no longer increasing at the rate it used to, and as a result, hypercompetition is on the rise. The growth rate has unquestionably slowed; wealth creation has not kept pace proportionally with population growth. The low-hanging fruit has been plucked, and complexity continues its upward spiral. Economic gains are still present and will continue, but not at the pace and with the ease they had before. We're reaching a point of diminishing returns. There has been a good run economically for some two hundred years, most notably from 1950 to 1975. The last thirty years, however, have featured just as much wealth transfer to the already rich as they have wealth creation for all. Human nature dictates that a diminishing pool of goods will cause an increasing population to fight competitively and uncooperatively to attain those goods. Hypercompetition leads humans to acquire aggressively—*sharing* the economic pie is a thing of the past, disdained as downright Pollyannaish.

Keynesian props and bailouts—used by FDR (arguably effective) and by Bush and Obama (arguably ineffective)—presuppose growth continuing at a robust rate. As growth continues, says the ideological construct, the debt will be repaid. Consequently, growth must be served at all costs. Neither Bush nor Obama has been a proponent of conservation—minimizing resource consumption for the sake of *sustainable* development. Full-bore consumerism is needed for continued growth. If, however, the growth is not robust, then we are all hoodwinked, because the debt will continue to expand. Future generations will be forced to cover the previous generations' inability to live with reasonable constraint. The mythical religion of commerce, materialism, and consumption bolstered by the philosophical commitment to unlimitedness, has forced us into a corner. If our current rates of consumption continue, we'll need multiple planets to feed our unsatiated appetites for further growth.[56] We have only one planet, however, and currently, we're not able to order anymore on eBay or Amazon.

Sustainable development is at the heart of economic democracy. Quality over quantity, consideration of the needs of future generations, heightened emphasis on efficiency (to serve resource conservation), and the recognition that the carrying capacities of ecological systems must be respected are some of the characteristics that define sustainable development.[57] A lot of businesses, however, still operate with a worldview and mindset that hasn't changed since the industrial era began: resources are inexhaustible, and harmful waste streams are simply a cost of doing business (making profits). But changing realities of scarcity—the limited nature of resources and waste stream "sinks" (receptors)—will continue to create new opportunities for those able to adapt and develop. These are the businesses that will make it into the new era.[58] It's time to change the emphasis from short-term profit making as the most important factor in commercial endeavor. The broadcasting of a bastardized version of Adam Smith's invisible hand—that profits can be divorced from communal common good—needs to be further exposed as a self-serving mantra that destroys long-term health, well-being, and survival.

Common Good

The common good is the fifth and final characteristic of economic democracy and integral to a capitalist economic system governed by shared power. Friedrich Hayek was awarded the Nobel Prize for Economics in 1974 (sharing the prize with Swedish economist Gunnar Myrdal). Hayek, born in Austria-Hungary in 1899, was a libertarian whose social understandings and convictions were forged in a Europe that was a proving ground for democracy, socialism, and fascism. Like theologian Paul Tillich, he served in World War I and was suspicious of the growing Nazi movement (he became a British subject in 1938); those experiences contributed to his lifelong love and investigation of liberty.

During World War II Hayek wrote *The Road to Serfdom*, his classic diatribe against governmental central planning and its control of economic production and distribution. In the 1970s, he published a three volume set under the heading *Law, Legislation and Liberty*; the second volume had the transparent title of *The Mirage of Social Justice*. Hayek, obviously, was not opposed to societal justice; he was entirely skeptical that social or distributive justice could be pursued without the corruption of personal liberty. Milton Friedman agreed wholeheartedly: intentional pursuit of the common good was to be resisted on the basis of its potential destructiveness to personal liberty. In this regard, Hayek and Friedman follow the tradition of the liberty strain attributed to Alexander Hamilton: the cart can't lead the horse—societal virtues are products of market dynamics. Personal liberty is the greatest of all goods, predominant over all other considerations. Hayak and Friedman went farther than Hamilton within the liberty strain: the outcomes of the capitalistic market are "beyond justice." Outcomes are not to be *managed*; the market system will dictate winners and losers. These results may be tragic and seemingly unfair, but they are not unjust. This is what Hayek meant by the title of his book: social justice is not an economic goal.[59]

John Rawls, the late Harvard political philosopher, is categorized as a social contract theorist, following in the tradition of Thomas Hobbes, John Locke, and Immanuel Kant. The idea behind social contract theory is that people will give up some freedoms in order that they might live together in a civilized fashion. It's a trade-off where anarchy and tyranny are rejected in order to obtain an agreed-upon political order. The plank upholding democracy (and to a degree, modern economy) is civil freedom—negotiated, practiced, and maintained. The US Declaration of Independence, written primarily by Thomas Jefferson, is a document drenched in social contract understandings. Rawls published his influential *A Theory of Justice* in 1971; it serves as a counterbalance to the works of Hayek and Friedman. Rawls brought a moral dimension back to economic considerations, one that Friedman and Hayek were willing to cast aside as they elevated the importance of personal liberty.[60]

Harvard political philosopher Michael Sandel furthers this debate between those who recognize individual rights and choices as primary and those who advocate an ethic of the common good. "The most fateful change that unfolded during the past three decades was not an increase in greed. It was the expansion of markets, and of market values, into spheres of life where they don't belong." The expansion of market values—bolstered by the works of Hayek and Friedman— has let greed run free without significant counterbalances in the last three decades. Sandel elaborates: "Economists often assume that markets are inert, that they do not affect the goods they exchange. But this is untrue. Markets leave their mark. Sometimes, market values crowd out nonmarket values worth caring about."[61]

Economists Friedman, Hayek, Keynes, Galbraith, and Samuelson all came from the era when economics as a discipline was trying to put itself on equal footing with the hard sciences. Aspiring to a certain status is one thing, achieving it another. Robert Nelson is an economist who served a lengthy tenure in the US Department of the Interior and currently teaches in the University of Maryland's School of Public Policy. He has an alternative view on economics: *it's more like a religion than anything else*. Yes, economics deals with numbers, specifically the empirical data of production and consumption, on scales large and small. The discipline works with the critical markers of inflation and unemployment rates and incentives— financial, social, and moral—to describe the broad world of interactions between people, goods, services, and mediums of exchange. But ultimately, science is progressive in terms of knowledge accumulation, whereas financial economics are cyclical in terms of outcomes.[62]

Economic theories aid in determining public policies that are implemented at local, national, and international levels. Nelson argues that the greatest influence economists have is in their defense of a particular "set of values." Paul Krugman, Raghuram Rajan, Hernando de Soto, Elinor Ostrom (deceased 2012), and Jeffrey Sachs are just a few of the recognized contemporary economists whose proposals wield considerable policy influence. Like the myriad religions of the world, there exists among these economists a wealth of differences in their deliberations and convictions. In the computation of their theories, they all use numbers and figures, but a set of values underlies and girds the entire structure.[63]

In no way do I disparage the discipline; economics is incredibly diverse, important, and far reaching. Like sociology and psychology in their attempt to explain and describe a wide breadth of human experience and circumstance, economics is not able to be value neutral. Neither is religion. Paul Heyne was an American economist who taught at the University of Washington during the last quarter of the previous century. Heyne also had a graduate degree in theology. He argued that the practice of economics is never value neutral and is infused with religious leanings; in their attempt to make the world of human interactions more effective (by advocating their specific recommendations), economists operate with a "theological vision." Is it Krugman or Ben Bernanke or Arthur Laffer that we are to believe in and follow?[64]

Nelson explains that religions seek to change a person's or a community's preference structure. "Thou shalt not kill" and "Thou shalt not steal" are value-laden constructs that seek to change (or maintain within the community) a given preference structure. Religion teaches adherents be happy with what they have or to desire worthier things (spiritual joys instead of material riches, for example). Economics, on the other hand, typically assumes a preexisting preference structure and works with it as is. [65] Economics is differentiated from religion in this sense. If people prefer to buy bananas over raspberries, that ordering of alternatives is accepted and is used in the formation of choice or demand models. People will buy food and purchase phones—preexisting preference structures—good economic theorizing helps producers and suppliers determine strategies based on consumer wants. Religion seeks to change the way people think and act; economics seeks to understand that behavior via the categorization and description of the buying, selling, and consuming.

Economics becomes more like a religion when it gets involved in changing or influencing preference structure. Economics morphs into religion not with the purchasing choices, for example, between the iPhone 6 or the Galaxy S4—that's marketing—but rather with the exaltation of a particular value set. All economic systems from Marxism to capitalism come equipped with their own set of values. Capitalism is best at creating wealth; its great moral dilemma is the ethical balance between self-interest and societal good.[66] Self-interest, for better and for worse, is capitalism's primary value set.

In 1958 Canadian economist John Kenneth Galbraith wrote about the "atmosphere of private opulence and public squalor." Galbraith implied the two were intimately connected, with the common good in play between their sway. Self-interested *consumers*, lacking a counterbalance, have no responsibilities or obligations to fellow consumers. Citizens, in contrast, have duties to one another and to society. The adoption of and sellout to market values in the short era of excess has led to an eclipse of citizen or communal values.* Citizens are more likely to be in touch with intrinsic values such as duty, honor, and accountability. Consumers are more likely to be in touch with extrinsic values such as wealth, possessions, and appearances. Do neighbors today know each other better than was the case thirty-five years ago? Usually not; our neighborhoods suffer as a result. As social critic Benjamin Barber says, "Markets flatter our solitary egos but leave our yearnings for community unsatisfied."[67]

Selfish capitalism, described by British psychologist Oliver James, includes the related emphases of business success and elevated share prices, minimal business regulation and limited taxation of the rich, and the conviction that consumption and market forces will meet all of society's needs. This last characterization encompasses the premise that internal human deficiencies (loneliness, hurt) can be alleviated by external means (a new sofa). Once again, strength and weakness are two inseparable sides of the same coin. Market activity has created wealth and lifted many from poverty, yet in the last thirty-five years, hubristic market values have made people turn away from public life to private devices and desires. People are increasingly self-absorbed and expectant of entitlements. Obligation to great causes is fleeting; the cult of self-interest has created a society of individuals who lack commitment to one another. James is not a pessimist; he alternatively envisions the *unselfish* capitalist: "Meet your needs, not your wants; be, don't have; cooperate as well as compete."[68]

Social capital, the potential or actual resources related to social networks and structures leading to cooperation and mutual benefits between actors, is essential for the existence of a well-ordered capitalism. Social capital is not always created by individuals motivated solely by self-interested aims; many other motivations from altruism to self-sacrifice spur its creation. Social capital is the result of positive contacts; it has individual and communal aspects affecting actors and their communities directly and indirectly. Usually, but not always, the effects are favorable. (A person with criminal intent who, with the help of a friend, locates a gun and then uses it to rob a bank is an example of unfavorable effects of social capital.)[69]

The Berlin Wall tumbled in 1989, burying controlled economies' attempts to prevail over capitalism. For Russia, coming out of communism and dealing with the secession of various lands from the former Soviet Union, a capitalistic economy would undoubtedly need some time to become established. Now that twenty-five years have passed, how are things faring economically in Russia? Money

---

* President Kennedy's famous 1961 inaugural entreaty "Ask not what your country can do for you—ask what you can do for your country" has been almost thoroughly eroded by market values.

is prevalent and Moscow is the haven of Russia's handful of *billionaires*. The concentration of wealth, however, is wholly disproportional. Journalist Chrystia Freeland describes contemporary Russia as sustaining economic inequalities worse than the time of the tsars. Crony or criminal capitalism dominated by Russia's oligarchs—created by the fire sale of state-owned companies in the 1990s—has also been described by the Russian term *prykhvatizatsiya*, translated "grabification." The fire-sale bids were essentially fixed; Russia's ratio of billionaires to GDP and national population is the world's most unbalanced—by far. Russia not only lacks a sizable middle class, but it also lacks a millionaire class. Lack of social capital is a main reason for capitalism's uneven debut in Russia and has led to excessive wealth by political connection and not by industry.[70]

Norwegian political scientist Jon Elster points to the prominence of traits such as duty and honesty in countries like the United States as evidence of robust social capital: "If people always engaged in opportunistic behavior when they could get away with it, civilization as we know it would not exist."[71] Russia is not made up principally of bad actors; as a society, it has few egalitarian traditions and a fragile concept of the common good. The egalitarian values of American society are among the strongest in the history of the world, yet the current competition with the market values–infused religion of self-interest increasingly hastens the depletion of America's precious social capital.

Many and various factors contribute to the perpetuation of a society's common good. The practice of greed management, reverse hierarchical dominance, egalitarianism, and other efforts that keep plutocratic, aristocratic, and corpocratic tendencies in check are crucial. The proliferation of economic inequalities, as exhibited currently in the United States for almost two generations, erodes the common good. Irony: the economy produced by unchecked overemphasis on personal liberty in the end collapses in on itself. "The new emphasis on uninhibited self-expression for individual gain meant that traditional ethical commitments to honesty, personal sacrifice, duty to country, civic participation, political involvement, and so forth would have a declining role in society."[72] Robert Nelson's description in 2000 is unfortunately on target more than a decade later.

Coexistence and Cooperation

Coexistence and cooperation are characteristics of an economy that is more democratic—of the people—than one controlled by concentrated power.

Coexistence and cooperation inform and instruct the five previous mentioned characteristics of economic democracy.

New Orleans attracts many American visitors and foreign tourists. The food, the culture, the nightlife, and the music are big draws. Not too many travelers, however, venture out into the Mississippi River Delta region that extends south and east of the city. For five thousand years, the deltaic forces have advanced the fragile coastline out into the gulf. An estuary is the geographical and ecosystem convergence of freshwater and saltwater. Bays, harbors, lagoons, inlets, bayous, and sounds are sometimes technically categorized as estuaries—salinity of 0.5–3.0 percent defines the grouping (seawater typically is 3.5 percent saline). The main channel of the Mississippi River estuary fans out thirty miles, supporting a network of subchannels and streams. Close to five million gallons of Mississippi River water discharge per second into the Gulf of Mexico. At the very mouth of the river, this estuary consists of river water flowing on top of a foundation of saline ocean water. Farther out, however, the mixing of fresh and saline waters is constant and ever changing. Ocean tides, storms, and winds also contribute to the waters' blending.[73]

We might typically think that bodies of water, by definition, fall into either the fresh or the saline category. Typically, they do. The plant, animal, and marine life they support generally adhere to the same separation. The mixing of fresh and saline bodies, however, provides a most unique and fertile environment. Estuaries, the coexistence of fresh and salt water, are among the most highly productive and abundant ecosystems on the earth, boasting stunning biodiversity. Estuaries— much more common than typically realized—not only provide critical sanctuary for myriad plants and wildlife, they also protect coastal regions from storms and floods, while providing the nursery grounds for two-thirds of the commercial fish and shellfish production in the United States.[74] Acting as a filter or trap, estuaries also retain pollutants.[75] While the retention of pollutants is harmful for the life supported by an estuary, it is beneficial for the surrounding environments.

Balance is the principle that allows for dynamic and vigorous public life, while simultaneously creating an atmosphere for the common good to flourish. With balance, ample wiggle-room exists for diverse understandings and practices. Balance doesn't necessarily mean middle of the road; balance implies a state of non-domination by one side. As with a pendulum—the distance traversed between the opposite end points of the arc creating its fluidity—a graceful sway to and fro includes all points in between. Estuaries are a manifestation of the fundamental polarities or phenomena in nature that produce jointly what can't be produced individually: sexual reproduction from male and female representatives; the atomic structure of positive and negative charges producing electricity, magnetism, and thermal conductivity; primary colors as seen in a rainbow blending to form every other possible color and hue.

The strains of American thought as represented by Alexander Hamilton and Thomas Jefferson—respectively, liberty and egalitarianism—need not strive against each other as if in a concerted struggle to the death. One side does not have to win out over the other. Preferably, as it has been for most of American history, coexistence of the two contenders creates a climate that is fertile and robust for its social, economic, and political realms. An underlying coexistence of the two, like an estuary or like the two sides of the brain working separately yet in tandem simultaneously, makes for a society unmatched in freedoms and function.

Were you born in the United States after 1980? If so, you've grown up in an environment and era where the devotion to *excess* and its demonstrations— profit margins, work hours, growth as dogma, hyper-partisanship, winner-take-all bias—have dominated to the point of hegemony (dominance over all others). The short era of excess posits itself as normal: nine-figure severance packages for CEOs; restaurants offering no charge if you can eat a 4 lb. burger or 7 lb. burrito in less than an hour; the lionizing of a Wall Street criminal like Jordan Belfort (*The Wolf of Wall Street*), replete with the adoration of wealth, status, and greed.[76] But don't be fooled; like the other short eras of excess in US history—the Gilded Age and the 1920s—this current one is unsustainable and will eventually crash.

The current short era of excess entices us to believe that competition is the highest expression of our human nature and endeavor. While competition does inspire and demand greatness, cooperation is competition's balancing trait that has not only enabled the human species to survive, but to thrive in ways unimagined by our ancestors.[77] Our advances and discoveries impress, and cooperation is to be lauded for the progress just as much as is competition. Simply put: we wouldn't be alive without cooperation's harmonizing and compensating exertions alongside competition. Nature—from colonies of ants and bees, to flocks of birds flying in unison and schools of fish swimming collectively—gives countless examples of life's sustainability due to cooperation. Present day America undervalues cooperation at its own peril; cooperation is the thumb working together with competition's forefinger.

Where will we go from here? Capitalism has given us so much, but in the process, it has robbed us of the consciousness of knowing when and what is enough. Like Rockefeller, we all want just a little bit more—and our children and grandchildren are easily indoctrinated into the same value system. Our religious devotion to the god of excess coincides with a time where we have lost the ability to have significant moral and spiritual discourse on the matter; the mantra of more growth, more consumption, and more *Market* loudly drowns out other rivals.[78]

Yet the two grandest virtues of the American experience, democracy and egalitarianism, have shown themselves to be undeterred by previous eras of excess. That didn't happen naturally; it happened because democracy and egalitarianism—mutually dependent entities—*had the support of the people*. It's been that way since the late 1700s, and it will be that way as we move forward.

ENDNOTES

INTRODUCTION

[1] Adam Smith, *The Wealth of Nations*, Thrifty Books (2009), 186.

[2] Muhammad Yunus, *Banker to the Poor: Micro-Lending and the Battle Against World Poverty*, Public Affairs (1999), 248.

CHAPTER 1

[1] Ron Chernow, *Titan: The Life of John D. Rockefeller, Sr.*, Vintage (1998), 344.

[2] Ibid., 6.

[3] Ibid., 19.

[4] Ibid., 44–51.

[5] Niall Ferguson, *The Ascent of Money: A Financial History of the World,* Penguin (2008), 61–62.

[6] Charles Tabb, "A Brief History of Bankruptcy Law" derived from "The History of Bankruptcy Laws in the United States," American Bankruptcy Institute Law Review, (1995).

[7] Charles Morris, *The Tycoons: How Andrew Carnegie, John D. Rockefeller, Jay Gould, and J.P. Morgan Invented The American Supereconomy,* Holt (2006), 13–16.

[8] Ibid., 21–24, 230.

[9] Ibid., 28.

[10] Ibid., 289.

[11] Herodotus, *The Histories* (rev.), Penguin Classics (2003), 627.

[12] *Plutarch's Lives*, John Dryden (tr.), Arthur Clough (ed.), vol. 1, Modern Library (2001), 750.

[13] Ferguson, 53–54.

[14] Stuart Blumin, *The Emergence of the Middle Class,* Cambridge University Press (1989), 1–2.

[15] Chernow, 77, 133.

[16] Daniel Yergin, *The Prize: The Epic Quest for Oil, Money, and Power*, Simon & Schuster (1991), 80. One of Edison's major financial backers was J. P. Morgan; Henry Ford worked for Edison Illuminating Company from 1891 to 1899.

[17] Chernow, 255.

[18] Ibid., 153, 191.

[19] Ibid., 189–90.

[20] Ibid., 469.

[21] Ibid., 313, 590.

[22] Ibid., 314. Field donated the original land for the University of Chicago; Armour would start what is known today as the Illinois Institute of Technology.

[23] Kevin Phillips, *Wealth and Democracy: A Political History of the American Rich,* Broadway (2003), xv.

[24] Morris, 28.

[25] Phillips, 22–24.

[26] Ibid., 26, 39.

[27] Morris, 33–39 (the unique culture of nineteenth century American innovation is superbly highlighted by Morris); Phillips, 42–43.

[28] Chernow, 352.

[29] Ibid., 339–41.

[30] Ferguson, 203.

[31] Census Records website, http://www.censusrecords.com/content/1900_census? utm_medium=cpc&utm_campaign=B_1900census&utm_source=bing&utm_term= census+1900+census, retrieved January 1, 2014.

[32] David Wagner, *Ordinary People: In and Out of Poverty in the Gilded Age*, Paradigm (2008), 11, 39, 45.

[33] Morris, 161–62, 177.

[34] Donald Miller, *City of the Century*, Simon & Schuster (1996), 244–48. My father, who grew up on a farm in rural Minnesota in the 1940s and '50s, always has had a strong fondness for Ward's; the company has served five generations of our family.

[35] Morris, 164–77.

[36] Ibid., 183.

[37] Daniel Gross, "No Rest for the Wealthy," *New York Times*, July 5, 2009.

[38] Sven Beckert, *The Monied Metropolis: New York City and the Consolidation of the American Bourgeoisie 1850–1896,* Cambridge University Press (2003), 1; Doug Henwood, "Our Gilded Age," *The Nation*, June 30, 2008.

[39] Phillips, 38.

[40] Charles Mann, *1491: New Revelations of the Americas before Columbus*, Vintage (2005), 56.

[41] Theodore Roosevelt Association website, www.theodoreroosevelt.org/TR%20Web% 20Book/TR_CD_to_HTML365.html, retrieved January 23, 2012.

[42] Edmund Morris, *Theodore Rex*, Random House (2001), 233–34.

[43] Daniel Okrent, *Last Call: The Rise and Fall of Prohibition*, Scribner (2010), 46–48.

[44] Ibid., 2–4.

[45] Ibid., 48–49.

[46] Ibid., 54, 92.

[47] W. Elliot Brownlee, *Federal Taxation in America: A Short History*, 2nd ed., Wilson/ Cambridge (2004), 60, 65.

[48] Ibid., 65–67, 72–73.

[49] Ibid., 74.

[50] Henwood, *The Nation*, June 30, 2008.

[51] Frederick Lewis Allen, *The Lords of Creation*, Harper & Brothers (1935), 222.

[52] David Cannadine, *Mellon: An American Life*, Knopf (2006), 349.

[53] Liaquat Ahamed, *The Bankers Who Broke the World*, Penguin (2009), 439–40.

[54] Allen, 222–23.

[55] Ibid., 223–32.

[56] Edwin Burrows and Mike Wallace, *Gotham: A History of New York City to 1898*, Oxford University Press (1999), 939–40, 1046.

[57] Steve Fraser, *Every Man a Speculator: A History of Wall Street in American Life*, Harper Collins (2005), 171–74.

[58] Brownlee, 43–44, 49.

[59] Ahamed, 140–43, 162.

[60] Justin Kaplan, *Mr. Clemens and Mark Twain: A Biography*, Simon & Schuster (1966), 95–96.

[61] Robert Putnam and David Campbell, *American Grace: How Religion Unites Us and Divides Us*, Simon & Schuster (2010), 83.

[62] Fraser, 397, 399–400.

[63] Ibid., 394, 398.

[64] Ibid., 384.

[65] Ibid., 375.

[66] Ibid., 385.

[67] Ibid., 375.

[68] Phillips, 63–64.

[69] Ibid., 65–68.

CHAPTER 2

[1] Texas State Historical Association website, http://www.tshaonline.org/handbook/online/articles/hlp39, retrieved June 25, 2013.

[2] Dave Harmon, "Austin financial advisor's death sparks inquiry into loans he solicited from wealthy investors," May 28, 2013, *Austin American-Statesman* website, http://www.mystatesman.com/news/news/local/austin-financial-advisers-death-sparks-inquiry-int/nX5Yp/, retrieved June 25, 2013; Dave Harmon and Shonda Novak, "New details emerge in dead investment manager's financial dealings," June 19, 2013, *Austin American-Statesman* website, http://www.mystatesman.com/news/news/new-details-emerge-in-dead-investment-managers-fin/nYQDt/, retrieved June 25, 2013; Dave Harmon, "Powell's creditors bank on insurance," *Austin American-Statesman*, January 26, 2014, A1.

[3] CNBC website, "Missing Millions in Austin," May 30, 2013, http://www.nbcnews.com/video/cnbc/52047728/#52047728, retrieved June 27, 2013.

[4] Ecclesiastes 5:10.

[5] Merriam-Webster website, www.merriam-webster.com/dictionary/greed, retrieved February 3, 2012.

[6] Tony Hendra, *The Book of Bad Virtues*, Pocket (1994), 57.

[7] Rush Limbaugh radio archive website, www.rushlimbaugh.com/daily/2011/11/28/question_what_has_fed_more_hungry_mouths_greed_self_interest_or_charity, retrieved February 6, 2012.

[8] David Kessler, *The End of Overeating: Taking Control of the Insatiable American Diet*, Rodale (2009), 43–44.

[9] Peter Whybrow, *American Mania: When More Is Not Enough*, Norton (2006), 1–11, 278–79; Michael Lewis, *Boomerang: Travels in the New Third World*, Norton (2011), 203–6; Peter Whybrow, "Dangerously Addictive," *The Chronicle Review*, March 13, 2009, and Judith Waren, "Dysregulation Nation," *New York Times*, June 14, 2010, http://www.peterwhybrow.com/whatsnew.html, retrieved July 1, 2013.

[10] James Stewart, *Den of Thieves*, Touchstone (1991), 40–41, 261.

[11] Jeff Madrick, *Age of Greed: The Triumph of Finance and the Decline of America, 1970 to the Present*, Knopf (2011), 87–89.

[12] Ari Goldman, "Boesky Studying Hebrew and Talmud at Seminary," July 23, 1987, *The New York Times* website, www.nytimes.com/1987/07/23/nyregion/boesky-studying-hebrew-and-talmud-at-seminary.html, retrieved February 11, 2012.

[13] Madrick, 77–82.

[14] Sam Pizzigati, *Greed and Good: Understanding and Overcoming the Inequity That Limits Our Lives*, Apex Press (2004), 52–55.

[15] Bethany McLean and Peter Elkind, *The Smartest Guys in the Room: The Amazing Rise and Scandalous Fall of Enron*, Penguin (2003), 2–3.

[16] Ibid., xxi, 39, 55.

[17] Bob Dylan, "Not Dark Yet," *Time Out of Mind* (1997), Columbia.

[18] McLean and Elkind, 122, 125, 239–40.

[19] Michael Kinsley, "Private-Equity Pigs," July 19, 2007, *Time* website, www.time.com/time/magazine/article/0,9171,1645146,00.html, retrieved February 13, 2012.

[20] Reinhart and Rogoff, *This Time Is Different: Eight Centuries of Financial Folly*, Princeton University Press (2009), 291–92.

[21] Steve Fishman, "The Madoff Tapes," February 27, 2011, *New York Magazine* website, nymag.com/news/features/berniemadoff-2011-3/, retrieved February 14, 2012. Other reports claim Madoff established his firm with $5,000 when he started out in 1960.

[22] Ibid.; *The Great Hangover: 21 Tales of the New Recession from the Pages of Vanity Fair*, Graydon Carter (ed.), Harper Perennial (2010), 337–66.

[23] Ibid., 337–66; Fishman, "The Madoff Tapes."

[24] Raj Patel, *The Value of Nothing*, Picador (2009), 88.

[25] Charles Young, "Justice," in *A Companion to Aristotle*, Georgios Anagnostopoulos (ed.), Wiley-Blackwell (2009), 465–66.

[26] Paul Hawken, from the Forward in *Hooked: Buddhist Writings on Greed, Desire, and the Urge to Consume*, Stephanie Kaza (ed.), Shambhala (2005), viii.

[27] Ragheb El-Sergany (ed.), "Qarun the Wealthy," June 20, 2010, Islam Story website, www.islamstory.com/en/node/29976, retrieved February 16, 2012.

[28] Shadi Hamid, "An Islamic Alternative? Equality, Redistributive Justice, and the Welfare State in the Caliphate of Umar(rta)," www.renaissance.com.pk/Augvipo2y3.html, retrieved February 16, 2012.

[29] Chandra Muzzafar, "God or Greed? A Muslim View," September 27, 2011, International Movement for a Just World website, www.just-international.org/index.php/component/content/article/171-in-focus/index.php?option=com_content&id=923:chandra-muzaffar&catid=22:sep&Itemid=37, retrieved February 16, 2012.

[30] Tess Vigeland, "Muslim Mortgages," American Public Media Marketplace website, March 8–9, 2008, http://www.marketplace.org/topics/business/middle-east-work/muslim-mortgages, retrieved February 18, 2012; Lindsay Wise, "Islamic mortgages in US seem to be booming in recession," April 23, 2009, *Houston Chronicle* website, www.chron.com/life/houston-belief/article/Islamic-mortages-in-U-S-seem-to-be-booming-in-1738159.php, retrieved February 16, 2012.

[31] Paul Johnson, *A History of the Jews*, Harper and Row (1987), 172–73; Susan Thistlethwaite, *#Occupy the Bible: What Jesus Really Said (and Did) About Money and Power*, Astor + Blue Editions (2012), 43.

[32] Deirdre Good, *Jesus the Meek King*, Trinity Press (1999), 74; author interview with Peter Steinke, February 28, 2012.

[33] Ray Pickett, "You Cannot Serve God and Mammon," Brawley Lecture paper (unpublished) presented at Lutheran School of Theology, Chicago, November 14, 2011, 13.

[34] Ferguson, 37–38, 42–45.

[35] David Jones, *Reforming the Morality of Usury: A Study of the Differences That Separated the Protestant Reformers*, University Press of America (2004), 4.

[36] G.H. Cohen Stuart, *The Struggle in Man Between Good and Evil: An Inquiry into the Origin of the Rabbinic Concept of Yaser Hara*, Campen (1984); author interview with Whit Bodman, February, 17, 2012.

[37] Basil Johnston, *The Manitous*, Minnesota Historical Society Press (2001), 222–25.

[38] "Wal-Mart pepper-spray attack involved Xbox, Wii games, witnesses say," November 25, 2011, *The Los Angeles Times* website, http://latimesblogs.latimes.com/lanow/2011/11/wal-mart-pepper-spray-attack-involved-xbox-wii-games-witnesses-says.html, retrieved October 1, 2012. The woman turned herself in the following day to the Los Angeles police, but was never charged in the incident. Self-defense and fear of safety in the midst of a chaotic crowding situation were mitigating factors in her case.

[39] "Violence mars Black Friday," November 25, 2011, CNN website, http://www.cnn.com/2011/11/25/business/money-black-friday-incidents/?hpt=us_c1, retrieved October 1, 2012.

[40] Jason Zweig, *Your Money and Your Brain: How the New Science of Neuroeconomy Can Make You Rich*, Simon & Schuster (2007), 6, 66–67.

[41] Raj Patel, *The Value of Nothing: How to Reshape Market Society and Redefine Democracy*, Picador (2009), 32.

CHAPTER 3

[1] George Orwell, *Animal Farm*, Harcourt, Brace, Jovanovich (1946), 33, 123.

[2] Christopher Boehm, *Hierarchy in the Forest: The Evolution of Egalitarian Behavior*, Harvard University Press (1999), 1–3.

[3] Ryan Early, "Balance of Power," March–April 2000, *American Scientist* website, www.americanscientist.org/bookshelf/pub/balance-of-power, retrieved February 25, 2012.

[4] Boehm, 4.

[5] Margaret Atwood, *Payback: Debt and the Shadow Side of Wealth*, Anansi (2008), 12–20.

[6] Michael J. Thompson, *The Politics of Inequality: A Political History of the Idea of Economic Inequality in America,* Columbia University Press (2007), 32–47; quote from 47.

[7] Phillips, 4.

[8] Thompson, 6, 61.

[9] Pizzigati, 416–17.

[10] Thompson, 60.

[11] Ibid., 75, 77.

[12] Ibid., 176–77.

[13] Ibid., 197.

[14] Pizzigati, 417.

[15] Phillips, 16–17.

[16] Thompson, 121–23.

[17] Ibid., 123–25. It's ironic that Sumner is partly remembered as a proponent of "inequality"; he was a vociferous opponent of imperialism and its accompanying annexation, by force, of territories. He coined the term *ethnocentrism* and mentored Thorstein Veblen at Yale.

[18] Pizzigati, 339–40; John Rawls, *A Theory of Justice* (rev. edition), Belknap Press (1999).

[19] Chernow, 664–67.

[20] Brownlee, 90.

[21] Pizzigati, 437–40.

[22] Ibid., 441.

[23] Phillips, 220, 315.

[24] Pizzigati, 442–43.

[25] Phillips, 76.

[26] Daniel Bell, *The Cultural Contradictions of Capitalism*, Basic Books (1978), 287–89.

[27] Gil Rendle, *The Multigenerational Congregation: Meeting the Leadership Challenge*, Alban Institute (2003), 56–63; Phillips, xii.

[28] Phillips, xxii.

[29] Ibid., 76–79.

[30] Bell, 21.

[31] Rendle, 65–69.

[32] M. J. Stephey, "A Brief History of: Credit Cards," *Time* website, April 23, 2009, http://content.time.com/time/magazine/article/0,9171,1893507,00.html, retrieved March 6, 2012; Ben Woolsey and Emily Starbuck Gerson, "The History of Credit Cards," CreditCards.com website, www.creditcards.com/credit-card-news/credit-cards-history-1264.php, retrieved March 6, 2012.

[33] Rendle, 65–69. The tea party movement, which developed in response to the 2007–08 financial crisis, has emphasized limiting government spending. A good argument can be made that part of the tea party lineage includes the GI generation and its emphasis on frugality and personal responsibility.

[34] Thomas Merton, *The Spring of Contemplation: A Retreat at the Abbey of Gethsemani*, Ave Maria Press (1997), 110.

[35] Yves Smith, *Econned: How Unenlightened Self Interest Undermined Democracy and Corrupted Capitalism*, Palgrave MacMillan (2010), 112.

[36] George Carlin, "Dumb Americans," *Life's Worth Losing* (2006), Laugh.com.

[37] Gary Dorrien, *Economy, Empire, Difference: Social Ethics for Social Justice*, Columbia University Press (2010), 150, 160.

[38] Ibid., 143.

[39] Nicolaus Mills, "Why Downton Abbey is a Hit in America," February 25, 2012, CNN website, www.cnn.com/2012/02/25/opinion/mills-downton-abbey-compassion/index.html, retrieved March 12, 2012.

[40] American Social History Project website, http://historymatters.gmu.edu/d/5105/, retrieved January 7, 2014.

CHAPTER 4

[1] Paul Tillich, *Theology of Culture*, Oxford University Press (1959), 7–8.

[2] Ibid.

[3] Erich Fromm, *To Have or To Be?*, Continuum (1976), 111.

[4] Marcus Borg, *The Heart of Christianity: Rediscovering a Life of Faith*, Harper Collins (2003), 12, 26–29.

[5] Robert Burton, *On Being Certain: Believing You Are Right Even When You're Not*, St. Martin's Press (2008), xiii, 9–11,157–58.

[6] H. Allen Orr, "A Mission to Convert," *The New York Review of Books* website, January 11, 2007, *The New York Times* website, www.nybooks.com/articles/archives/2007/jan/11/a-mission-to-convert/, retrieved March 15, 2012.

[7] Tillich, 25. "Genuine religion without an element of atheism cannot be imagined."

[8] Quoted in Huston Smith, *Why Religion Matters: The Fate of the Human Spirit in an Age of Disbelief*, Harper Collins, (2001), 68.

[9] Huston Smith, 34–35. Additionally, "Adam" comes from the Hebrew word better translated as "human," meaning "from the earth." This is an intriguing religious insight perpetuated long before the advent of abiogenesis.

[10] Quoted in Borg, *The Heart of Christianity*, 50.

[11] Eric Michael Mazur, *The Encyclopedia of Religion and Film*, ABC-CLIO (2011), 338.

[12] Ibid., 339.

[13] Pete Hamill, *Why Sinatra Matters*, Little, Brown & Company (1998), 37.

[14] Peter Guralnick, *Last Train to Memphis: The Rise of Elvis Presley*, Little, Brown & Company (1994), 248.

[15] Guralnick, 416, 426, 499–501, 620. The BNDD was a predecessor agency of the federal Drug Enforcement Administration.

[16] David Itzkoff, "Thriller Video Added to US Film Registry," December 30, 2009, *The New York Times* website, www.nytimes.com/2009/12/31/arts/music/31arts-THRILLERVIDE_BRF.html?_r=1, retrieved March 18, 2012.

[17] J. Randy Taraborelli, *Michael Jackson: The Magic and the Madness*, Citadel (1991), 518–20.

[18] Smithsonian National Postal Museum website, http://www.postalmuseum.si.edu/artofthestamp/SubPage%20table%20images/artwork/rarities/Elvis%20Ballot/elvisballot.htm, retrieved January 2, 2014.

[19] Huston Smith, 51.

[20] Robert Putnam and David Campbell, *American Grace: How Religion Divides Us and Unites Us*, Simon & Schuster (2010), 534–39; Borg, *The Heart of Christianity*, xi.

[21] Business Pundit website, "Goldman Sachs Earnings: $13.4bn for 2009; Compensation: $16.2bn," January 21, 2010, www.businesspundit.com/goldman-sachs-earnings-13-4bn-for-2009-compensation-16-2bn/, retrieved March 12, 2012; Jonathan Weil, "Blankfein Invokes God and Man at Goldman Sachs," November 11, 2009, Bloomberg website, www.bloomberg.com/apps/news?pid=newsarchive&sid=aqPYJqlCzOHo, retrieved March 23, 2012.

[22] Christine Harper, "Goldman Sachs's Top Managers to Get All-Stock Bonuses," December 10, 2009, Bloomberg website, www.bloomberg.com/apps/news?pid=newsarchive&sid=aZZpuBhMHTbo&pos=1, retrieved March 23, 2012.

[23] Bell, 5.

[24] Boston Collaborative Encyclopedia of Western Theology website, *Paul Tillich*, Wesley Wildman (ed.), http://people.bu.edu/wwildman/bce/tillich.htm, retrieved March 25, 2012. Tillich's host Niebuhr is widely credited with having penned the Serenity Prayer, used extensively by the 12-step movement.

[25] Tillich, 44.

[26] Necrometrics website, www.necrometrics.com/20c5m.htm#WW1, retrieved March 26, 2012.

[27] Quoted in Bell, 166.

[28] Tillich, 46.

[29] Quoted in Morris Berman, *A Question of Values*, Berman (2010), 185.

[30] Philip Goodchild, *Theology of Money*, Duke University Press (2009), 258.

[31] Quoted in Goodchild, George Savile (1726–1784), English politician, 39.

[32] Ibid., 4, 56, 106, 110.

[33] Ibid., 11–12.

[34] Ibid., 106, 170, 179, 216, 218.

[35] Ibid., 110.

[36] Ibid., 121.

[37] "Having less, giving more: The influence of social class on prosocial behavior," Paul Piff, et al; *Journal of Personality and Social Psychology*, Vol. 99(5), November 2010, 772.

[38] Goodchild, 237.

[39] Ibid., 58.

CHAPTER 5

[1] Dave Jamieson, "Join the Booming Dollar Store Economy! Low Pay, Long Hours, May Work While Injured," August 9, 2013, Huffington Post website, http://www.huffingtonpost.com/2013/08/29/dollar-stores-work_n_3786781.html, retrieved September 3, 2013; Kent Patterson, "Activists Accuse Family Dollar Stores of Anti-Labor Practices," November 8, 2010, Texas Civil Rights Project website, http://www.texascivilrightsproject.org/2644/activists-accuse-family-dollar-stores-of-anti-labor-practices/, retrieved September 3, 2013; US Department of Labor document, http://www.dol.gov/whd/regs/compliance/fairpay/fs17a_overview.pdf, retrieved September 3, 2013; Kent Patterson, "Dollar Stores: Top Link in Sweatshop Chain," October 6, 2010, CorpWatch website, http://www.corpwatch.org/article.php?id=15629, retrieved September 3, 2013; Jack Hitt, "The Dollar Store Economy," August 18, 2011, *The New York Times Magazine* website, http://www.nytimes.com/2011/08/21/magazine/the-dollar-store-economy.html?pagewanted=all&_r=1&, retrieved September 3, 2013.

[2] Richard Donkin, *Blood, Sweat and Tears: The Evolution of Work*, Texere (2001), 46–47.

[3] Economic Policy Institute, "Work and Leave Policies," February 14, 2011, State of Working America website, http://stateofworkingamerica.org/charts/comparison-of-total-statutory-leave-time-and-average-weeks-worked-per-year/, retrieved April 8, 2012; Catherine Rampell, "Koreans Put in the Most Hours," May 12, 2010, *The New York Times* website, economix.blogs.nytimes.com/2010/05/12/s-koreans-put-in-most-hours/, retrieved April 8, 2012.

[4] Gar Alpoveritz, *America Beyond Capitalism: Reclaiming Our Wealth, Our Liberty, and Our Democracy*, Wiley & Sons (2005), 197–98; Chrystia Freeland, *Plutocrats: The Rise of the New Global Super-Rich and the Fall of Everyone Else*, Penguin Press (2012), 86; John De Graaf, David Wann, and Thomas Naylor, *Affluenza: The All-Consuming Epidemic*, Berrett-Koehler Publishers (2001), 42.

[5] Marshall Sahlins, *Stone Age Economics,* Aldine Transaction (1974), 1–2; Donkin, 4.

[6] Donkin, 17, 25–26.

[7] Ibid., 32.

[8] Ibid., 30; Bell, xvi.

[9] Ibid., 62–66.

[10] Ibid., 73–77. The name Luddite came from Ned Ludd, perhaps a legendary figure, who was said to have smashed an earlier version of a knitting frame in a fit of passion in the 1780s, a generation before the uprising bearing his name.

[11] Stephen Nissenbaum, *The Battle for Christmas*, Random House (1996), 5–9.

[12] Ibid., 62, 84.

[13] Donkin, 79.

[14] Ibid., 79–81.

[15] Kathleen Strange, *Climbing Boys: A Study of Sweeps' Apprentices*, Allison & Busby, (1982), 31.

[16] Donkin, 82.

[17] Morris, 272.

[18] R.W. Tawney, *Religion and the Rise of Capitalism*, Harcourt, Brace & World (1926), 231, 234–35.

[19] Donkin, 130.

[20] Miller, 224–40; Donkin, 122–31.

[21] Donkin, 147–52.

[22] Chernow, 611–12.

[23] Donkin, 138–44.

[24] Morris, 301–14.

[25] Donkin, 158.

[26] Aldous Huxley, *Brave New World*, Harper Perennial Classics (1932), 4, 33, 50, 92.

[27] Donkin, 215–16.

[28] Naomi Klein, *No Logo: Taking Aim at the Brand Bullies*, Picador (2000), 200–5, 212.

[29] Jemima Kiss, "The real price of an iPhone 5: life in the Foxconn factory," September 13, 2012, *The Guardian* website, http://www.guardian.co.uk/technology/2012/sep/13/cost-iphone-5-foxconn-factory, retrieved September 15, 2013.

[30] Arun Devnath, "Bangladesh Building Collapse Death Toll Reaches 1,000," May 9, 2013, Bloomberg website, http://www.bloomberg.com/news/2013-05-09/fire-at-bangladesh-garment-factory-kills-at-least-7-people.html, retrieved September 15, 2013.

[31] US Department of Labor, Bureau of Labor Statistics website, http://data.bls.gov/pdq/SurveyOutputServlet, retrieved April 16, 2012.

[32] Eric Schlosser, *Fast Food Nation: What the All-American Meal is Doing to the World*, Penguin (2002), 149–54.

[33] US Department of Labor, Bureau of Labor Statistics website, http://www.bls.gov/news.release/union2.nr0.htm, retrieved January 2, 2014.

[34] Schlosser, 154–64.

[35] Ibid., 169–74.

[36] Ted Genoways, "Cut and Kill," *Mother Jones*, July–August 2011, 27–37, 67.

[37] Tawney, 218–24.

[38] Dorrien, 341.

[39] Alexander Thomas, "Ronald Reagan and the Commitment of the Mentally Ill: Capital, Interest Groups, and the Eclipse of Social Policy," *Electronic Journal of Sociology* (1998), www.sociology.org/content/vol003.004/thomas_d.html, retrieved April 22, 2012.

[40] Ibid.

[41] Yves Smith, 109; "How Many People Experience Homelessness?", July 2009, National Coalition for the Homeless website, www.nationalhomeless.org/factsheets/How_Many.html, retrieved April 22, 2012; Phillips, xviii.

[42] Tavis Smiley and Cornel West, *The Rich and the Rest of Us: A Poverty Manifesto*, SmileyBooks (2012), 17, 24–25, 28–29.

[43] Ahamed, 441.

[44] Paul Krugman, "Who Was Milton Friedman?", February 15, 2007, *The New York Review of Books* website, www.nybooks.com/articles/archives/2007/feb/15/who-was-milton-friedman/?pagination=false, retrieved April 23, 2012; Yves Smith, 34–38. Neoliberalism as a term is somewhat disputed. Some maintain that its use is strictly pejorative.

[45] Madrick, 245–46.

[46] Yves Smith, 292.

[47] Reinhart and Rogoff, 162.

[48] Paul Kedrosky and Dane Stangler, "Financialization and Its Entrepreneurial Consequences," *Kauffman Foundation Research Series*, March 2011, 2–3, www.kauffman.org/uploadedFiles/financialization_report_3-23-11.pdf, retrieved April 7, 2012.

[49] Andrea Seabrook, "Who's Weighing Tax on Rich? Congress' Millionaires," September 20, 2011, National Public Radio website, www.npr.org/2011/09/20/140627334/millionaires-in-congress-weigh-new-tax-on-wealthy, retrieved June 4, 2012.

[50] Nomi Prins, *It Takes a Pillage: An Epic Tale of Power, Deceit, and Untold Trillions*, Wiley (2009), 141–42.

[51] Charles Lindblom, *The Market System: What It Is, How It Works, and What To Make of It*, Yale (2001), 236, 247–49.

[52] Ibid., 8–15.

[53] Ibid., 41–42, 47.

[54] Ibid., 10, 65, 237.

[55] Ibid., 168.

[56] Bill Moyers, "Encore: How Big Banks Are Rewriting the Rules of our Economy," March 16, 2012, Moyers and Company website, billmoyers.com/episode/encore-how-big-banks-are-rewriting-the-rules-of-our-economy, retrieved May 10, 2012.

[57] Katrina Brooker, "Citi's Creator, Alone With His Regrets," January 2, 2010, *The New York Times* website, www.nytimes.com/2010/01/03/business/economy/03weill.html?pagewanted=all, retrieved May 10, 2012.

[58] Madrick, 309–13.

[59] Moyers, "Byron Dorgan on Making Banks Play by the Rules," March 16, 2012, Moyers and Company website, http://billmoyers.com/segment/byron-dorgan-on-making-banks-play-by-the-rules/, retrieved May 10, 2012; Madrick, 313–15.

[60] Nomi Prins and Andy Kroll, "9 Wall Street Execs Who Cashed in on the Boom—and the Bust," November 7, 2011, *Mother Jones* website, www.motherjones.com/politics/2011/11/9-wall-street-execs-who-got-off-scot-free, retrieved May 13, 2012.

[61] Madrick, 317; Moyers, "John Reed on Big Banks' Power and Influence," March 16, 2012, Moyers and Company website, http://billmoyers.com/segment/john-reed-on-big-banks-power-and-influence/, retrieved May 10, 2012.

[62] Phillips, 154.

[63] Thomas Frank, *One Market Under God: Extreme Capitalism, Market Populism, and the End of Economic Democracy,* Anchor (2000), xiv; Whybrow, xvii, 260.

[64] Quoted in Frank, 87.

[65] Lindblom, 224.

[66] William T. Cavanaugh, *Being Consumed: Economics and Christian Desire*, Eerdmans (2008), 16, 32. Shopping addicts: upward of 10 percent of society, including 20 percent of women.

[67] Ibid., 32, 36.

[68] David Loy, "The Religion of the Market," *Journal of the American Academy of Religion*, 1997, vol. 65, issue 2, 275.

[69] Yves Smith, p. 42–44; George Akerlof and Robert Schiller, *Animal Spirits: How Human Psychology Drives the Economy, and Why It Matters for Global Capitalism*, Princeton University Press (2009), 1, 45, 168.

[70] Loy, 277–78.

[71] Akerlof and Schiller, xi, 146.

[72] Karl Polanyi, *The Great Transformation: The Political and Economic Origins of Our Times*, Beacon Press (2001), 60.

[73] Barbara Ehrenreich, *Nickel and Dimed: On (Not) Getting By In America*, Henry Holt and Company (2001), 119–20.

[74] Quoted in James Childs, *Greed: Economics and Ethics in Conflict*, Augsburg Fortress (2000), 6–7, 141.

[75] Matthew Taibbi, *Griftopia: Bubble Machines, Vampire Squids, and the Long Con That Is Breaking America*, Spiegel & Grau (2010), 29.

[76] "Social Mobility and Inequality: Upper Bound," April 15, 2010, *The Economist* website, www.economist.com/node/15908469, retrieved May 18, 2012.

[77] Richard Wilkinson and Kate Pickett, *The Spirit Level: Why Greater Equality Makes Societies Stronger*, Bloomsbury Press (2009), 157–63.

[78] "Pew Commissioned Poll Finds Americans Optimistic About Prospects for Economic Mobility Despite the Recession,"* March 12, 2009, The Pew Charitable Trusts website, www.pewtrusts.org/news_room_detail.aspx?id=50022, retrieved May 20, 2012.

[79] Dorrien, 146, 166.

[80] Childs, 126.

[81] Tawney, 221–22.

[82] Frank Deford, "Seasons of Discontent," *Newsweek*, December 29, 1997.

[83] Michael Sandel, *What Money Can't Buy: The Moral Limits of Markets*, Farrar, Straus, and Giroux (2012), 173–74.

[84] James Farrell, *One Nation Under Goods: Malls and the Seductions of American Shopping*, Smithsonian Exposition Books (2004), xi; International Council of Shopping Centers website, www.icsc.org/srch/faq_category.php?cat_type=research&cat_id=3, retrieved May 22, 2012.

[85] Paco Underhill, *The Call of the Mall: The Author of 'Why We Buy' on the Geography of Shopping*, Simon & Schuster (2004), 21. An argument can be made for Disney World to be considered an American "place of worship," according to our functional definition of

religion. Like newer sports stadiums, it also is in the category of cathedral. Its prohibitive costs, however, for a large number of Americans negates its inclusion.

[86] Malcolm Gladwell, "The Terrazo Jungle," March 15, 2004, *The New Yorker* website, www.newyorker.com/archive/2004/03/15/040315fa_fact1, retrieved May 17, 2012; Jeffrey Hardwick, *Mall Maker: Victor Gruen, Architect of an American Dream*, University of Pennsylvania Press (2004), 3–5; Farrell, 8–11.

[87] Lizabeth Cohen, *A Consumers' Republic: The Politics of Mass Consumption in Postwar America*, Vintage (2004), 337; Hardwick, 5.

[88] Underhill, 14.

[89] Wells Dunbar, "Highland Mall Hysteria Over Texas Relays," April 10, 2009, *Austin Chronicle* website, www.austinchronicle.com/news/2009-04-10/764651/, retrieved May 25, 2012.

[90] Farrell, 122.

[91] Ibid., 119, 122, 124, 129, 132, 133.

[92] Ibid., 76, 80, 81, 86, 90, 99, 108, 109.

[93] Karen Stabiner, "New Lives for 'Dead' Suburban Malls," *The New York Times*, January 21, 2011, http://newoldage.blogs.nytimes.com/2011/01/21/new-lives-for-dead-suburban-malls/, retrieved May 25, 2012.

[94] Johan Nylander, "World's biggest mall a China 'ghost town'," March 3, 2013, CNN website, www.edition.cnn.com/2013/03/03/business/china-worlds-largest-mall, retrieved May 28, 2013; Robert Marquand, "China's supersized mall," November 24, 2004, *Christian Science Monitor* website, www.csmonitor.com/2004/1124/p01s03-woap.html, retrieved May 28, 2013.

[95] Peter Sedgwick, *The Market Economy and Christian Ethics*, Cambridge University Press (2008), 109.

[96] Lindblom, 236.

[97] Wilkinson & Pickett, 33–36.

[98] Akerlof & Schiller, 128–29.

CHAPTER 6

[1] Carlin, *Life's Worth Losing*.

[2] CNN.com/Transcripts, October 6, 2011; http://transcripts.cnn.com/TRANSCRIPTS/0110/06/smn.26.html, retrieved June 1, 2012; "Transcript of Bush Conference—Americas—International Herald Tribune, *New York Times*, December 20, 2006, www.nytimes.com/2006/12/20/world/americas/20iht-web.1220bushtext.MAIN.3964806.html?pagewanted=all, retrieved June 1, 2012.

[3] Lawrence Wright, *The Looming Tower: Al-Qaeda and the Road to 9/11*, Knopf (2006), 368.

[4] David Alsup, "1 dead, 16 injured in Tennessee crashes involving 176 cars," December 1, 2011, CNN website, http://www.cnn.com/2011/12/01/us/tennessee-crashes/, retrieved June 2, 2012.

[5] James McMurtry, "Racing to the Red Light," *Walk Between the Raindrops* (1998), Sugar Hill Records.

[6] Kessler, 3–6; "Overweight and Obesity," Centers for Disease Control and Prevention website, www.cdc.gov/obesity/data/databases.htm, retrieved June 2, 2012; "F as in Fat: How Obesity Threatens America's Future, 2011," Trust for America's Health, Robert Wood Johnson Foundation, July 2011, 8; www.healthyamericans.org/reports/obesity2011/Obesity2011Report.pdf, retrieved June 3, 2012; "Diabetes Public Health Resource", Centers for Disease Control and Prevention website, http://www.cdc.gov/diabetes/surveillance/index.htm, retrieved November 5, 2013.

[7] Kessler, 7, 173.

[8] Wilkinson & Pickett, 90–92.

[9] Kessler, 12–14.

[10] Ibid., 19, 37–38, 60, 68; United States Department of Agriculture, Economic Research Center, "Food Expenditures," July 13, 2011, www.ers.usda.gov/data-products/food-expenditures.aspx#26636, retrieved June 5, 2012.

[11] Kessler, 67–71.

[12] Ellen Ruppel Shell, *Cheap: The High Cost of Discount Culture*, Penguin (2009), 12–14. Wanamaker is credited with the innovation of seasonal sales, such as January white sales. For this specific sale, he wanted to combat the post-Christmas slowdown and keep his workforce intact, not having to lay them off.

[13] Ibid., 15.

[14] Ibid., 16.

[15] Charles Fishman, *The Wal-Mart Effect: How the World's Most Powerful Company Really Works—and How It's Transforming the American Economy*, Penguin (2006), xii, xxiv, xxxi.

[16] Ibid., 31, 37.

[17] Ibid., 33–34.

[18] Quoted in Ibid., 141–45, 163–66.

[19] Ibid., 80–84.

[20] Ibid., 39–40, 42, 46–48.

[21] Quoted in Ibid., 22.

[22] Ibid., 48.

[23] Ibid., 9–10, 27. Fishman tells of employees being locked inside stores overnight to work against their will and being forced to clock out and then return during their "off" hours to work unpaid. Dawn Hughey and Abel Lopez (chapter 5) can relate.

[24] Ibid., 15; Karen Blumenthal, *Mr. Sam: How Sam Walton Built Walmart and Became America's Richest Man*, Viking (2011), 160–64.

[25] Shell, 70–72. Compulsive shoppers and hoarders seem to be unable to distinguish between present or future buying, acting from a "mounting pressure or anxiety that can seemingly be relieved only by buying." Tim Kasser, *The High Price of Materialism*, The MIT Press (2002), 85.

[26] Ibid., 72–75.

[27] Ibid., x–xi.

[28] Ibid., 2-3.

[29] Ibid., ix, 14, 18, 24, 28.

[30] Ibid., 30.

[31] Morris, 13; Madrick, 89, 227; McLean & Elkind, 4.

[32] Kasser, 29, 42, 44–45.

[33] Ibid., 53–54.

[34] Neil Postman, *Amusing Ourselves to Death: Public Discourse in the Age of Show Business*, Penguin (1985), 60.

[35] Ibid., 41, 92.

[36] Quoted in Ibid., 111, 121.

[37] Quote from a NBC instructional video for advertisers, Cohen, 302; Thomas Mann & Norman Ornstein, *It's Even Worse Than It Looks: How the American Constitutional System Collided with the New Politics of Extremism*, Basic Books (2012), 59–60.

[38] "60 Years of News on NBC," www.youtube.com/watch?v=mFvTrGDTCYU, retrieved June 23, 2012.

[39] Neil Postman & Steve Powers, *How to Watch the TV News*, Penguin (1992, revised 2008), 4–5.

[40] Mann & Ornstein, 60–61.

[41] Shaun O'Connell, "Tip O'Neill: Irish-American Representative Man," *New England Journal of Public Policy*, vol. 18, issue 2 (2003).

[42] Olivia Katrandjian, "Golf Summit: President Obama and the Speaker Boehner Tee Off," June 18, 2011, ABC News website, www.abcnews.go.com/Politics/golf-summit-president-obama-boehner-tee-off/story?id=13874970, retrieved June 24, 2012; "Hank Williams, Jr. Compares Obama to Hitler," Fox & Friends, October 3, 2011, www.youtube.com/watch?v=YdrJGjhmEes, retrieved June 25, 2012.

[43] Richard Hasen, "Why Washington Can't Be Fixed," May 9, 2012, *Slate* website, www.slate.com/articles/news_and_politics/politics/2012/05/thomas_mann_and_norman_ornstein_s_ideas_won_t_solve_washington_s_gridlock_.html, retrieved June 22, 2012.

[44] Mann & Ornstein, 44–45.

[45] Ibid., xii, 4, 33–43. The 2011 disapproval rating was surpassed in the fall of 2013 on the heels of a government shutdown. Polling Report website, http://www.pollingreport.com/CongJob.htm, retrieved December 14, 2013.

[46] Jacob Hacker & Paul Pierson, *Winner Take All Politics: How Washington Made the Rich Richer—And Turned Its Back on the Middle Class*, Simon & Schuster (2010), 46, 49.

[47] Ibid., 62.

[48] Alan Dunn, "Average America vs. the One Percent," March 21, 2012, *Forbes* website, http://www.forbes.com/sites/moneywisewomen/2012/03/21/average-america-vs-the-one-percent/, retrieved June 27, 2012.

[49] Hacker & Pierson, 62–63.

[50] Chris Roush, *Inside The Home Depot: How One Company Revolutionized an Industry Through the Relentless Pursuit of Growth*, McGraw-Hill (1999), 1.

[51] Geoff Colvin, "Nardelli's Downfall: It's All About the Stock," January 3, 2007, CNN Money website, www.money.cnn.com/2007/01/03/news/companies/colvin_nardelli.fortune/, retrieved June 30, 2012.

[52] Hacker & Pierson, 61–62.

[53] Madrick, 353–67.

[54] Ibid., 366–70; Aaron Glantz, "Mortgage Settlement: Many Are Left Behind," *The New York Times*, November 10, 2011, www.nytimes.com/2011/11/11/us/mortgage-settlement-many-are-left-behind.html, retrieved July 1, 2012.

[55] Ben Protess, "Long After Fall, Countrywide's Mozilo Defended His Legacy," *The New York Times*, February 17, 2011, http://dealbook.nytimes.com/2011/02/17/long-after-fall-countrywides-mozilo-defended-his-legacy/?_r=0, retrieved January 2, 2014.

[56] Brian Grow, "Out at Home Depot," January 9, 2007, NBC News website, www.msnbc.msn.com/id/16469224/ns/business-us_business/t/out-home-depot/, retrieved July 3, 2012; Charles Herman & Reynolds Holding, "Chrysler Owner Won't Disclose Total Pay for $1 CEO," February 17, 2009, ABC News website, www.abcnews.go.com/Business/Economy/story?id=6894813&page=1, retrieved July 3, 2012.

[57] Madrick, 370.

[58] Ibid., 410–13; Geoffrey Moore, *Crossing the Chasm: Marketing and Selling High-Tech Products to Mainstream Customers,* HarperBusiness (1991), 71–72; author interview with Bob Batlan, a former IBM marketing manager, on August 24, 2012.

[59] Brownlee, 49, 223–26; Darien Jacobson, Brian Raub, Barry Johnson, "The Estate Tax: Ninety Years and Counting," www.irs.gov/pub/irs-soi/ninetyestate.pdf, retrieved July 6, 2012; William Gates Sr., "The Estate Tax: What's At Stake," *Washington Post*, February 16, 2001, A.25.

[60] The Giving Pledge website, www.givingpledge.org, retrieved February 11, 2012.

[61] Nathaniel Parish Flannery, "Carlos Slim Consolidates Telecom Empire, Attracts Attention from Anti-Trust Regulators," August 22, 2012, *Forbes* website, www.forbes.com/sites/nathanielparishflannery/2012/08/22/carlos-slim-consolidates-telecom-empire-attracts-attention-from-anti-trust-regulators/, retrieved August 25, 2012; Kerry A. Dolan, "Mexico's Carlos Slim Joins Ranks Of World's Biggest Philanthropists," May 20, 2011, *Forbes* website, http://www.forbes.com/sites/kerryadolan/2011/05/20/mexicos-carlos-slim-joins-ranks-of-worlds-biggest-philanthropists/, retrieved August 25, 2012; Oliver Lee, "Dark Knights Rising? 8 Super Rich, Real-Life Bruce Waynes," Yahoo! News website, www.news.yahoo.com/dark-knights-rising-8-super-rich-real-life-223008480.html, retrieved August 25, 2012.

[62] McLean & Elkind, 1; Peter Coy, "How Houston Gets Along Without Zoning," October 1, 2007, Bloomberg Business Week website, www.businessweek.com/the_thread/hotproperty/archives/2007/10/how_houston_gets_along_without_zoning.html, retrieved August 28, 2012; Steven Bertoni, "America's Fastest Growing Millionaire Cities," July 14, 2011, *Forbes* website, www.forbes.com/sites/stevenbertoni/2011/07/14/americas-fastest-growing-millionaire-cities/, retrieved August 28, 2012.

[63] Pratap Chatterjee, *Halliburton's Army: How a Well-Connected Texas Oil Company Revolutionized the Way America Makes War*, Nation Books, 2009, xi, 41–42, 49.

[64] Mark Abramson, "McChrystal orders AAFES scaled back," February 10, 2010, Stars and Stripes website, www.stripes.com/news/mcchrystal-orders-aafes-scaled-back-1.98854, retrieved August 30, 2012; author interview with Rene DeLeón, September 16, 2012. The Army and Air Force Exchange Service (AAFES) has been serving military personnel for more than one hundred years—a joint military venture under the auspices of the Department of Defense.

[65] Chatterjee, 5–7, 10–12, 219; DeLeon interview, September 16, 2012; Stiglitz & Bilmes, 15.

[66] Smedley Butler, *War is a Racket*, Feral House, (2003), p. 1.

[67] Peter Elkind, "The Truth About Halliburton," April 18, 2005, CNN Money website, www.money.cnn.com/magazines/fortune/fortune_archive/2005/04/18/8257012/index.htm, retrieved September 1, 2012; Chatterjee, 215, 219.

[68] Stephen Ambrose, *Eisenhower: Soldier and President*, Simon & Shuster (1990), 536–37.

[69] "Recent Trends in Military Expenditure," Stockholm International Peace Research Institute, 2012, www.sipri.org/research/armaments/milex/resultoutput/trends, retrieved September 2, 2012.

[70] US Navy website, "Status of the Navy," www.navy.mil/navydata/nav_legacy.asp?id=146, retrieved September 2, 2012.

[71] James Carroll, *House of War: The Pentagon and the Disastrous Rise of American Power*, Mariner Books (2006), 108, 140.

[72] Ibid., 234, 605.

[73] Paul Kennedy, *The Rise and Fall of the Great Powers: Economic Change and Military Conflict from 1500 to 2000*, Vintage Books (1987).

[74] Dana Priest & William Arkin, *Top Secret America: The Rise of the New American Security State*, Little, Brown & Company (2011), 39, 51.

[75] Ibid., 86–87, 99–100, 177–78, 238.

[76] Carroll, 445–46, 605; Priest & Arkin, 98.

[77] Priest & Arkin, 162, 176, 181, 190.

[78] Melody Petersen, *Our Daily Meds: How the Pharmaceutical Companies Transformed Themselves into Slick Marketing Machines and Hooked the Nation on Prescription Drugs*, Picador (2008), 9–10.

[79] Ibid., 115–19.

[80] Ibid., 118–21. George Merck and streptomycin discoverer Selman Waksman (Rutgers University) cooperated to give its patent to a university trust fund that then licensed its rights to various producers. The antibiotic remedies tuberculosis. (It was determined, however, to be very toxic to children. Some patients were cured but rendered deaf. Streptomycin's use was eventually discontinued.) Also, Jonas Salk famously didn't patent his polio vaccine when introduced in 1955.

[81] "The Use of Medicines in the United States," Report by the IMS Institute for the Healthcare of Informatics, April 2010, http://www.imshealth.com/ims/Global/Content/Insights/IMS%20Institute%20for%20Healthcare%20Informatics/IHII_Medicines_in_U.S_Report_2011.pdf, retrieved September 9, 2012.

[82] Petersen, 90, 121.

[83] Ibid., 115–17, 119–25, 141.

[84] Ibid., 146–47.

[85] Ibid., 152–53.

[86] Ibid., 24, 155; Gene Stone (ed.), "Forks Over Knives: The Plant-Based Way to Health," *The Experiment* (2011), 12.

[87] Viagra website, www.viagra.com/index.aspx, retrieved September 1, 2012.

[88] John Abramson, *Overdo$ed America: The Broken Promise of American Medicine*, Harper Perennial (2004), xvi–xxi, 58, 70–71; Petersen, 158–70, 198–205.

[89] Centers for Medicare and Medicaid Services, "National Health Expenditures 2011 Highlights," http://www.cms.gov/Research-Statistics-Data-and-Systems/Statistics-Trends-and-Reports/NationalHealthExpendData/Downloads/highlights.pdf, retrieved September 2, 2012; "Health Care Spending in the United States and Selected OECD Countries," April 2011, Kaiser Family Foundation website, http://www.kff.org/insurance/snapshot/OECD042111.cfm, retrieved September 2, 2012; Wilkinson and Pickett, 79–85.

[90] US Census Bureau website, http://www.census.gov/hhes/www/hlthins/data/incpovhlth/2011/highlights.html, retrieved September 4, 2012; Center for Economic and Policy Research website, "Over 20 Million Working Americans Lack Health Insurance Coverage," March 22, 2010, http://www.cepr.net/index.php/press-releases/press-releases/over-20-million-workers-lack-health-insurance/, retrieved September 3, 2012.

[91] Maggie Mahar, *Money Driven Medicine: The Real Reason Health Care Costs So Much*, HarperCollins (2006), xii–xv; Sophie Quinton, "Gallup: Fewer Americans Covered by Employer-Based Insurance," November 11, 2011, *National Journal* website, http://www.nationaljournal.com/healthcare/gallup-fewer-americans-covered-by-employer-based-insurance-20111111, retrieved September 6, 2012.

[92] Commonwealth Fund website, http://www.commonwealthfund.org/, retrieved September 9, 2012; Mahar, pp. xvi–xvii; Karen Davis, "Uninsured in America: Problems and Possible Solutions," February 16, 2007, Commonwealth Fund publication, http://mobile.commonwealthfund.org/Publications/In-the-Literature/2007/Feb/Uninsured-in-America--Problems-and-Possible-Solutions.aspx, retrieved September 9, 2012; "Health Care Bill Bankruptcies," December 18, 2008, FactCheck.Org website, http://factcheck.org/2008/12/health-care-bill-bankruptcies/, retrieved September 9, 2012.

[93] Mahar, xvi–xvii.

[94] Wilkinson and Pickett, 81–87; Max Fisher, "U.S. Ranks Near Bottom on Income Inequality," September 19, 2011, *The Atlantic* website, http://www.theatlantic.com/international/archive/2011/09/map-us-ranks-near-bottom-on-income-inequality/245315/, retrieved July 13, 2012; "U.S. Ranks Last Among Seven Countries on Health Care Performance Based on Measures of Quality, Efficiency, Access, Equity, and Healthy Lives," June 23, 2010, Commonwealth Fund website, http://www.commonwealthfund.org/News/News-Releases/2010/Jun/US-Ranks-Last-Among-Seven-Countries.aspx, retrieved July 13, 2012. The six other countries in the study: Australia, Canada, Germany, the Netherlands, New Zealand, the United Kingdom.

[95] Florence Williams, *Breasts: A Natural and Unnatural History*, W.W. Norton & Company (2012), 57, 66, 70–71.

[96] Ibid., 72–73; www.google.com/finance?client=ob&q=NASDAQ:RICK, retrieved July 20, 2012.

[97] Williams, 73–77, 79.

[98] Ibid., 82.

[99] John Hoberman, *Testosterone Dreams: Rejuvenation, Aphrodisia, Doping*, University of California Press (2005), 55, 183, 188, 260.

[100] Ibid., 20, 26, 32, 191, 210, 228, 278–79.

[101] Hoberman, 213. At the 2001 Tour de France, sanctioned doctors tending to racers had official permission to use up to three hundred drugs and other substances for treatment purposes.

[102] BBC Sport Cycling website, "Lance Armstrong & Oprah Winfrey interview transcript," January, 18, 2013, http://www.bbc.co.uk/sport/0/cycling/21065539, retrieved August 16, 2013.

[103] Associated Press, "1994 strike was a low point for baseball," http://sports.espn. go.com/mlb/news/story?id=1856626, retrieved July 17, 2012.

[104] Ed Bouchette, "Haslett Admits to Using Steroids," *Pittsburgh Post-Gazette*, March 24, 2005, www.archive.apsportseditors.org/contest/2005/writing/100-250/ 100-250_breaking_fourth1.html, retrieved July 18, 2012; Hoberman, 275

[105] USA Today Sports Hoopshype website, www.hoopshype.com/salaries.htm, retrieved July 20, 2012.

[106] Associated Press, "NBA Average Ticket Price Increases," February 1, 2012, ESPN NBA website, www.espn.go.com/nba/story/_/id/7529476/nba-average-ticket-price-increases-first-time-three-years, retrieved July 20, 2012.

[107] Joseph Tainter & Tadeusz Patzek, *Drilling Down: The Gulf Oil Debacle and Our Energy Dilemma*, Springer (2012), 65, 67, 79.

[108] Ibid., 190–91.

[109] Ibid., 3–5, 87–89, 200, 209.

[110] Yves Smith, 2–3; Frank Partnoy, *F.I.A.S.C.O.: Blood in the Water on Wall Street*, W.W. Norton & Company (1997), 30–32.

[111] Joseph Stiglitz, *The Price of Inequality*, W.W. Norton & Company (2012), 165.

[112] Zinta Lundborg, "UT's Nobel physicist takes measure of his field," *Austin American-Statesman*, July 10, 2011.

[113] Nassim Nicholas Taleb, *Fooled by Randomness: The Hidden Role of Change in Life and the Markets*, Random House (2004), 29; Kevin Roose, "Wall Street Protests Inspire Ire Over Bank Recruiting," October 11, 2011, *The New York Times* Dealbook website, http://dealbook.nytimes.com/2011/10/11/wall-street-protests-inspire-ire-over-bank-recruiting/, retrieved July 25, 2012; Lynn Parramore, "The Best and the Greediest? Ivy League Students Are Still Heading to Wall Street," May 27, 2012, AlterNet website, www.alternet.org/story/155535/the_best_and_the_greediest_ivy_league_students_are_still_heading_to_wall_street?page=0%2C0, retrieved July 25, 2012.

[114] Joshua Ritchie, "Why Wall Street Is Recruiting Poker Players," May 26, 2010, Mintlife website, www.mint.com/blog/trends/wall-street-poker-05262010/, retrieved July 26, 2012.

[115] Peter Lattman & Azam Ahmed, "Hedge Fund Billionaire is Found Guilty of Insider Trading," May 11, 2011, *The New York Times* Dealbook website, http://dealbook.nytimes.com/2011/05/11/rajaratnam-found-guilty/, retrieved August 12, 2012; Susan Pulliam & Chad Bray, "Trader Draws Record Sentence," October 13, 2011, *The Wall Street Journal* website, http://online.wsj.com/article/SB100014240529702039143045766271910818762 86.html, retrieved August 12, 2012.

[116] Partnoy, p. 43; Michael Lewis, *Liar's Poker: Rising Through the Wreckage on Wall Street*, W.W. Norton & Company (1989), 202.

[117] Greg Smith, "Why I Am Leaving Goldman Sachs," March 14, 2012, *The New York Times* website, www.nytimes.com/2012/03/14/opinion/why-i-am-leaving-goldman-sachs.html?pagewanted=all&_r=1&, retrieved August 15, 2012.

[118] Stiglitz, 33.

[119] Ibid., 33–34.

[120] Whybrow, 7, 207, 213, 225, 227; Jack Russell Weinstein, Internet Encyclopedia of Philosophy website, http://www.iep.utm.edu/smith/#SH2a, retrieved August 24, 2013.

[121] Yves Smith, 4.

[122] Lindblom, 59–60.

[123] Partnoy, *Infectious Greed: How Deceit and Risk Corrupted the Financial Markets*, Henry Holt & Company (2003), 2.

[124] Dan Fitzpatrick, Gregory Zuckerman, and Pat Rappaport, "J.P. Morgan's $2 Billion Blunder," May 11, 2012, *The Wall Street Journal* website, www.online.wsj.com/article/ SB10001424052702304070304577396511420792008.html, retrieved August 24, 2013; "JP Morgan's trading loss: $5.8 billion," July 13, 2012, CNN Money website, http:// money.cnn.com/2012/07/13/investing/jpmorgan-earnings/index.htm, August 24, 2013.

[125] A word about Nassim Nicholas Taleb's concepts of Mediocristan and Extremistan is necessary at this point. According to Taleb, physical quantities belong to the realm of Mediocristan–human height and weight, income levels of laborers, mortality rates. They are entirely predictable and follow a bell curve rate of distribution. They are non-scalable; natural boundaries and constraints cannot be overcome. Some social quantities belong to the realm of Extremistan–wealth of the ultra-rich, book sales of the most successful authors, damage caused by natural disasters, company size (Rockefeller's Standard Oil and Walmart, as examples). These quantities are not predictable and do not conform to a bell curve pattern of distribution. Their returns are scalable, often resulting in winner-take-all inequalities. Taleb warns about confusing the two, or more specifically, treating the events of Extremistan with the intuitions of Mediocristan (for example, the idea that 9/11 could have been prevented if we had more precise knowledge of the terrorists' plans). This type of confusion, according to Taleb, leads to errors in understanding the past and present, and predicting the future.
The examples of excess discussed in this book, to use Taleb's terminology, are from both Mediocristan and Extremistan. I want to emphasize that the eras of excess (long era since 1900, short era since the late 1970s) have created an atmosphere of similar confusion. The examples of Extremistan's excesses–the wealth of Rockefeller and Gates, the gains (and losses) on Wall Street—are mistakenly understood to be guides for how things are to operate in Mediocristan: more food consumed, more hours worked, more oil drilled for, hyper-partisanship in politics, bigger breasts, etc. Limits are entirely natural and necessary. Due to excess's sway, however, limits (further discussed in chapter 8) are increasingly seen as antiquated and unnecessary. See Nassim Nicholas Taleb, *The Black Swan: The Impact of the Highly Improbable*, Random House (2010), 32–37.

CHAPTER 7

[1] Chernow, 527–29.

[2] Mazur, 338.

[3] Barbara Rossing, *The Rapture Exposed: The Message of Hope in the Book of Revelation*, Basic Books (2004), 104–107.

[4] Tim De Chant, "Income Inequality in the Roman Empire," December 16, 2011, Per Square Mile website, http://persquaremile.com/2011/12/16/income-inequality-in-the-roman-empire/, retrieved August 15, 2012. De Chant, a researcher at the Kellogg School of Management at Northwestern University, claims that wealth inequality is worse in today's United States than it was in the Roman Empire; in the United States the top 1 percent controls 40 percent of the wealth whereas in the Roman Empire the top 1 percent controlled 20 percent. Preindustrial societies created significantly less wealth, but Rome boasted a large number of slaves in its lowest economic class.

[5] Quote from Brandeis University website, www.brandeis.edu/legacyfund/bio.html, retrieved March 12, 2012.

[6] Tami Luhby, "The One Percenters in Congress," May 8, 2012, CNN Money website, www.money.cnn.com/2012/05/08/news/economy/congress-net-worth/index.htm, retrieved August 15, 2012; Robert Frank, "Who, Me? A One Percenter?", July 26, 2012, CNBC website, www.cnbc.com/id/48338035/Who_Me_A_One_Percenter, retrieved August 16, 2012.

[7] Edwin Durgy, "What Mitt Romney is Really Worth: An Exclusive Analysis of his Latest Finances," May 16, 2012, *Forbes* website, www.forbes.com/sites/edwindurgy/2012/05/16/what-mitt-romney-is-really-worth/, retrieved August 16, 2012.

[8] "Says Mitt Romney told university students in Ohio that to start a business, they should 'borrow money if they have to from their parents'," September 5, 2012, *Austin American-Statesman* website, http://www.politifact.com/texas/statements/2012/sep/05/julian-castro/julian-castro-says-mitt-romney-advised-college-stu/, retrieved September 12, 2012; Felicia Sonmez, "Mitt Romney: Wife Ann drives 'a couple of Cadillacs'," February 24, 2012, *Washington Post* website, www.washingtonpost.com/blogs/election-2012/post/mitt-romney-wife-ann-drives-a-couple-of-cadillacs/2012/02/24/gIQAMBz6XR_blog.html, retrieved August 16, 2012; Lam Thuy Vo, "What America Owes in Student Loans," April 23, 2012, NPR Planet Money website, http://www.npr.org/blogs/money/2012/04/18/150909686/what-america-owes-in-student-loans, retrieved August 17, 2012.

[9] Bill Bishop, *The Big Sort: Why The Clustering of Like-Minded America is Tearing Us Apart*, Houghton Mifflin Company (2008), 6, 9.

[10] Stiglitz, 143, 162, 200.

[11] Jeffrey Stout, *Blessed Are the Organized: Grassroots Democracy in America*, Princeton University Press (2011), 63.

[12] Annie E. Casey Foundation, Kids Count website, www.datacenter.kidscount.org, retrieved August 20, 2012.

[13] "Measuring Child Poverty," UNICEF report, May 2012, www.unicef-irc.org/publications/pdf/rc10_eng.pdf, retrieved August 20, 2012.

[14] Mary E. Corcoran & Ajay Chaudry, "The Dynamics of Childhood Poverty," *The Future of Children,* Vol. 7, No. 2, 1997, http://www.futureofchildren.org/futureofchildren/publications/docs/07_02_02.pdf, retrieved August 21, 2012; Mark Hugo Lopez & Gabriel Velasco, "Childhood Poverty Among Hispanics Sets Record, Leads Nation," September 28, 2011, Pew Research Center website, www.pewhispanic.org/2011/09/28/childhood-poverty-among-hispanics-sets-record-leads-nation/, retrieved August 21, 2012.

[15] Wilkinson & Pickett, 1–4.

[16] Ibid., 1–10, 17–19.

[17] Ibid., 5, 215–16; Tainter & Patzek, 87–89.

[18] Wilkinson & Pickett, 5–6.

[19] Sean Scallon, "Carter Conservatism," April 6, 2009, *The American Conservative* website, www.theamericanconservative.com/articles/carter-conservatism/, retrieved August 25, 2012.

[20] "Crisis of Confidence," speech by President Jimmy Carter, July 15, 1979, PBS American Experience website, www.pbs.org/wgbh/americanexperience/features/primary-resources/carter-crisis/, retrieved August 25, 2012.

[21] "Examining Carter's 'Malaise Speech,' 30 Years Later," July 12, 2009, NPR Books website, http://www.npr.org/templates/story/story.php?storyId=106508243, retrieved August 25, 2012.

[22] Wilkinson & Pickett, 253.

[23] Reinhart & Rogoff, 171.

[24] Joel Kotkin, "Are Millenials the Screwed Generation?" July 16, 2012, The Daily Beast website, http://www.thedailybeast.com/newsweek/2012/07/15/are-millennials-the-screwed-generation.html, retrieved August 28, 2012.

[25] US Energy Information Administration website, September 27, 2012, www.eia.gov/dnav/pet/pet_pnp_pct_dc_nus_pct_m.htm, retrieved October 5, 2012.

[26] Tainter & Patzek, 38–40, 132–33, 188–89.

[27] Wilkinson & Pickett, 204–5.

[28] Morris, 196–206; Chernow, 571–83.

[29] Wilkinson & Pickett, 134–44.

[30] Quoted in Ibid., 133.

[31] Bell, 189.

[32] Carmen DeNavas-Walt, Bernadette D. Proctor, Jessica C. Smith, "Income, Poverty, and Health Insurance Coverage in the United States: 2010," US Census Bureau publication, September 2010, 14, www.census.gov/prod/2011pubs/p60-239.pdf, retrieved September 6, 2012.

[33] Ibid., 133–41, 150.

[34] Daniel B. Wood, "US Crime Rate at Lowest Point in Decades. Why America is Safer Now," January 9, 2012, The Christian Science Monitor website, www.csmonitor.com/USA/Justice/2012/0109/US-crime-rate-at-lowest-point-in-decades.-Why-America-is-safer-now, retrieved September 8, 2012.

[35] Wilkinson & Pickett, 148–50; "2010 Census Shows Nation's Population Is Aging," US Census Bureau news release, May 26, 2011, http://www.census.gov/2010census/news/releases/operations/cb11-cn147.html, retrieved September 8, 2012.

[36] Wilkinson & Pickett, 40, 225.

[37] Ibid., 222–25.

[38] Stiglitz, 53–57; Gary Dorrien, "Crisis, Economic Justice, and the Divine Commonwealth," speech given in Austin, Texas, April 27, 2012; Brownlee, 155, 174; Wilkinson & Pickett, 223.

[39] Graeme Wood, "Secret Fears of the Super-Rich," April 2011, The Atlantic website, www.theatlantic.com/magazine/archive/2011/04/secret-fears-of-the-super-rich/308419/#, retrieved September 12, 2012.

[40] Yunus, 42.

[41] Muhammad Yunus, "Adam Smith Lecture at Glasgow University," Yunus Centre website, http://muhammadyunus.org/index.php/media/speeches/210-adam-smith-lecture-at-glasgow-university, retrieved September 14, 2012; Herman Daly & John Cobb, Jr., For The Common Good: Redirecting the Economy toward Community, the Environment, and a Sustainable Future, Beacon Press (1989), 89.

[42] Yunus, 249; Daly & Cobb, 6.

[43] Quoted in Daly & Cobb, 36.

[44] Ari Berman, "The .000063% Election: How the Politics of the Super Rich Became American Politics," February 16, 2012, Huffington Post website, www.huffingtonpost.com/ari-berman/super-pacs-2012_b_1281716.html, retrieved September 15, 2012.

[45] Wilkinson & Pickett, 7, 17; Sam Pizzigati, "Joe the Plumber, We Miss You!" October 22, 2012, Nation of Change website, www.nationofchange.org/joe-plumber-we-miss-you-1350914654, retrieved October 24, 2012.

[46] *Democracy in Japan,* Takeshi Ishida & Ellis Krauss (eds.), University of Pittsburgh Press (1989), 10.

[47] "Suicide Rates per 100,000 by Country, Year, and Sex," 2011, World Health Organization website, www.who.int/mental_health/prevention/suicide_rates/en/, retrieved September 17, 2012; Jared Diamond, "Three Reasons Japan's Economic Pain is Getting Worse," April 25, 2012, Bloomberg website, www.bloomberg.com/news/2012-04-25/three-reasons-japan-s-economic-pain-is-getting-worse.html, retrieved September 17, 2012.

[48] "Energy imports, net (% of energy use)," 2012, The World Bank website, http://data.worldbank.org/indicator/EG.IMP.CONS.ZS, retrieved September 18, 2012.

[49] Wilkinson & Pickett, 7, 52, 91–92, 145, 159–60, 174–77.

[50] Bruce Cockburn, "Call It Democracy," *World of Wonders* (1986), True North Records.

[51] Jonathan Sacks, *Future Tense: Jews, Judaism, and Israel in the Twenty-First Century,* Schocken (2009), 81.

CHAPTER 8

[1] Robert Dahl, *A Preface to Economic Democracy*, University of California Press (1985), 1. Dahl claims economic democracy is what Tocqueville encountered in American society in 1831.

[2] "Results from the 2010 National Survey on Drug Use and Health: Summary of National Findings," US Department of Health and Human Services, http://www.samhsa.gov/data/NSDUH/2k10NSDUH/2k10Results.htm, retrieved October 2, 2012.

[3] Ernie Kurtz, "Not-God: A History of Alcoholics Anonymous," Hazelden (1979), 171–72.

[4] Richard Heinberg, *The End of Growth: Adapting to Our New Economic Reality*, New Society Publishers (2011), 7, 20.

[5] Ha-Joon Chang, *23 Things They Don't Tell You About Capitalism,* Bloomsbury Press (2010), 144–45.

[6] Quoted in Heinberg, 155.

[7] Heinberg, 107, 125–26, 131, 135; Tainter & Patzek, 22, 116.

[8] Thomas I. Palley, "Financialization: What It Is and Why It Matters," The Levy Economic Institute and Economics for Democratic and Open Societies, December 2007, 2, www.levyinstitute.org/pubs/wp_525.pdf, retrieved October 5, 2012.

[9] Reinhart & Rogoff, 210.

[10] Chang, 235.

[11] Ibid., 239.

[12] Daly & Cobb, 6, 140; T. S. Eliot, *Collected Poems, 1909–1962*, Harcourt Brace Jovanovich (1991), 160.

[13] Yves Smith, 4.

[14] Daly & Cobb, 138–39.

[15] Stiglitz, 6.

[16] Ben Stein, "In Class Warfare, Guess Which Class Is Winning," November 26, 2006, *The New York Times* website, http://www.nytimes.com/2006/11/26/business/yourmoney/26every.html/?_r=0, retrieved January 16, 2014.

[17] Yunus Centre, "Adam Smith Lecture at Glasgow University."

[18] "World Bank Sees Progress Against Extreme Poverty, But Flags Vulnerabilities," February 29, 2012, The World Bank website, www.worldbank.org/en/news/2012/02/29/world-bank-sees-progress-against-extreme-poverty-but-flags-vulnerabilities, retrieved October 8, 2012.

[19] James Buchan, *Frozen Desire: The Meaning of Money,* Farrar, Straus, Giroux (1997), 10.

[20] Madrick, 27; Daly & Cobb, 140; Yunus, "Adam Smith Lecture at Glasgow University."

[21] Robert Dahl, 1, 162–63.

[22] Ibid., 3, 7–8.

[23] Robert A. G. Monks, *Corpocracy: How CEOs and the Business Roundtable Hijacked the World's Greatest Wealth Machine—and How to Get It Back*, Wiley & Sons (2008), 39–40.

[24] Robert Falkner, "Biography of Adam Smith," April 12, 2008, Liberal Democratic History Group website, www.liberalhistory.org.uk/item_single.php?item_id=37&item=biography, retrieved October 15, 2012.

[25] Monks, 22–23.

[26] Ibid., 42.

[27] Daly & Cobb, 215.

[28] Steve Coll, *Private Empire: ExxonMobil and American Power*, Penguin Press (2012), 71, 82–83, 327, 496, 623.

[29] Ibid., 623.

[30] Monks, 20.

[31] Monsanto website, http://www.monsanto.com/whoweare/Pages/default.aspx, retrieved September 2, 2013; Donald L. Barlett and James B. Steele, "Monsanto's Harvest of Fear," May 2008, *Vanity Fair* website, http://www.vanityfair.com/politics/features/2008/05/monsanto200805, retrieved September 2, 2013; Marie-Monique Robin, *The World According to Monsanto* (translated by George Holoch), The New Press (2010), 11–12, 162–64, 311–12. Supreme Court Justice Clarence Thomas worked as a Monsanto Company lawyer before his appointment to the high court; assistant administrator of the EPA (Environmental Protection Agency) Linda Fisher later became Monsanto's vice president for governmental affairs; and Clinton cabinet members Dan Glickman and Mickey Kantor had cozy relationships with Monsanto executives.

[32] Monks, xii.

[33] Heinberg, 38.

[34] Quoted in Monks, 209.

[35] Daly & Cobb, 71–73.

[36] Quoted in Daly & Cobb, 109.

[37] Burton, 141–42.

[38] Daly & Cobb, 408–9, 413.

[39] Ibid., 413.

[40] Ibid., 72.

[41] Heinberg, 19.

[42] David Wessel, *Red Ink: Inside the High-Stakes Politics of the Federal Budget*, Crown Business (2012), 26–28. Wessel says that (in 2010) Americans paid about 25% of their income as tax. Japan paid 27%, Canada 31%, the U.K. 35%, Germany 36%, and France 43%.

[43] Ibid., 50–52.

[44] Ibid., 135.

[45] Ibid., 150–52.

[46] Ibid., 151–52; Peter Peterson interviewed by Bill Moyers, September 26, 2003, PBS Now website, www.pbs.org/now/transcript/transcript236_full.html, retrieved October 14, 2012.

[47] "Guarding the American Dream," Interview of Peter Peterson, April 2011, Leaders Magazine website, www.leadersmag.com/issues/2011.2_Apr/New%20Frontiers%20in%20Doing%20Good/LEADERS-Peter-Peterson-Peter-G.-Peterson-Foundation.html, retrieved October 15, 2012.

[48] Clive Hamilton, *Growth Fetish*, Griffin Press (2003), 3; Donella Meadows, Jorgen Randers, Dennis Meadows, *Limits to Growth: The 30 Year Update*, Chelsea Green (2004), 12.

[49] Monks, 117; Michael Sandal, "A New Citizenship: Market and Morals," The Reith Lectures, June 9, 2009, 10, BCC website, www.bbc.co.uk/programmes/b00kt7sh, retrieved October 22, 2012. Sandal notes a British study by the late sociologist Richard Tittmus that compared blood donation practices in the U.K., where donors were not compensated, and in the US, where commercialization had been allowed. Tittmus concluded the US system to be inferior: more incidence of blood shortage and contamination. Titmuss, "The Gift Relationship: From Human Blood to Social Policy," The New Press (1997).

[50] Heinberg, 40; Chang, 95.

[51] Erich Fromm, *To Have or To Be?*, Continuum Books (1976), 6, 17, 19–20, 23, 89, 143.

[52] Hamilton, 209, 225.

[53] Center for the Advancement of a Steady State Society website, http://steadystate.org/discover/definition/, retrieved October 25, 2012.

[54] Hamilton, 66.

[55] Walmart corporate website, http://corporate.walmart.com/our-story/locations#/, retrieved October 27, 2012; McDonald's franchising website, http://www.aboutmcdonalds.com/mcd/franchising/international_franchising.html, retrieved October 27, 2012; Burger King international website, http://www.bk.com/en/us/international/index.html, retrieved October 27, 2012.

[56] Meadows, Randers, Meadows, 122.

[57] Ibid., 255–60.

[58] Paul Hawken, Amory Lovins, L. Hunter Lovins, *Natural Capitalism: Creating the Next Industrial Revolution*, Back Bay Books (1999); Natural Capitalism website, www.natcap.org, retrieved October 30, 2012.

[59] Daniel Bell, Jr., *The Economy of Desire: Christianity and Capitalism in a Postmodern World*," Baker Academic (2012), 102, 110.

[60] Martha Nussbaum, "The Enduring Significance of John Rawls," The Chronicle Review, July 20, 2001, Evatt Foundation website, http://evatt.org.au/papers/enduring-significance-john-rawls.html, retrieved November 3, 2012.

[61] Sandel, 7, 9.

[62] Robert H. Nelson, *Economics as Religion: from Samuelson to Chicago and Beyond*, The Pennsylvania State University Press (2001), xxii; Alex J. Pollock, "Is Economics a Science?", November 2, 2010, The American website, http://www.american.com/archive/2010/november/is-economics-a-science, retrieved November 7, 2012.

[63] Nelson, xvi.

[64] Ibid., 117.

[65] Ibid., xviii, 71.

[66] Ibid., 105, 120, 287.

[67] John Kenneth Galbraith, *The Affluent Society*, Mariner Books (1998), 191; Barber quoted in DeGraaf, Wann, Naylor, 60–61, 110, 200.

[68] Oliver James, *Affluenza: How to be Successful and Stay Sane*, Vermillion (2007), xiv, 11, 329; Sacks, 197. The rash of hit-and-run vehicular incidents and offending drivers who flee is indicative of two trends—decreased communal commitments and distracted driving due to smart phones. Gloria Hillard, "Hit-And-Run Deaths Increase, But Culprits Hard To Capture," January 3, 2013, NPR website, http://www.npr.org/2013/01/03/168545915/hit-and-run-deaths-increase-but-culprits-hard-to-capture, retrieved December 4, 2013.

[69] Robert Putnam, *Bowling Alone: The Collapse and Revival of American Community*, Simon & Schuster (2000), 20–21.

[70] Freeland, 193; Linette Lopez, "How Russia's Billionaire Oligarchs Got So Very Rich," March 24, 2013, Business Insider website, http://www.businessinsider.com/what-is-a-russian-oligarch-2013-3, retrieved November 13, 2012; Ezra Klein, "The billionaires list," June 24, 2012, *Washington Post* website, http://www.washingtonpost.com/blogs/wonkblog/wp/2012/06/24/the-billionaires-list/, retrieved November 13, 2012.

[71] Jon Elster, *Solomonic Judgments: Studies in the Limitations of Rationality*, Cambridge University Press (1989), 179.

[72] Nelson, 232.

[73] Oceana website, http://oceana.org/en/explore/marine-places/mississippi-estuary, retrieved April 23, 2013.

[74] Donald McLusky, Michael Elliot, *The Estuarine Ecosystem: Ecology, Threats, and Management*, Oxford University Press (2004), 1–2; US Environmental Protection Agency website, "Coastal Watershed Factsheets–Estuaries and your Coastal Watershed, http://water.epa.gov/type/oceb/fact5.cfm, retrieved January 24, 2014. Most salmon are anadromous, able to live in both fresh- and saltwater environments.

[75] Water encyclopedia website, http://www.waterencyclopedia.com/En-Ge/Estuaries.html, retrieved April 23, 2013.

[76] See Coupon Sherpa website, "Place Your Bets Again: 83 Gut-Busting Restaurants Challenges for Free Food," February 23, 2011, http://blog.couponsherpa.com/place-your-bets-40-gut-busting-restaurant-challenges-for-free-food/, retrieved January 30, 2014; Christina McDowell, "An Open Letter to the Makers of *The Wolf of Wall Street*, and The Wolf Himself," December 26, 2013, *LA Weekly* website, http://www.laweekly.com/

informer/2013/12/26/an-open-letter-to-the-makers-of-the-wolf-of-wall-street-and-the-wolf-himself?page=2, retrieved January 30, 2014. McDowell reveals some of the dark consequences suffered as a result of Belfort's excesses.

[77]Jason Voss, "Capitalism: It's as Much About Cooperation as Competition," July 16, 2012, CFA Investor Blog website, http://blogs.cfainstitute.org/investor/2012/07/16/capitalism-it-is-as-much-about-cooperation-as-competition/, retrieved February 4, 2014.

[78]Sandel, 202; Sacks, 15–16; Robert and Edward Skidelsky, *How Much is Enough?: Money and the Good Life*, Other Press (2013), 69.

INDEX